D1572820

# Stagings

# Stagings

## Short Scripts for Middle and High School Students

*Written and Illustrated*
*by*

## Joan Garner

1995
TEACHER IDEAS PRESS
A Division of
Libraries Unlimited, Inc.
Englewood, Colorado

TEACHER IDEAS PRESS
A Division of
Libraries Unlimited, Inc.
P.O. Box 6633
Englewood, CO 80155-6633
1-800-237-6124

*Production Editor,* Louisa M. Griffin
*Copy Editor,* D. Aviva Rothschild
*Proofreader,* Tama J. Serfoss
*Layout and Design,* Pamela J. Getchell

**Library of Congress Cataloging-in-Publication Data**

Garner, Joan.
    Stagings : short scripts for middle and high school students /
written and illustrated by Joan Garner.
    xiii, 233p. 22x28 cm.
    ISBN 1-56308-343-4 (pbk.)
    1. Acting.   2. One-act plays, American.    3. American drama--20th
century.    I. Title.
    PN2080.G38    1995
    812'.54--dc20
                                                        95-19013
                                                        CIP

# Contents

# INTRODUCTION

## WHAT IS STAGINGS?

The term "stagings" suggests the variety and progression in which each play may be approached:

For a simple reading exercise to enhance cold reading skills and diction.

For a classroom dramatization where dramatic skills are observed and critiqued by other students and instructors.

For a fully staged production that incorporates props, costumes, sets, and lighting.

For its progression (or stages) in sophistication, intricacy, form, and intent from the first play to the last in this series.

*Stagings* strives to accomplish three objectives:

1) Not *Our Town* again! Today's drama coaches, theatre instructors, and literature teachers are faced with the great challenge of bringing material into the classroom that is not only appropriate for the maturity level of the students, but is also interesting. The traditional method of teaching drama—of telling students to find a play and perform a scene from it—is becoming more difficult and, I dare say, risky due to the increasing number of new plays that contain controversial or inappropriate subject matter or dialogue. Although controversy has always made for compelling drama, it tends to complicate training a middle or secondary school student in the mechanics of acting and play production. Langford Wilson's *Burn This* is a riveting piece of theatre, but would a responsible adult be comfortable watching two sixth-graders act out the scenes between Anna and Pale? And would the students themselves even know what needs to be expressed? With such a dilemma at hand, the instructor often returns to the reliable classics, but this presents its own problems. How many times can a student converse with Harvey before becoming bored with the big white rabbit? And how many times can an instructor sit through the same scene from *Our Town* without screaming? The plays in *Stagings* provide instructors and students with new and age-appropriate material.

2) *Stagings* scripts are short in length (approximately 15 to 25 minutes each). But they are also complete plays with beginnings, middles, and ends. A few middle schools and many high schools produce a half dozen or so full-length plays per school year, but this limits the number of students who have an opportunity to participate. A *Stagings* play is a lesser endeavor that still teaches all the standards for theatre. For example, a promising actor can take a role through the entire process of character development without having to memorize the kind of large part usually found in a full two-hour production. The short plays also present the extra challenge of establishing a clearly defined character in a limited amount of time. This especially holds true for the more sophisticated *Stagings* plays, where character definitions and stimuli may be studied and explored. *Stagings* plays will not only challenge the actor, but also give budding theatre artists an opportunity to create and carry through the concepts of style, color, and execution of design required in a complete production. Yet *Stagings* scripts are carefully engineered not to be too difficult for the inexperienced designer. Each play requires only one permanent set. And of the approximately 113 characters in the nine *Stagings* plays, only 10 roles call for an actor to change into a second costume.

By introducing *Stagings* plays between major productions, an increasing number of students can be involved in more ways. Thus, more students will accomplish the suggested National Standards for Arts Education.

3) *Stagings* plays have been written simply to entertain. Many of the plays are set in the future or in outer space—settings easily related to by today's students. Also, *Stagings* scripts have been written using modern humor while dealing with current morals and ideals. In other words, *Stagings* plays have been specially created for the savvy and bravado demonstrated by today's teenagers (grades 6-12).

## NATIONAL STANDARDS FOR ARTS EDUCATION

*Stagings* scripts strive to assist educating students in the theatre discipline based on the National Standards for Arts Education (what students should know and be able to do by the time they have completed secondary school). In compliance, *Stagings* scripts focus on four of the seven Content Standards suggested for grades 6-12: acting, design, directing, and research.

**Acting**. When students read or act in a *Stagings* play, their proficiency increases with practice and performance.

**Design**. The brevity and simplicity of a *Stagings* script encourages students to design costumes, sets, and more at an earlier grade level. Students can also be placed in charge of specific tasks that carry greater responsibility (e.g., set design and construction) at higher grade levels.

**Directing**. A *Stagings* script allows students to be assigned the responsibility of directing. Students have the opportunity to direct an entire play and see the production process through from start to finish, yet the responsibility is not as great as with a full-length play, and less time is required to produce a *Stagings* script.

**Research**. Designing for and producing a short *Stagings* play requires an extensive amount of research to create the proper ambiance and look for each play. (The real test, and in-depth study, may come in designing the art for the science fiction plays.) Although imagination can be turned up all the way, an idea usually begins with observing that which has come before. As theatre is a visual art, students should be encouraged to find photographs and watch film and video presentations of similar productions for ideas and art styles to emulate.

## ABOUT THE PLAYS

Fantasy and science fiction themes have been selected for this series of *Stagings* plays. Because middle and high school students seem especially interested in these two genres, they will be particularly receptive to these types of plays. Some of the fantasy and science fiction plays have been adapted from familiar fairy tales, while the remaining plays are original stories. A brief perusal of the *Stagings* plays also shows their diversities in style. They range from the dramatic *Opposing Forces* to the farcical *The Quib Blaster from Zantar*, the straightforward *Beauty and the Beast*, to the highly stylized *Koba and the Red Lion*. A couple of the plays have parallel plots so character development can be studied. Other plays are structured to emphasize the production aspects of theatre. All have been created to give the instructor and students as much flexibility and freedom in producing and performing as possible.

## ADDITIONAL MATERIAL PROVIDED

The first three pages of this book consist of brief play synopses of the nine *Stagings* plays. In addition, at the beginning of each play, the following is provided:

**Cast of Characters**. A list of characters in the play in order of appearance. A male/female designation (suggestion) is included.

**Character and Costume Descriptions**. A one- or two-line personality description is given with a brief description (suggestion) of costuming and makeup for each character.

**Set**. A diagram of the stationary set.

**Props**. A list of props required.

**As a Study Lesson**. Suggestions on how to use the play in the classroom environment.

**As Performance**. Suggested staging of the play indicating target audience (e.g., children, parents, general) or whether it is designed to best serve as a road show to elementary schools, as a class project, or as a term assignment.

**Considerations, Effects, and Affects**. How to handle and implement special effects easily. Suggestions on styles and ways of presenting the play for maximum effect and affect.

# WHAT YOU CAN DO, WHAT YOU CAN'T DO, WHAT YOU NEED TO DO

## Copyright

The author, Joan Garner, holds copyright to each play in this book. All rights are reserved on story and content.

Poster illustrations at the front of each play are exclusively owned by the author and may not be copied and used for advertising or promotional purposes.

## Copying Scripts

For rehearsal purposes, *Stagings* scripts may be copied and distributed to each cast member of a play being produced. (The publisher and author do not provide individual scripts for each play in this book.) Students finding this book in a library may copy the scripts or sections of the script for scene performing or classroom exercise purposes.

Scripts cannot be copied and given to another instructor or school to use.

Scripts cannot be copied and distributed throughout a school district for general use.

## Videotaping and Sound Recording

Videotaping or sound recording your production of a *Stagings* play is permissible for private use only.

Videotaping or sound recording your production of a *Stagings* play for the intent of viewing for profit is *not* permitted unless arrangements are made with and permission is granted by the author.

## Royalties

*Stagings* plays performed not for profit (e.g., in a classroom environment, for parents and family, for elementary schools, as a program to acquire funds for charity) will not require a royalty fee.

A production of *The Tinder Box, Casings, The Pied Piper of Hamelin, The Quib Blaster from Zantar, Beauty and the Beast, Opposing Forces, Koba and the Red Lion,* or *The Phantom of the Crystal Chasms* will not require a royalty fee if the play is performed alone (even if performed for profit).

For profit performances of multiple *Stagings* plays may require a minimal royalty fee along with other considerations as stated below. (The royalty fees listed below are figured to accommodate a normal production run of two to six performances. These fees may increase or change depending on individual needs and desires [e.g., if a large number of performances are planned and for what purpose]. These variants will be considered and agreed upon by the author and instructor/school/producer when permission to stage is requested.)

The performances of two plays at one showing (to comprise a full production) requires permission from the author, acknowledgment of this permission in any printed material distributed (e.g., posters, advertising, programs), and a royalty fee of $25.00.

The performances of three plays at one showing (to comprise a full production) requires permission from the author, acknowledgment of this permission in any printed material distributed (e.g., posters, advertising, programs), and a royalty fee of $30.00.

The performances of four plays at one showing (to comprise a full production) requires permission from the author, acknowledgment of this permission in any printed material distributed (e.g., posters, advertising, programs), and a royalty fee of $35.00.

Performance of *Winds of Silk* requires permission from the author, acknowledgment of this permission in any printed material distributed (e.g., posters, advertising, programs), and a royalty fee of $50.00.

Permission for producing a *Stagings* play and instructions on how to pay the required royalties may be obtained by writing to the author in care of Libraries Unlimited. Write to:

Joan Garner
c/o Libraries Unlimited
P.O. Box 6633
Englewood, Colorado 80155-6633

Theatre is magic. It is hoped that the plays in *Stagings* help encourage interest in this enchanting milieu and inspire young talents.

# PLAY SYNOPSES

## THE TINDER BOX
*(A Fairy Tale)*

At the end of the Napoleonic Wars, a professional soldier who goes by the name of Gunner finds himself out of work. He meets an old hag who asks him to enter a hollow tree to fetch her tinder box. Inside the tree, Gunner discovers three doors. Behind the first door is a treasure of copper coins guarded by a big dog. Behind the second door are silver coins guarded by a larger dog. And behind the third door are gold coins guarded by an enormous dog. The old hag tells Gunner that he may keep all the treasure he can carry as long as he brings her the tinder box. True to his word, Gunner delivers the tinder box to the old hag, who then reveals that she is a witch. She attempts to kill Gunner by placing an evil spell on him, but he kills her first by cutting off her head with his sword.

Gunner proceeds into town with his fortune and spends his money generously and freely. He hears stories of the lovely and kind Princess Ann, whom he wishes to meet. But Ann is kept behind palace walls and is not allowed to see anyone, so Gunner can do nothing but spend his money until it is all gone. Then he discovers that the tinder box is magical; when he strikes it, the dogs who had guarded the treasure below the tree appear to do his bidding. Gunner asks the dogs to bring Ann to him. Soon he and the princess fall in love, but the king opposes the romance because Gunner is not of royal blood. The king tries to hang Gunner, but the dogs magically lift the king up in the air and transport him over the countryside. Gunner becomes king and marries Ann, and they live happily ever after.

## CASINGS
*(A Space Yarn)*

Above Saturn, a war rages between the Northern Hemisphere and the Southern Hemisphere for mineral rights to the particle rings around the planet. With his fighting ship out of commission, the Captain is forced to stay a few weeks at the Star Relief Space Station. He visits the solarium, where he agrees to climb down a sinkhole to fetch the Professor's casings. In the sinkhole he finds three Olaks, furry aliens who guard a quarry of rubies, emeralds, and diamonds. The Captain befriends the Olaks, and his friendship and honesty are rewarded when the Olaks share their gemstones with him. With the gems, the Captain is able to live in high style on the space station, and with the assistance of the Olaks, he meets Shalon, the Commander's daughter. The Captain and Shalon fall in love, but soon the Captain is called back to his squadron, and Shalon is afraid the Captain will be killed in action. However, the Olaks arrange to have the Commander promoted and have the Captain put in charge of the space station. A celestial twist on *The Tinder Box*, *Casings* also ends happily ever after.

## THE PIED PIPER OF HAMELIN
*(A Little Comedy)*

In the German town of Hamelin, circa 1284, all is pleasant and fine until, quite unexpectedly, a couple of rats (the advance team) come visiting. The rats (Heidi and Felix) create havoc by their mere presence, and when the rest of the rats come to party, the townspeople demand the Burghermeister do something about it. Word is sent out, and the Pied Piper comes calling. The Piper strikes a deal with the rats and rids the town of the vermin, but the Burghermeister refuses to pay the Piper for his services, so the Piper takes away all the children. Because this is a comedy, many humorous elements have been added to this familiar story. For one, Heidi (not that Heidi) insists she's a lemming—higher class, you know. Also, there is Felix the rat (no, you're thinking of another character) and the two children, Hansel and Gretel (not that Hansel and Gretel). And the Pied Piper's real name is Orkin (that's Orkin, ma'am . . .). The Piper arranges for the rats to be boated up the Weser River to a time-sharing community, and he talks the children into going up to Köppen Hill where Disneyworld is located (this is a comedy—go with it). Hamelin returns to normal only after a lot of high jinks and nonsense.

## THE QUIB BLASTER FROM ZANTAR                                   *(A Space Farce)*

On the planet Picatell (population puny), all are celebrating 25 years of colonization. Colony 3.7 is holding a picnic. Although one of the young people suggests they clean up their picnic mess before going to the pond—well, purification plant—to watch the fireworks, the others decide to clean up the mess in the morning. Almost immediately, Quibs zero in on the foodstuffs left behind. (Quibs are pesky little insects that fly through space looking for litter.) Soon the entire planet is swarming with Quibs and it is decided to bring in an exterminator to get rid of them. Enter Jade, the Quib Blaster from Zantar, who offers to blast the Quibs back into space—for a fee, of course. A deal is made, and Jade blasts the Quibs away, but the planet officials renege on the deal, so Jade gets her revenge by blasting the two young people of Colony 3.7 to a more exciting planet. The citizens of Picatell are rather dense, the Quibs are rather pesky, and the whole affair is rather silly. Great fun.

## BEAUTY AND THE BEAST                              *(A Romantic Tale of Enchantment)*

When Papa leaves home on business, he promises to bring gifts to his grown children. Beauty asks for a rose. On his way home, Papa is caught in a storm and seeks shelter in a castle. He finds a note saying he may dine and warm himself by the fire, but not to take anything from the place. As Papa is about to leave, he sees a bouquet of roses in a vase and decides to take a rose home to Beauty. Then Papa is confronted by the owner of the castle—a horrifying beast. Having broken the law set forth by taking the rose, Papa is sentenced to death by the Beast. However, the Beast allows Papa to return to his family to say good-bye as long as Papa returns to the castle the next night to face his punishment. (If Papa does not return, the Beast will kill all of Papa's children.) Back home, Papa tells his children about the Beast and of his appointment with death. Feeling responsible for her father's terrible fate, Beauty follows Papa to the castle to plead for her father's life. The Beast agrees to let Papa go if Beauty stays with him forever. Beauty reluctantly agrees. She hates the Beast at first but eventually warms to his gentle manner.

Then Beauty, sensing that Papa is sick and dying, longs to return home. Having fallen in love with Beauty, and not wanting to cause her pain, the Beast lets her go. Once home, Beauty realizes that she loves the Beast and decides to return to the castle once her father is well. But upon returning to the castle, Beauty finds the Beast brokenhearted, weak, and dying. Although she confesses her love for him, it is too late. The Beast leaves the room to die alone, but miraculously returns as a handsome prince. It's the classic tale retold simply and sympathetically.

## OPPOSING FORCES                                              *(A Space Drama)*

Lieutenant Jenny Lo crashes on Starcrest, an uninhabited planet—at least, a planet *thought* to be uninhabited. However, she finds two individuals living there: Borrel, a gruff and rude man who wears an eye patch, and Collan, a creature who keeps herself covered with a sweeping red cape. Borrel chains Jenny to prevent her from entering his shack. Already hurt and sore from the crash, Jenny is forced to spend the night out in the elements without food or drink. Later, Jenny's brother, Brighton, comes to rescue her, but Borrel overpowers the smaller man and chains him as well. While the two are held captive, Collan tells the story of how she came to be, and what she and Borrel are doing on the planet. Borrel is conducting experiments trying to turn Collan back into the human being she once was. In the course of events, one of the experiments blows up, and Collan appears to die in the explosion. However, the explosion transforms the creature back into a beautiful young woman, or was it the experiment, or was it . . . ? Playing on the *Beauty and the Beast* theme, *Opposing Forces* focuses on the ugliness of behavior and the beauty of gentleness and compassion.

## KOBA AND THE RED LION

*(A Jungle Fable)*

In Old Africa, the rains have not come for two seasons. The animals and humans are having a hard time of it, with food scarce and water more so. To make matters worse, a large red lion has begun stalking the village. Koba's father, Attar, and his uncle, Jaca, leave to hunt the lion. Koba's cousin, Sutu, follows the two men, and Koba feels he must go with Sutu to protect her from the jungle. They come upon a zebra, a cobra, a vulture, and a monkey before returning home to find that Jaca has been badly injured by the Red Lion. Wanting to help his family, Koba sets out again to kill the lion. This time he has the help of Vorasee, a medicine woman from the village. She turns Koba's spear into a magical weapon. Now unafraid, Koba hunts down the Red Lion and kills it with his magic spear. *Koba and the Red Lion* is a story about growing up, about learning to live in peace with all creatures of the Earth, and about the balance of nature.

## THE PHANTOM OF THE CRYSTAL CHASMS

*(A Space Masque)*

A group of mountain climbers go to the planet Chaseon to climb its famous crystal rock formations. There are stories of a Phantom who lives at the bottom of the chasms, and when the young mountain climber Ryan falls into the depths of the chasms, he comes upon the Phantom: a magnificently dressed woman who wears a mask over most of her face. The Phantom tries to kill the already badly injured Ryan but is stopped by her daughter, Passell. Passell also wears a beautiful costume and a mask that covers her face, but she is much nicer than her mother and says she can heal Ryan's broken bones with the power of the crystals if he promises to stay with her in the chasms. In great pain, Ryan promises to stay with Passell, only to change his mind once he is well again. Very much like grand opera, *The Phantom of the Crystal Chasms* plays as tragedy as well as pageant.

## WINDS OF SILK

*(A Minispectacle)*

On a small Japanese island in the 1870s, a girl is saddened by the way her sisters treat her. Although she loves her sisters, they make fun of her and won't let her play with them because she is different. While the other sisters have names like May-Lee, Bay-Lee, and Day-Lee, the young girl's name is Selma. Selma prays to the Great Sea Spirit for guidance, and the Spirit appears to tell Selma to dive for a giant pearl. The Spirit explains that by risking her life to dive for the pearl, Selma should gain the respect of her sisters. When Selma does so and shows her sisters the giant pearl, her older sister, Tay-Lee, grabs the pearl and claims she is the one who found it and that she is in favor with the Great Sea Spirit. The village holds a celebration to gives thanks to the Great Sea Spirit and to honor Tay-Lee for being in favor with the gods. Selma should be upset with the undeserved attention given to Tay-Lee, but she is happy because a few of her sisters have befriended her, and now she has someone to play with.

After a few days, a gang of comical pirates lands on the island to steal the giant pearl and sneak off with it. The Great Sea Spirit is angered that his pearl is missing and creates a great wind that blows the pirates back to the island. When confronted, the pirates deny taking the pearl, so the Great Sea Spirit creates a bigger, fiercer wind that begins to blow the island apart. The villagers beg for mercy and ask Tay-Lee to pray to the Great Sea Spirit for forgiveness. However, not being truly in favor, Tay-Lee's prayers go for naught. The other sisters declare that Selma really found the pearl and when Selma prays to the Great Sea Spirit, he turns the mighty winds into winds of silk.

This is a sweet and often humorous story of differences, love, and honesty. Told in the Kabuki theatre style, *Winds of Silk* is a feast for the eyes, yet easily staged.

# THE

# TINDER

# BOX

# The Tinder Box

*A Fairy Tale by Joan Garner*
*Based on the story by Hans Christian Andersen*

## CAST OF CHARACTERS (m=male   f=female)

| | | | |
|---|---|---|---|
| NARRATOR (m/f) | COPPER DOG (m/f) | INNKEEPER (f) | QUEEN (f) |
| GUNNER (m) | SILVER DOG (m/f) | PRINCESS ANN (f) | GUARD #1 (m) |
| FARMER (m) | GOLD DOG (m/f) | KING (m) | GUARD #2 (m) |
| HAG/WITCH (f) | | | |

## CHARACTER AND COSTUME DESCRIPTIONS

(The following costume suggestions are for a realistic production. If a fantasy-style production is done, costumes may be as simple or as elaborate as the designer likes—accuracy in period and detail needn't be a concern.)

**GUNNER:** Gunner is a brave soldier with a good heart. A typical hero, Gunner is straightforward and mannerly to all. Gunner wears the uniform of a Prussian Gunner of the Guards Mounted Artillery. The blue jacket is short with tails—collar and cuffs are black with red piping and gold insignia. The trousers are gray with a red stripe down the pant leg. The shako (optional) is black with gold cording and insignia and a white plume. The leather belting is white, and the pouch is black. The sword is straight-bladed and on a shoulder belt. The boots are black.

**FARMER:** The Farmer is a nice man who is fairly plain in looks and nature. He wears simple breeches of the period (brown, most likely). The tailcoat should be of the same color. The waistcoat may be of another neutral color, and the shirt should be white with no collar or cravat. Tall boots to the knee and a floppy cap.

**HAG/WITCH:** The Witch is evil and shrewish. She should be ugly in both appearance and deportment. The Witch wears a ragged dark blouse and long skirt, a large black cape or shawl to cover her entire body, and a black or gray waist apron. Black stockings and slippers. Makeup considerations are a gray or white wig ratted to stick out, warts, and a long nose.

**COPPER DOG:** The Copper Dog is a likable, cool character. He (she) can wear a dog costume, but a simpler outfit might be just as effective—solid tan shirt and slacks. A piece of metallic copper material can be draped over the shoulder, and lighting gel (filter) material of an amber color may be cut out and affixed like glasses to make the small round eyes. Tan gloves and socks.

**SILVER DOG:** The Silver Dog is a likable, cool character. He (she) can wear a dog costume, but a simpler outfit might be just as effective—solid gray shirt and slacks. A piece of metallic silver material can be draped over the shoulder, and lighting gel (filter) material of a gray or blue color may be cut out and affixed like glasses to make the medium-sized round eyes. Gray gloves and socks.

**GOLD DOG:** The Gold Dog is a likable, cool character. He (she) can wear a dog costume, but a simpler outfit might be just as effective—solid yellow shirt and slacks. A piece of metallic gold material can be draped over the shoulder, and lighting gel (filter) material of a yellow color may be cut out and affixed like glasses to make the large round eyes. Yellow gloves and socks.

**INNKEEPER:** The Innkeeper is an ordinary person, but kind of a busybody. The Innkeeper wears a brightly colored blouse with long skirt—no lace or frills—and should have a shoulder-length white apron. Neutral color stockings and slippers.

**PRINCESS ANN:** Princess Ann is a very nice, almost meek person. She is sincere and honest. Princess Ann wears an elegant, elaborately trimmed, white, short-sleeved chemise gown of the empire era. Over it is a light blue satin sleeveless waistcoat with long train. Diamond tiara, long white gloves, white hose, and soft slippers. Hair should be of ringlets and a chignon.

**KING:** The King is pompous and egotistical. He likes to throw his weight around and believes the opinions of everyone else are wrong. The King wears a fancy red spencer jacket over a black tailcoat. He wears a high collar, brightly patterned cravat, and long, tight-fitting pantaloons. A dignitaries' sash from shoulder across chest to waist with metals. Dark, tall hat and black, soft shoes.

**QUEEN:** The Queen is rather wimpish and indecisive. She cowers and whimpers at the King's command. The Queen wears an elegant empire dress of light green with a darker green outdoor pelisse over it. A sash from over the shoulder to across the breast and down to the waist should be worn to signify royalty. This white satin sash may be ornately decorated with gold and silver insignia and jewels. Neutral stockings and soft slippers.

**GUARDS:** The Guards are nondescript. They do what they are told up to a point. The Guards wear uniforms similar to, but not of the ornateness of Gunner's. Belts, pouches, and swords.

**Scene Design for *The Tinder Box***

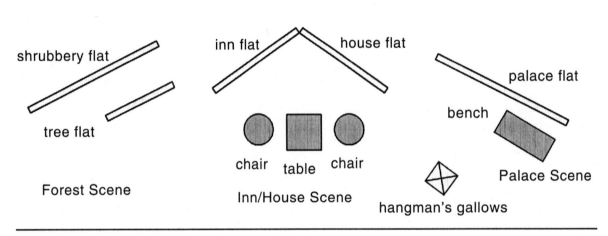

Blue Sky Drop

shrubbery flat — tree flat — **Forest Scene**

inn flat — house flat — chair — table — chair — **Inn/House Scene**

palace flat — bench — hangman's gallows — **Palace Scene**

Apron

## SET

The set as suggested above consists of one-dimensional flats. Realistic scenery may be used but might be more difficult to construct.

## PROPS

sack of apples, ropes, lamp, coins, matches, tinder box, food on plate, stein, sacks of coins, buckets, paintbrushes, candle, noose.

## AS A STUDY LESSON

*The Tinder Box* is written specifically for reading, with minimal action and props required to tell the story. This makes the play ideal for a classroom scene or for cold reading practice.

The characters in this play are one-dimensional and superficial. Gray areas are of a gossamer consistency and need not be addressed (or bothered with).

All the characters are familiar to young actors, who can easily grasp and portray their parts. This allows the actor to concentrate on stage presence and dialogue delivery without having to explore the character's inner conflict, understand antagonist/protagonist contentions, or find the motivation involved. Although there are emoting properties, they need not be expounded to clearly convey the classic story.

## AS PERFORMANCE

As stated, *The Tinder Box* is best as a reading vehicle. If performed fully and traditionally, the target audience is obviously children, but this could also be a nice, entertaining piece for peers and parents.

*The Tinder Box* will play nicely as a small road show taken to elementary schools or as a community project.

## CONSIDERATIONS, EFFECTS, AND AFFECTS

As this is a fairy tale, a fantasy/picture-book style is suggested. A cutout-like set will also travel better if the play is taken on the road. Because the play is relatively short, it has been written for smooth, continual flow direction without the incorporation of physical scene changes. To best achieve this continual flow, a stationary set is suggested. The country road and street scene may be played downstage in front of the stationary set.

For the sake of simplicity, one stand-alone door can be used for depicting all three doors that are under the tree. This door may be wheeled in from the wings as Gunner makes his way down into (behind) the tree, and the appropriate dog need only enter and exit on cue. Of course, the easiest way to depict this scene is to have the dogs enter and exit without a door.

If the fantasy/picture-book style is incorporated, the characters should be played more broadly or more exaggeratedly.

# The Tinder Box

**SET:** The stage is divided into three distinct playing areas:
1) At stage right is the Forest Scene, which consists of one large, dead tree flat with a shrubbery flat behind it. A blue sky drop follows behind and off from right to stage left.
2) At center stage is the Inn/House Scene, which is a flat showing the interior of an inn on the right side of the flat and the interior of a house on the left side of the flat. A small table with two chairs on either side sits down from the flat.
3) At stage left is the Palace Scene, which can be a half flat from the floor to three or four feet in height. A bench or throne and a small decorative accessory table sit downstage from the palace flat. Between the Inn/House Scene and the Palace Scene downstage is a box large enough and strong enough for a person to stand on.

**AT RISE:**
Afternoon, September 7, 1815. A pleasant day in the Prussian countryside. The stage is empty, and normal lighting is up on all three playing areas.

**NARRATOR:**
One calm and pleasant fall afternoon, a tired and hungry Prussian soldier walked down a dirt road. The Napoleonic Wars that had lasted for years were finally over, and the roads and byways found many a soldier on his way home to his family. But the Prussian soldier on this road—the one called Gunner—had no family to go home to. He was headed somewhere; he just didn't know where.

*(**GUNNER** enters stage left and crosses to center stage while the **NARRATOR** speaks. **GUNNER** is a brave soldier with a good heart. A typical hero, **GUNNER** is straightforward and mannerly to all.)*

**NARRATOR:** *(Continued.)*
Trees lined both sides of the path, providing nice shade, and a gentle breeze swept past with a hint of gunpowder in the air—or that's what Gunner thought he could smell. Having been a member of the mounted artillery and having been around the cannon for so long during battle, the handsome soldier could smell nothing but gunpowder thereafter. So dedicated had he been to his post, everyone called him Gunner, and so long had he been called Gunner, he could scarcely remember his own name. When a farmer met him on the edge of an apple orchard, the soldier readily answered when the man called out to him.

*(The **FARMER** enters stage right to center stage where **GUNNER** is already standing. The **FARMER** is a nice man who is fairly plain in looks and nature. The **FARMER** has a sack of apples.)*

**FARMER:**
Say there, Gunner, on your way home, are you?

**GUNNER:**
Yes, sir, I am.

**FARMER:**
You look mighty tired there, son. You must be happy all the fighting is finally over.

**GUNNER:**
Yes, sir, but to be truthful, I'm a bit sad as well.

**FARMER:**
Why is that?

**GUNNER:**
I'm a soldier. I make my living fighting in wars. Now I have no job and no money.

**FARMER:**
Huh. I never thought of it that way. But I'm sure you'll find something else soon. I'd offer you work myself, but I already have all the help I can afford. Still, will you take this sack of apples from my orchard? You can eat them on the way to wherever it is you're going.

**GUNNER:** (*Taking the sack of apples.*)
You're very kind. Yes, thank you, I'll enjoy the apples very much.

**FARMER:**
Thank *you*, son. Thank *you*.

(*The* **FARMER** *exits stage right.*)

**NARRATOR:**
And the farmer went back to picking his apples, and Gunner strolled on down the lane.

(**GUNNER** *crosses to the Forest Scene.*)

**NARRATOR:** (*Continued.*)
Moments later, the trees along each side of the road became thicker, almost blocking the sun out entirely.

(*An old* **HAG** *[the* **WITCH***] jumps out from behind the tree or into the Forest Scene stage right and startles* **GUNNER** *with her loud, harsh voice. The* **HAG/WITCH** *is evil and shrewish. She is ugly in both appearance and deportment. The* **HAG/WITCH** *has a rope in her hand.*)

**HAG:**
Boy! Soldier boy!

**GUNNER:** (*Stepping back.*)
Madame—what is it?

**HAG:**
I need . . .
(*Changing her train of thought after eyeing* **GUNNER***.*)
My, what a handsome soldier you are with your shiny boots and flashy sword.

**NARRATOR:**
On the other hand, the old hag was especially repulsive, with bulging eyes, a long crooked nose, several warts, and wild hair sticking out everywhere. Gunner would have preferred not to have looked at her at all, but he thought the woman might be alone and in need of help. So he stopped and let the hunched-over hag approach him.

**GUNNER:**
May I help you, madame?

**HAG:**
Why, yes you can.
(*Pointing to the tree.*)

Do you see this dead tree here? It's hollow and has a hole at the top. If you climb up the tree, you can then drop down inside. I have a rope. We can tie it around your waist and when you're ready, I'll pull you back up.

**GUNNER:**
What do I do at the bottom of the tree?

**HAG:**
You can find money down there. At the bottom of the tree is a wide tunnel that leads down under the earth. There should be a lamp and flint there to use in lighting your way. Follow the tunnel until you come to three doors. Behind the first door is a room with a large chest in it. On the chest sits a dog with eyes as big as cup saucers. He may growl at you, but you needn't be afraid.
*(Unfastening her apron and handing it to him.)*
Take my apron with you. Spread the apron on the floor and place the dog on it. Then you may take all the money you want from the chest, which is full of copper coins. If you like silver coins, go into the second room. On the chest in the second room is another big dog with eyes the size of dinner plates. He might bark at you and bare his teeth, but you needn't be afraid. Simply spread the apron on the ground again and put the dog on it. Then you may take all the silver coins you can carry. However, if you fancy gold coins, proceed to the third room. Inside on the chest is a huge dog with eyes nearly the size of water wheels. He will bristle and bark ferociously, but you needn't be afraid. Pick up the dog and place him on the apron and all the gold coins you desire are yours.

**GUNNER:**
It sounds too good to be true. But what do *you* want out of this?

**HAG:**
I want the tinder box my dear departed mother left down there. It's the only thing she ever owned, and I'd like to have it to remember her by.

**GUNNER:**
All right. Are you sure you wouldn't like any of the money?

**HAG:**
No, no—just the tinder box, please.

**GUNNER:**
Very well. Tie the rope around my waist and I'll go down and get your box.

*(The **HAG/WITCH** ties the rope around **GUNNER,** who will climb up/walk around the tree cutout.)*

**NARRATOR:**
Gunner hoisted himself up the tree and then lowered his body through the hole and down to the tree's hollow interior.

*(From behind the tree cutout, **GUNNER** unties himself and picks up a lamp.)*

**NARRATOR:** *(Continued.)*
There he found the tunnel and a lamp sitting on the ground nearby. Gunner had wondered if the old woman was just tricking him with her claims of riches waiting below. But there was the tunnel, and there was the lamp. So he thought she might be telling him the truth after all, and he decided to go on. He untied the rope from his waist, lit the lamp, and began walking through the dark tunnel until he came upon three doors.

*(The **COPPER DOG** enters the Forest Scene stage right. He [she] may move in a freestanding door or door frame with a cutout chest attached to the side. **GUNNER** will go through the door or frame when mentioned by the **NARRATOR**. The **COPPER DOG** is a likable, cool character.)*

**GUNNER:** *(Yelling back.)*
I see the doors!

**HAG:**
Good, good. Now go inside the first door!

**GUNNER:**
Wouldn't it save time to just go in the third door where the gold is and skip the copper and silver?

**HAG:**
No, you can't do that.

**GUNNER:**
Why not?

**HAG:**
Because that's the way it is. If you don't follow the rules, nothing will work.

**GUNNER:**
Well, it doesn't make much sense, but I'll do as you say!

*(**GUNNER** steps through the door.)*

**NARRATOR:**
Gunner walked through the first door, and in the room was a large chest with a dog resting on top of it with eyes as big as cup saucers.

**COPPER DOG:**
Grrrrrrrr . . .

**GUNNER:**
Whoa, fella. Easy there.

*(**GUNNER** spreads the apron on the floor on the other side of the chest that the **COPPER DOG** is sitting on [standing behind]. He then moves the **COPPER DOG** onto the apron as the **NARRATOR** speaks.)*

**NARRATOR:**
Gunner spread the old hag's apron on the ground and lifted the dog onto it. When he opened the chest, Gunner found it full of copper coins. Delighted, he quickly emptied his sack of apples and filled it with coins.

*(**GUNNER** acquires the copper coins from behind the chest.)*

**NARRATOR:** *(Continued.)*
He then picked up the apron and stepped back into the tunnel.

*(As **GUNNER** picks up the apron and steps back out in front of the door, the **COPPER DOG** exits stage right, while the **SILVER DOG** enters stage right and assumes the **COPPER DOG'S** position on top of the chest. The **SILVER DOG** is a likable, cool character.)*

**GUNNER:** *(Yelling back to the **HAG/WITCH**.)*
I have the copper coins!

**HAG:**
Wonderful. Now go through the second door.

**GUNNER:**
All right. It still doesn't make any sense, but—all right.

*(**GUNNER** steps back through the door.)*

**NARRATOR:**
So Gunner went into the second room and found a dog resting on top of a chest. This dog was bigger than the first, with eyes the size of dinner plates, and when he saw Gunner, he stood up on the chest growling and watching Gunner closely.

**SILVER DOG:**
Grrrrrrrr . . .

**GUNNER:**
All right, big laddie. I've got a nice apron here for you to lie on. You'll like the nice apron.

*(**GUNNER** spreads the apron on the floor on the other side of the chest that the **SILVER DOG** is sitting on [standing behind]. He then moves the **SILVER DOG** onto the apron as the **NARRATOR** speaks.)*

**NARRATOR:**
As before, Gunner spread out the apron and managed to lay the dog on it.

*(**GUNNER** acquires the silver coins from behind the chest.)*

**NARRATOR:** *(Continued.)*
In the chest were more silver coins than Gunner had ever seen and he happily emptied his sack of copper coins, along with his soldier's pouch, and filled them to the brim with silver coins. He then swept up the apron and flipped it over his shoulder while returning to the tunnel.

*(**GUNNER** steps back through the door. The **SILVER DOG** exits stage right, while the **GOLD DOG** enters stage right and assumes the **SILVER DOG'S** position. The **GOLD DOG** is a likable, cool character.)*

**GUNNER:** *(Yelling back to the **HAG/WITCH**.)*
I have all the silver coins I could want, old woman!

**HAG:**
Marvelous. You can go through the third door now!

**NARRATOR:**
By now Gunner had stopped questioning the old hag. So far, everything that she had told him would happen had happened. Joyfully he walked into the third room, ready to handle the dog inside.

*(**GUNNER** steps through the door.)*

**NARRATOR:** *(Continued.)*
But oh, what a frightening dog it was! The mutt stood as tall as Gunner, and although its eyes weren't quite the size of water wheels, they were big and round.

**GUNNER:** *(Saluting the dog—unconcerned.)*
Good afternoon big, ferocious doggy. How are you today?

**NARRATOR:**
Cheerfully Gunner busied himself. He spread the apron out and commanded the big dog to lie upon it.

*(**GUNNER** spreads the apron on the floor on the other side of the chest that the **GOLD DOG** is sitting on [standing behind]. He then points for the **GOLD DOG** to move onto the apron as the **NARRATOR** speaks.)*

**NARRATOR:** *(Continued.)*
Then he went over to the chest and loaded everything he had with gold coins. He stuffed his apple sack, soldier's pouch, boots, hat, and pockets with gold coins.

*(**GUNNER** acquires the gold coins from behind the chest.)*

**GUNNER:**
Gosh, all of this gold is heavy. I can barely move. I hope the old woman will be able to pull me up out of the tree. Wait, I promised to get that tinder box for her.
*(Looking around.)*
I wonder where it is.

*(**GUNNER** acquires the tinder box from behind the chest.)*

**NARRATOR:**
Gunner looked about and found a small metal tinder box sitting on a table in the corner of the room. It was a pretty little tinder box, elegantly painted and in good shape.

**GUNNER:** *(Picking up the box.)*
What a nice tinder box. I wouldn't mind owning it myself to use with my pipe. Oh well, it belongs to the old woman—I best get back above ground and give it to her.

*(The **GOLD DOG** exits stage right, taking the door with him [her]. **GUNNER** steps back behind the tree with the lamp and ties the rope around himself again.)*

**NARRATOR:**
With his work done, Gunner traveled back through the tunnel and tied the rope around his waist, ready to be hoisted up.

**GUNNER:**
I'm all finished down here. Help me out of this tree!

**HAG:**
Do you have my tinder box?

**GUNNER:**
Yes, ma'am. I have it.

**HAG:**
Good, I'll pull you up then.

*(The **HAG/WITCH** pulls on the rope from the other side of the tree.)*

**NARRATOR:**
As Gunner climbed down the outside of the tree, he thought it strange how anxious the old hag was to get her little tinder box.

*(**GUNNER** steps to the other side of the tree with the **HAG/WITCH** and begins to untie himself.)*

**HAG:**
My box—my box! Give me my box!

**GUNNER:** *(Handing the tinder box to the **HAG/WITCH**.)*
Here it is. It's a pretty little box. You can cherish the memory of your dear departed mother now.

**HAG:**
My mother? Oh, yes, my mother.
*(Laughing wildly.)*
You foolish man, I have no dear departed mother. This is *my* tinder box. I wanted it so badly because it's a magic box. And I'm not a poor old woman, I'm a witch! And now, with the magic tinder box in my hands, I'm a very powerful witch—so powerful, I can cast a spell on you and kill you!

**GUNNER:**
Wait a minute here . . .

**HAG:** *(Conjuring a spell.)*
Eyes of the wolf, teeth of the jaguar, I put this death spell . . .

**GUNNER:** *(Pulling out his sword.)*
WAIT!

**NARRATOR:**
Gunner had no time to lose. He had to act quickly before the Witch could finish her evil spell. Having no choice, Gunner drew his sword and chopped off the Witch's head.

*(The **HAG/WITCH** screams, ducks her head under her cape as if it has been cut off, and stumbles off stage right.)*

**NARRATOR:**
Though terribly upset by it all, Gunner managed to pull himself together. He picked up the tinder box the Witch had dropped and carried it into town.

*(**GUNNER** crosses to center stage into the Inn/House Scene.)*

**NARRATOR:** *(Continued.)*
It was quite late by the time he found a small roadside inn, but there were still people there eating and drinking, so Gunner went inside to inquire about lodgings for the night.

*(The **INNKEEPER** enters the Inn/House Scene stage right. The **INNKEEPER** is an ordinary person with a little busybody in her.)*

**GUNNER:**
Good evening, ma'am—might you have a room for me?

**INNKEEPER:** *(Not terribly thrilled to see him.)*
Aye, I have rooms, but not for returning soldiers with no money.

**GUNNER:** *(Pulling out a few gold coins from his pocket.)*
But I have money. See?

**INNKEEPER:** *(Now delighted.)*
Ooooo! Well, come in, come in! I can give you the best room at the inn.
*(The **INNKEEPER** takes the coins and leads **GUNNER** over to the table and chair setting.)*
Sit yourself right down, sir.
*(Moving the plate and stein nearer to **GUNNER**.)*
Have some sumptuous fruits and delicious meats. Drink? Would you like a good lager? Here, have all you want.

*(**GUNNER** eats and drinks while the **INNKEEPER** sits on the other side of the table and talks.)*

**INNKEEPER:** *(Continued.)*
You'll like it here. The countryside is beautiful, and so is our little town. Come daylight, I'll take you around and show you the sights. I'll also acquaint you with the merchants of the town. You'll be wanting to purchase new clothes and such. . . . Say, there's a lovely house for sale next door. Have you enough money to buy a house?

**GUNNER:**
I suspect I do.

**INNKEEPER:**
How marvelous. Of course, the most stupendous sight this region has to offer is the princess of the kingdom. Of Princess Ann, they say no man could ever want to feast his eyes on one so lovely and nice.

**GUNNER:**
Is there some way I can meet her?

**INNKEEPER:**
Oh, no. I'm afraid not. She's kept away from the public. Princess Ann spends all day behind the walls and gardens of the palace. Only the King and Queen are allowed to see her. But the princess is so modest, with a gentle and loving heart, it is said that she would be perfectly happy marrying a common soldier like yourself. Naturally, the King insists she marry a prince, or at least a duke or lord—royal blood, you know.

**GUNNER:**
That's too bad. I would've liked to have met the Princess if she's as lovely as you say.

*(**GUNNER** and the **INNKEEPER** rise and cross to stage left, over to stage right, and then back to center stage as the **NARRATOR** speaks.)*

**NARRATOR:**
The next day the Innkeeper escorted Gunner through town, where he spent his money freely. Soon the whole town was talking about the handsome young soldier who was so nice and rich. Gunner even bought the large house by the inn. He led a lively and happy life going to the theater and attending parties. He also gave a lot of his money to the poor because he remembered what it was like not to have money and to be hungry. But in the middle of all this gaiety, Gunner felt quite alone. Ever since the Innkeeper had told him about Princess Ann, Gunner couldn't stop thinking of the young woman. He wondered what she looked like and if she would speak to him if they ever met. If the Princess was as nice as they said, surely she wouldn't mind talking to him. Still, the people of the town were most willing to help Gunner spend his money while telling him how wonderful he was and what good friends they were. He liked that, but soon the gold coins were gone, and all the people who had called him their friend when he had money stopped coming around.

*(**GUNNER** sits at the table. The **INNKEEPER** exits stage right.)*

**NARRATOR:** *(Continued.)*
Gunner had to move out of his big house and into a small room at the inn. He mended his own clothes and cooked his own meals when he could scrape together enough to eat. He was cold and miserable. But he didn't blame anyone. He knew he had been fortunate to find the treasure and foolish to spend it all so quickly. One cold and lonely night, when things were looking pretty grim, Gunner remembered he had one candle left in his soldier's pouch. He took it out and also removed the tinder box he had taken from the Witch. He was going to create a spark to light his candle, but the moment he struck the box, his apartment door opened and there stood the Copper Dog.

*(The **COPPER DOG** enters the Inn/House Scene stage right.)*

**COPPER DOG:**
What does my master desire?

**GUNNER:** *(Standing, surprised.)*
You can speak! A dog that can speak—how remarkable.

**COPPER DOG:**
Not remarkable, Master—magic. The tinder box is a magic box. Strike it once, and I appear to do your bidding. Strike the box twice, and the Silver Dog will come to you. And when you strike the magic tinder box thrice, the Gold Dog will be here.

*(**GUNNER** takes the tinder box and strikes it twice, then three times. The **SILVER DOG** and **GOLD DOG** enter stage right to join **GUNNER** and the **COPPER DOG**.)*

**SILVER DOG** and **GOLD DOG:**
What does our master desire?

**GUNNER:**
Can you get me some more money, please?

*(All three **DOGS** pull out a sack from behind their backs. The **COPPER DOG'S** sack is marked "copper," the **SILVER DOG'S** sack is marked "silver," and the **GOLD DOG'S** sack is marked "gold.")*

**GUNNER:** *(Taking the sacks.)*
This is truly wonderful. I have money again. But I won't spend it foolishly like I did before, on friends who are only my friends when I'm rich. And I'll take good care of you fellows, too. I promise.

**SILVER DOG:**
Do you mean we won't have to live underground anymore?

**GUNNER:**
No, sir. You can come live with me. We'll get the house back. It's a nice big house. You'll like it.

**GOLD DOG:**
How kind of you.

*(The other **DOGS** agree.)*

**NARRATOR:**
And Gunner bought back his house and was able to afford expensive clothing and food again. All in all, it was a grand life, with everything he wanted, and he should have been quite happy and content.

(*GUNNER sits back at the table and chair setting. The DOGS sit on the floor in front of him.*)

**NARRATOR:** (*Continued.*)
But something was missing, and one night, as Gunner sat before the fireplace with his dogs resting at his feet, he tried to figure out what was wrong.

**GUNNER:**
I don't understand it. Here I am living in the lap of luxury. I have all the fine things I could possibly want, and all the townspeople seem to like and respect me. But somehow I don't feel any better off than when I was a common soldier.

**SILVER DOG:**
A common soldier like Princess Ann once said she could love and would like to marry?

**GUNNER:**
The princess! Yes, I just know the princess would like me for who I am and not what I have. Oh, if I could only be with her and talk with her for a while.

**GOLD DOG:**
I could get her for you, Gunner. Any of us could fetch her.

**GUNNER:**
But she's hidden away in the palace.

**GOLD DOG:**
You forget that we're magical dogs. We could bring her here on a cloud of magic.

**GUNNER:**
To be with the princess. That would be the best thing that could ever happen to me. Yes, do it. Go bring the princess to me—hurry!

(*The DOGS stand and exit stage left.*)

**NARRATOR:**
The magical dogs stood and, puff, they were off in a cloud of dust. Then, moments later, they returned with Princess Ann.

(*The DOGS enter stage left with PRINCESS ANN. PRINCESS ANN is a very nice, almost meek person. She is sincere and honest.*)

**PRINCESS ANN:**
Where am I? How did I get here?

**GUNNER:**
Please, don't be frightened. I mean you no harm. The last thing I would want to do is frighten you.

**PRINCESS ANN:**
Who are you?

**GUNNER:**
I'm just a soldier who wanted to meet you very much. They told me you were so lovely and kind, and I was so lonely. I thought you wouldn't mind sitting down and talking with me awhile.

**PRINCESS ANN:**
What's your name?

**GUNNER:**
My name? Why, it's . . . Oh, Princess, I don't remember my name. Everyone has called me Gunner for so long—no one has ever wanted to know my real name.

**PRINCESS ANN:**
You poor, lonely man. All right, I'll sit with you awhile, but you must promise to get me back to the palace before they discover I'm gone.

**GUNNER:**
Yes, I promise, Princess. Yes—thank you.

*(GUNNER offers PRINCESS ANN a seat. He sits and they talk and laugh under the NARRATOR'S words.)*

**NARRATOR:**
And so Gunner and Princess Ann sat by the warm fire and talked for hours on end. They talked of the kingdom, of the town, and of the flowers and trees. Gunner told her of the dogs and how he came upon his fortune and how, by magic, the Princess could be sitting in her bedroom one moment and at his side the next. And when it grew late, as promised, Gunner commanded the dogs to return the Princess to the palace.

*(GUNNER and PRINCESS ANN stand as do the DOGS.)*

**GUNNER:**
This was the most delightful evening of my entire life. Might you come again?

**PRINCESS ANN:**
Yes, I would like that very much.

*(GUNNER smiles and kisses PRINCESS ANN'S hand. Then the DOGS escort PRINCESS ANN back to the Palace Scene. The DOGS stop short of completely entering the Palace Scene, allowing PRINCESS ANN to go alone and meet her parents—the KING and QUEEN, who enter the Palace Scene stage left. The KING is pompous and egotistical. He likes to throw his weight around and believes the opinions of everyone else are wrong. The QUEEN is rather wimpish and indecisive. She cowers and whimpers at the KING'S command.)*

**KING:**
Where have you been, young lady?!

**PRINCESS ANN:**
I was carried away by magical dogs to meet a young soldier in the town. Oh, Mama, he's so handsome and nice. My heart is beating so. I've fallen in love with him!

**QUEEN:**
Fallen in love? Oh, my. Oh, dear.

**KING:**
You can't be in love. I won't allow it. To be in love with a common soldier. Of all things!

**PRINCESS ANN:**
What difference does it make whether he's a common soldier or a king, as long as he's a good man and I love him?

**KING:**
It makes all the difference in the world! Because you're a princess. Because it's just not done!

**QUEEN:**
Who is this man? What's his name?

**PRINCESS ANN:**
I don't know his name. All I know is that I love him and I'm going to see him again tomorrow night.

**KING:**
Oh, no you're not. I forbid it!

**PRINCESS ANN:**
You can't stop me, Father. Even if you lock me in the highest room of the palace with 100 guards outside my door, his magical dogs will appear in a puff of smoke and take me away. You just wait and see.

(*PRINCESS ANN* storms offstage left in a huff.)

**QUEEN:**
Oh, dear. What will we do?

**KING:**
Tomorrow night we'll hide and wait for the dogs to come. Then we'll follow them and find out where this man lives. We'll mark his door with a white X. Come the morning, I can send my guards to find the door marked with the X and have them arrest the man who lives at that house. Yes, that should work. When they bring this soldier to me, I'll hang him, I will. We haven't had a good public hanging in a long time.

**QUEEN:**
Isn't hanging the man a little drastic, dear? Our darling Ann won't like you anymore if you hang the man she loves.

**KING:**
She'll get over it.

(The *KING* and *QUEEN* crouch down as if hiding from sight.)

[The *KING* grabs a bucket with a paintbrush in it as they crouch far downstage left.]

(The *DOGS* cross back to the Palace Scene as *PRINCESS ANN* reenters the Palace Scene. Then the dogs take *PRINCESS ANN* back to center stage with *GUNNER* as the *NARRATOR* speaks. They sit again and talk. At this time, the *KING* and *QUEEN* follow behind, but stay a distance to the left of center stage.)

**NARRATOR:**
The next night the magical dogs came back for Princess Ann. As soon as they began to sail away on their cloud of magic, the King and Queen followed, until all came to the center of town where Gunner's house was.

**QUEEN:**
So that's where this young man lives. It's a very nice house, dear. Maybe this man would be a good husband for our Ann. Shouldn't we at least get to know him before we hang him?

**KING:**
He's not of royal blood—it's quite impossible.

**QUEEN:**
But . . .

**KING:**
No "buts!"

*(The **KING** takes a step forward, dips the paintbrush in the bucket, and paints a large X on an imaginary door. Before he does so, the **DOGS** come around from the right and watch.)*

**NARRATOR:**
The King stepped up and marked Gunner's door with a big white X. Then he took the Queen back to the palace with him, confident his guards would find the house in the morning.

**COPPER DOG:**
Why do you suppose the King marked our master's door like that?

**SILVER DOG:**
I don't know, but I don't like it.

**GOLD DOG:**
Neither do I.

**COPPER DOG:**
What do we do?

**SILVER DOG:**
Let's mark all the doors in town with a big white X. Then no one will be able to tell our master's house from any of the others.

**GOLD DOG:**
Excellent idea.

**SILVER DOG:**
Why, thank you.

*(The **DOGS** cross stage right and retrieve buckets with paintbrushes from behind the Inn/House Scene and return to paint Xs on imaginary doors. Meanwhile, **GUNNER** stands and takes **PRINCESS ANN'S** hand once again.)*

**GUNNER:**
Princess, I so enjoyed myself. It's as if all the happiness in the world is mine when you're with me.

**PRINCESS ANN:**
I know, Gunner. I have never known such happiness myself. I must admit, though, it seems a trifle odd to call you Gunner and not by your real name.

**GUNNER:**
Well, what name do you like?

**PRINCESS ANN:**
I've always liked the name Hendrick.

**GUNNER:**
Then my name will be Hendrick, just for you.

*(**PRINCESS ANN** smiles and kisses **GUNNER** on the cheek. The **DOGS** reenter the Inn/House Scene and escort **PRINCESS ANN** stage left to the Palace Scene.)*

**NARRATOR:**
The next morning, the King and Queen hurried into town with the Guards to arrest the man who lived behind the door marked with the X.

*(The **KING**, **QUEEN**, and **GUARDS** step to just left of center stage. The **GUARDS** are nondescript. They do what they are told up to a point.)*

**KING:**
There! There's the door, men. Go arrest that man!

**QUEEN:**
But wait . . .
*(Pointing.)*
That door has an X painted on it, too . . . And that door, and that one.

**KING:**
What is this?

**QUEEN:**
Oh, dear. What do we do now?

**KING:**
We'll go back to the palace and insist Ann give us this man's name. It's against her nature to lie. If she knows his name, she'll tell us.

*(The **KING**, **QUEEN** and **GUARDS** cross back to the Palace Scene where **PRINCESS ANN** is waiting.)*

**KING:**
Ann, we insist you tell us that soldier's name!

**QUEEN:**
Yes, darling. If you're in love with this man, it would be nice for us to know his name.

**PRINCESS ANN:**
His name is Hendrick, Mother.

**KING:**
Success!
*(The **KING** turns so that he's yelling in the **GUARDS'** faces.)*
Guards!—Oh. . . . Go bring me every man in town whose name is Hendrick.

*(The **GUARDS** cross to stage right, then back to stage left and the Palace Scene.)*

**NARRATOR:**
The Guards busily rounded up all the men in the town named Hendrick. But when the King lined them all up and asked Princess Ann to pick out her Hendrick, she couldn't for he wasn't there. The townspeople only knew the handsome young soldier as Gunner, so when the Guards hunted down Hendricks, Gunner wasn't one of them.

_(The **GUARDS** and **PRINCESS ANN** exit stage left.)_

**KING:**
Foiled again. What are we to do?

**QUEEN:**
I have an idea. I'll fill a small cloth bag with flour and sew it into Ann's gown. If I poke a little hole in the bag, it should leave a trail of flour behind. We can follow the trail of flour, and it will lead us to the soldier.

**KING:**
Inspirational! How clever of you, my dear. Yes, quite clever. We'll do it!

_(The **KING** and **QUEEN** exit downstage left as **PRINCESS ANN** enters the Palace Scene upstage right. The **DOGS** cross to take **PRINCESS ANN** to the Inn / House Scene once again.)_

**NARRATOR:**
That night, just like the past two nights, the dogs appeared and carried Princess Ann away on their cloud of magic. But this time, the King and Queen followed the trail of flour left behind by Ann and went straight to Gunner's house.

_(The **KING**, **QUEEN**, and **GUARDS** enter upstage right and cross to slightly left of center stage.)_

**KING:**
The flour trail leads to that house. We've got him now, men. Go arrest the man inside that house!

_(The **GUARDS** pantomime breaking down the door. They then rush over and seize **GUNNER** on either side and drag him over to the **KING** despite **PRINCESS ANN'S** protest.)_

**KING:**
Think you're so smart, eh, with your magic dogs? Well, we've got you now.

**PRINCESS ANN:**
Father, don't! I love him!

**GUNNER:**
I love you, too, my darling Ann.

**KING:**
Take him to the public square and hang him immediately!

_(The **GUARDS** take **GUNNER** and stand him on top of the box. One **GUARD** removes a noose that has been hanging from his back pocket and places it over **GUNNER'S** head. As he does this, the **DOGS**, **FARMER**, and **INNKEEPER** enter to form the crowd.)_

**FARMER:**
You can't hang this man. What has he done?

**QUEEN:**
He's fallen in love with the princess.

**INNKEEPER:**
That's a crime punishable by hanging?

**PRINCESS ANN:**
Father, I beg you, please don't do this.

**FARMER:**
You're not a fair sovereign if you hang this man, Sire. And if you're not a fair sovereign, you shouldn't be king.

**INNKEEPER:**
The farmer's right.

*(Everyone agrees except the **KING**.)*

**KING:**
Enough with all of you. Hang this man right now. That's a royal command!

*(The **GUARDS** look at the **KING**, then at one another, then at **GUNNER**, then back to the **KING**, and shake their heads "no.")*

**KING:**
If you don't hang this man instantly, I'll hang you too.

**COPPER DOG** and **SILVER DOG** and **GOLD DOG:**
No, you won't!

**NARRATOR:**
Using all their magic, the dogs cast a spell on the King and sent him spinning high in the air.

*(The **KING** spins offstage right.)*

**NARRATOR:** *(Continued.)*
And the Guards released Gunner, to everyone's delight.

*(All cheer while **PRINCESS ANN** takes **GUNNER** over to the **QUEEN**.)*

**PRINCESS ANN:**
Mother, this is my Hendrick. I want to marry him.

**GUNNER:**
Yes, please. I love Ann very much and promise to make her happy.

**QUEEN:**
Oh, my. Oh, dear. But the princess can only marry a king.

**FARMER:**
So make him king.

**INNKEEPER:**
Yes. He's been a good and giving man to everyone in this town. Gunner deserves to be king. We all want him to be our king!

*(All agree.)*

**QUEEN:**
Well, that *would* solve the problem, wouldn't it?

*(**GUNNER** and **PRINCESS ANN** position themselves center stage. The **DOGS**, **QUEEN**, and **GUARDS** stand in the Palace Scene, and the **FARMER** and **INNKEEPER** stand in the Forest Scene where the **HAG/WITCH** will also enter and stand towards the end of the **NARRATOR'S** final words.)*

**NARRATOR:**
So Gunner became king and married Princess Ann. He was a good king who ruled wisely and fairly, and the kingdom flourished. He gave the Innkeeper his house so that she might expand her inn, and he made the Farmer the royal provider of apples for the palace. Princess Ann loved her handsome soldier very much because, even though Gunner was kept busy with the affairs of the land, he managed to find time every night to sit and talk with his lovely wife while the dogs rested peacefully at their feet. The Queen was content, knowing her daughter was happy, although she did peer into the sky every now and then to see if she could catch a glimpse of her husband, who had been seen from time to time tossing and turning over a hillside or church steeple.

*(The **KING** tumbles back in stage right and exits behind everyone stage left, but will reappear downstage left in the Palace Scene for curtain call.)*

**NARRATOR:** *(Continued.)*
And—oh, yes . . . In a room under heavy guard stood a small table. And on the table, placed ever so carefully and respectfully, was a small, elegantly painted, metal tinder box.

*(Curtain.)*

END OF THE TINDER BOX

CASINGS

# Casings

*A Space Yarn by Joan Garner*

## CAST OF CHARACTERS (m=male   f=female)

| | | | |
|---|---|---|---|
| NARRATOR (m/f) | PROFESSOR (f) | DIAMONDO (m/f) | COMMANDER (m) |
| CAPTAIN (m) | RUBY (f) | ZEPS (f) | DE MORA (f) |
| VIC (m) | EMERALDO (m/f) | SHALON (f) | |

## CHARACTER AND COSTUME DESCRIPTIONS

**CAPTAIN:** The Captain is your typical hero type, courageous, nice, and so on. The Captain wears a shirt and fatigue pants of matching color (preferably gray, black, or tan) with black combat/hiking boots. Star Fighter insignia on chest and upper arm sleeve.

**VIC:** Vic is an easygoing fellow, confident in his abilities and always willing to help. Vic wears mechanic's coveralls with a futuristic space emblem on the sleeve, a cap, and a greasy rag sticking out of his back pocket. Combat/hiking boots.

**PROFESSOR:** The Professor is somewhat absent-minded and is almost entirely focused on her solarium, but nice. The Professor wears a pant-suit or blouse and pants with a lab coat over them. Thick glasses and regular shoes.

**RUBY:** Ruby is a cool Olak—uptown, if you will. Ruby's costume may consist of a red blouse, pants, and socks with a piece of metallic red material draped over a shoulder. Long red wig and small, red-lensed glasses.

**EMERALDO:** Emeraldo is also a cool Olak. Emeraldo's costume may consist of a green blouse, pants, and socks with a piece of metallic green material draped over a shoulder. Long green wig and green-lensed glasses.

**DIAMONDO:** Diamondo is also a cool Olak. Diamondo's costume may consist of a white blouse, pants, and socks with a piece of metallic white material draped over a shoulder. Long, white wig and clear-lensed, underwater goggles.

**ZEPS:** Zeps is a salesperson, eager and a bit pushy. Zeps's costume can be a grab bag of fashion and should be as colorful as possible.

**SHALON:** Shalon is a nice, modern young woman who knows her mind, but isn't entirely turned off by the fairy tale/knight-on-a-white-horse dream. Shalon wears a nice sweater and skirt with a few decorations to suggest a futuristic style. Knee-high boots.

**COMMANDER:** The Commander is commanding and stern but fair. The Commander wears an outfit similar to the Captain's, but it should be of another color, and the emblem on the chest should be different. Black combat boots.

**DE MORA:** De Mora is a good mother and a loving wife, but probably has a high-paying, responsible job as well. De Mora also wears a nice sweater, skirt or slacks, and a blazer adorned with futuristic decorations. Knee-high boots.

## Scene Design for *Casings*

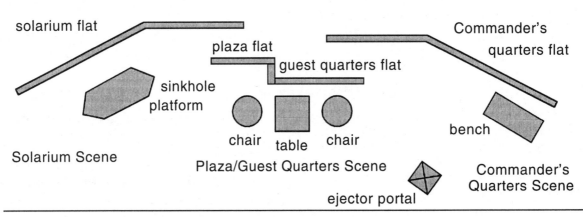

### SET

Because this play takes place inside a space station, specific breaks in the depiction of each scene area are not required (e.g., an outside forest scene as opposed to an indoor house scene). Therefore, it is suggested that a stage of continuous space station walls be constructed, and that these walls have windows that look out into a black outer space spattered with stars. And because the space station is supposed to be above Saturn, the planet should be shown somewhere in the windows. It is suggested that Saturn be seen through the windows of the Commander's Quarters because there isn't a great deal of action at stage left, so Saturn can be easily visible. A three-dimensional set of pipes and exposed I beams would suit this play the best, but such things can be simply painted onto a one-dimensional flat. [The table can be very small and round, and the two chairs can be small stools. This can make things very simple and save space, but the style of chair and table should also reflect a modern/futuristic flavor.]

### PROPS

spoon, medicine bottle, rubies, emeralds, diamonds, casings belt, plate, glass.

### AS A STUDY LESSON

Character development can be explored by taking *The Tinder Box* and *Casings* as two acting exercises. The plays parallel, and for every part in *The Tinder Box*, there is a corresponding part in *Casings*. By having the beginning actors play both parts (e.g., Gunner and the Captain), the actors will learn how to further separate their own personalities from the characters they are portraying, and their skill in creating two distinct personalities and performances for two similar characters will also be challenged.

### AS PERFORMANCE

Like *The Tinder Box*, this play will be best received by children, peers, and parents. Because the setting is outer space, it should have extra appeal to the younger set and prove to be an excellent road show.

Also, this play offers a refreshing new angle in producing a familiar story.

## CONSIDERATIONS, EFFECTS, AND AFFECTS

Because the location of this play is a factual space location—Saturn—and the time that the play occurs is not that far off—2084—costumes and sets do not have to be that different from those in the array of science fiction programs that are currently on film and television. In fact, similarity in style and design to these shows should help establish instant familiarity for the audience.

The sinkhole need only be a platform that the Captain can stand on, then jump down behind. He may then crawl some to the right before standing.

When he stands, an Olak can enter and sit to the side. If the Olak brings in a large beanbag chair to rest on (red for ruby, green for emerald, white for diamond), it will help convey the pile of gems the Olak is supposed to be sitting on. The narration will assist in establishing the area as the cavern.

Other nondefined areas (e.g., the repair shop, walking through the plaza) may be staged downstage in front of the stationary set.

# Casings

**SET:** The set consists of three stationary scenes:
1) At stage right is the Solarium Scene. Windows looking out into space are on the background flat, and a platform for the sinkhole is in front of it. Flowers and plants should be all about.
2) At center stage is the Plaza/Guest Quarters Scene. The right side of the flat should show the plaza; the left side should show the guest quarters. A small table and two chairs sits in front.
3) At stage left is the Commander's Quarters Scene. The back flat should also have windows looking out into space and at Saturn. A bench of some sort should be in front of it.

**AT RISE:**
Morning, the year 2084. The Star Relief Space Station above Saturn.

**NARRATOR:**
In the year 2084, a great war is being waged above the planet Saturn. The space colonies of Saturn's Northern Hemisphere have been at odds with the space colonies of the Southern Hemisphere as to which has territorial rights over the particle rings around the planet. On this day, a fierce spaceship dogfight has occurred between the Star Fighter Fleet of the Northern Hemisphere and the Devil Fighter Fleet of the Southern Hemisphere. A casualty of this great battle was the Captain's Class A Star Fighter ship, which sustained heavy damage. The Captain managed to guide his ship back to the Star Relief Space Station before the fighter ship broke down completely, and after hearing what repairs were needed, the Captain thought the situation looked pretty grim.

*(The **CAPTAIN** and **VIC** enter and cross to stand center stage. The **CAPTAIN** is your typical hero type, courageous, nice, and so on. **VIC** is an easygoing fellow, confident in his abilities and always willing to help.)*

**CAPTAIN:**
So what do you think, Vic? You're the best mechanic we have. If you can't fix my Star Fighter, no one can.

**VIC:**
I don't know, Captain. Your hydraulic system is shot, and half your fuel ejection system is fried.

**CAPTAIN:**
What will it take?

**VIC:**
A miracle. Basically, you have a piece of junk here, Cap. I'm afraid this baby isn't going anywhere any time soon.

**CAPTAIN:**
What am I supposed to do without my ship?

**VIC:**
Relax and take a nice vacation. It's going to be at least two weeks before your Fighter will be ready to fly again.

**CAPTAIN:**
Two weeks? What do I do on a relief station for two weeks? How boring.

**VIC:**

It's not so bad, Captain. Say, if you want to see the sights, take in the Commander's daughter. She's really something—and *unmarried*.

**CAPTAIN:**

Thank you, but I was thinking more of something like the mountains of Earth for my vacation. You know, forests and trees. I haven't seen a tree in five years.

**VIC:**

Hey, we have a solarium on Deck 3. It has trees and flowers—all that. Be cautious of the Professor there, though. She can grow posies like crazy, but she's a little weird, if you know what I mean.

**CAPTAIN:**

Thanks, I'll do that.

*(VIC exits stage left, while the CAPTAIN crosses over to the Solarium Scene. He comes upon the PROFESSOR, who has entered stage right. The PROFESSOR is somewhat absent minded and almost entirely focused on her solarium, but nice. The PROFESSOR has a large spoon in her hand. She feeds a spoonful of medicine to the flowers.)*

**PROFESSOR:**

Come along, dearies, take your medicine like good little geraniums so you can grow up big and pretty.

**CAPTAIN:**

Excuse me, are you the Professor?

**PROFESSOR:**

I surely hope so.

**CAPTAIN:**

Vic, the mechanic, told me I could visit here for a while.

**PROFESSOR:**

I guess that would be all right—just don't pick any of my flowers.

**CAPTAIN:**

Yes, ma'am—I mean, no ma'am, I won't.

**PROFESSOR:**

Say, maybe you can help me. I was at this sinkhole yesterday to see if it had grown any bigger when I dropped my casings of chemicals and plant food down it. There's an entire series of caverns underneath this ground, you know, and they say there are precious gems down there. You could collect some rubies and diamonds and become a very rich man.

**CAPTAIN:**

If there are diamonds down there, why hasn't anyone taken them already?

**PROFESSOR:**

Well, there's a slight problem in getting to them. Actually, they belong to the Olaks who live down there. They're furry things with big eyes.

**CAPTAIN:**

So, will I have to kill them to get the jewels? Forget it if I have to do that.

**PROFESSOR:**
I wouldn't know. It's a curious thing. Several people have gone down there to seek their fortune, but no one has ever returned. Now this makes me believe that these Olaks are very good at their job, or that they're especially fond of having fresh humans for dinner, if you catch my drift.

**CAPTAIN:**
Then what makes you think I'll be successful retrieving the diamonds?

**PROFESSOR:**
Because I think everyone who has gone down has just tried to steal the precious gems. I don't think anyone has ever bothered to talk with the Olaks. They may be *nice* things. I don't know. They've left me alone for years. Naturally, if someone tries to take what doesn't belong to them, there will be objections. Perhaps if you don't try to take any of the jewels and just go down to fetch my casings, they won't mind.

**CAPTAIN:**
Well, all right. I guess I could do that. I'm curious to meet these Olaks, now that you've described them to me.

**PROFESSOR:**
Oh, thank you, son—bless you.

**CAPTAIN:**
I'll need a flashlight or something . . .

**PROFESSOR:**
No, that's not necessary. The Olaks have equipped the caverns with indirect lighting.

**CAPTAIN:**
Good. See you later.

(*The **PROFESSOR** steps to the side of the Solarium Scene and tends to a few plants while the **CAPTAIN** climbs onto the platform and jumps down behind it. He will fully disappear behind the platform and eventually crawl out to the right of it to meet **RUBY**, who will enter stage right with her red beanbag chair, plop it down, and sit on it. All of this will be done upon the **NARRATOR'S** cue. **RUBY** is a cool Olak—uptown, if you will.*)

**NARRATOR:**
The Captain jumped into the sinkhole and crawled through a small opening until he was deep in the caverns underneath the ground. He then came to a large open space the size of a sports arena. There were several beautifully colored stalagmites coming up from the floor and stalactites hanging down from the ceiling, making the room appear magical and wondrous, and along the walls were three slim crevasses covered with curtains. The Captain stepped to the first curtain, which sparkled with red metallic glitters.

**CAPTAIN:** (*Yelling back.*)
Professor, I see a red curtain!

**PROFESSOR:**
That's where the ruby Olak lives. Go on in!

(***RUBY** should now be sitting on her chair. The **CAPTAIN** pantomimes opening the curtain and stepping inside.*)

**NARRATOR:**
The Captain stepped behind the red curtain to find a large cavern with a pile of rubies before him. And at the base of this pile sat an interesting creature—all furry, like the Professor said, with red, glowing eyes.

**RUBY:** *(Leery.)*
Hey, man, what do you want?

**CAPTAIN:**
Good morning. I'm looking for the Professor's casings. She said she dropped them down here yesterday.

**RUBY:**
Yeah, I've seen them around somewhere. . . . Are you sure you're not after my rubies?

**CAPTAIN:**
No, ma'am. They're beautiful rubies to be sure—stunning—and I'd certainly like to have a few, but they're not mine to have. So I'll just look for the Professor's casings if that's all right with you.

**RUBY:**
That's original. Are you *sure* you're not here to steal my rubies?

**CAPTAIN:**
Yes, ma'am.

**RUBY:**
But you'd like some, I bet.

**CAPTAIN:**
Well, sure. Who wouldn't?

**RUBY:**
Then take a few.

**CAPTAIN:**
Are you sure? You're not going to do anything to me if I take a couple, are you? I don't especially relish being your dinner.

**RUBY:**
Who says I'd have you for dinner?

**CAPTAIN:**
It's been rumored.

**RUBY:**
Far out. No, go ahead.

**CAPTAIN:** *(Taking a handful of gems [from a pocket in the chair] and putting them in his breast pocket.)*
Thank you. This is very generous of you.

**RUBY:**
Are you still going to look for the Professor's casings?

**CAPTAIN:**
Sure. It's what I came down for.

**RUBY:**
Maybe I better come along and square you with the others.

**CAPTAIN:**
Do you mean the emerald and diamond Olaks?

**RUBY:**
Right. They're not quite the sweetheart I am.

**CAPTAIN:**
That would be very nice of you. Thank you, Olak.

**RUBY:**
Call me Ruby—everybody does.

*(The emerald Olak known as* **EMERALDO** *enters stage right and plops down his green beanbag chair just beyond* **RUBY'S** *chair.* **EMERALDO** *is also a cool Olak.)*

**NARRATOR:**
The ruby Olak led the Captain to the green curtain that sparkled with green glitter and took him inside to another cavern filled high with dazzling emeralds. And at the bottom of the emerald pile sat an Olak with green eyes.

**EMERALDO:**
Hey, Ruby, what's happening?

**RUBY:**
This dude is looking for the Professor's casings—you seen them?

**EMERALDO:**
Not in here, man—only emeralds.

**RUBY:**
Why don't you give the Captain here some of your emeralds?

**CAPTAIN:**
May I?

**EMERALDO:**
You mean you're not going to just steal them?

**RUBY:**
No, he's not like the others. It's cool.

**EMERALDO:**
Go ahead, then. I have plenty. Fill your pockets up.

**CAPTAIN:**
Thanks. This is great. You guys are all right.

**EMERALDO:**
What did you expect? That we were going to eat you or something?

**CAPTAIN:** *(Looking very concerned.)*
Well. . . .

**RUBY:**
He's just joking—thinks he's a stand-up comic.

**CAPTAIN:**
Oh—yeah—funny.

**EMERALDO:** *(Knowing he wasn't funny.)*
I'll work on it.

*(The **CAPTAIN** fills his pockets with emeralds [from a pocket in the green beanbag chair].)*

**RUBY:**
We're going over to see if Diamondo has the Professor's casings. You want to come along?

**EMERALDO:**
Why not? There's nothing else to do down here.
*(Shaking the **CAPTAIN'S** hand.)*
The name's Emeraldo, Captain.

**CAPTAIN:**
Nice to meet you.

**NARRATOR:**
The Captain followed Ruby and Emeraldo to the last crevasse with the white curtain that sparkled with silver glitter. Inside was a huge cavern, and there at the base of a mountain of diamonds rested a big Olak with white eyes.

*(The diamond Olak, **DIAMONDO**, enters stage right and plops his white beanbag chair down just beyond the green one. **DIAMONDO** is another cool Olak.)*

**RUBY:**
Diamondo, this is the Captain. Captain, Diamondo.

**DIAMONDO:**
Hey, man, where's it at?

**CAPTAIN:**
We don't know. We thought maybe you did.

**DIAMONDO:**
No, man—I mean, how do you do?

**CAPTAIN:**
Oh, fine, thank you. We were wondering if you've seen the Professor's casings?

**DIAMONDO:**
Yeah, I've got them over there in the corner. They fell in a mud puddle, and I fished them out and put 'em in here so they wouldn't get ruined.

**EMERALDO:**
That's nice and considerate of you, 'Mondo—nice and considerate.

**DIAMONDO:**
We all do our part.

(***RUBY*** *steps to the edge of the solarium flat and retrieves the casings from behind it.*)

**RUBY:**
Here you go, Captain, the Professor's casings.

**CAPTAIN:**
Great. Thank you. I'll be leaving now.

**DIAMONDO:**
Do you mean to tell me that you came in here with all these diamonds and now you're leaving without any?

**CAPTAIN:**
They're *your* diamonds, not mine. I'd love to have a few, but not without your permission.

**DIAMONDO:**
Radical. Go on, then—load up on all the diamonds you want.

**CAPTAIN:**
That's very kind. Thanks.

**DIAMONDO:**
Well, you know how it is. Most of the time, all you have to do is ask.

**CAPTAIN:** (*Pocketing some diamonds [found in a pocket on the white chair].*)
I'm beginning to find that out . . . Well, it was nice meeting you.

**EMERALDO:**
Likewise, man. You come back and see us. It gets lonely with just us three down here.

**CAPTAIN:**
I'll do that. Thanks again.

(*The* ***OLAKS*** *exit stage right with their beanbag chairs, while the* ***CAPTAIN*** *crawls back behind the platform, then climbs up to stand on it.*)

**CAPTAIN:**
Here are your casings, Professor. You were right, those Olaks are great guys if you just take the time to get to know them. Look, they gave me some of their precious gemstones—just gave them to me.

**PROFESSOR:**
Well, what do you know about that? I guess it's true what they say—"a little kindness and understanding can go a long way." So, let's see if the compounds in these casings are still good. There's no telling what could happen should some of these chemical get mixed together.
(*The* ***PROFESSOR*** *looks in a casing and sneezes.*)
Gosh, I guess maybe . . .
(*Ah-choo!*)
I—uh—I didn't think . . .
(*Ah-choo!*)
Something must have . . .
(*Ah-choo!*)
Oh, dear. Excuse me, Captain . . .

*(The **PROFESSOR** continues to sneeze and exits stage right with the casings.)*

**NARRATOR:**
Not knowing what to do for the Professor, and feeling hungry, the Captain left the solarium and went up to Deck 1 to the People's Plaza—a plaza filled with restaurants and shops. There he came upon the Plaza host, a friendly little woman called Zeps from the planet Uranus.

*(The **CAPTAIN** crosses over to the Plaza / Guest Quarters Scene as **ZEPS** enters stage left. **ZEPS** is a salesperson, eager and a bit pushy.)*

**ZEPS:**
Hello, Captain. Is there something I can get for you?

**CAPTAIN:**
Yes, I'd like something to eat, please.

**ZEPS:**
Oh, we have a variety of foods to fit your fancy as long as you have money to pay for it. You fly-boys always come around without any money.

**CAPTAIN:**
Would you take a ruby?

**ZEPS:**
You have rubies?

**CAPTAIN:** *(Pulling some rubies out of his pocket.)*
I have a few.

**ZEPS:** *(Taking a ruby and eyeing it carefully.)*
Well, we'll be glad to accommodate you, Captain. Come sit yourself down and have a bite.

*(**ZEPS** leads the **CAPTAIN** over to the table and chair setting. The **CAPTAIN** sits.)*

**ZEPS:**
Our special today is Neptune squid.

**CAPTAIN:**
That sounds fine.

*(**ZEPS** moves the plate over to the **CAPTAIN**, who eats. **ZEPS** sits on the other side of the table.)*

**ZEPS:**
You'll be wanting a room. I have a luxury suite just behind us. It's big and spacious—you'll love it. You need a haircut—there's a good barber around the corner—and you'll definitely want to be getting out of that flying suit. I can fix you up in that department as well. For entertainment, there's a wonderful stellar band in the Luna Lounge, and if it's female companionship you desire, the infirmary is loaded with pretty doctors and nurses who would just love to meet a handsome Star Fighter pilot like yourself.

**CAPTAIN:**
I've been told of the Commander's daughter.

**ZEPS:**
Oh my, yes—Shalon. She's a lovely young woman—and nice . . . Lovely, simply lovely. But you might have a problem meeting her. The Commander doesn't like her associating with you fly-boys. I suppose he figures none of you will be around long enough to form a lasting relationship—always flying off to battle or elsewhere.

**CAPTAIN:**
I don't know, I may stay around for a while. I just met three cool Olaks.

**ZEPS:**
You were with the Olaks and they didn't tear you limb from limb and eject you out the ejector portal with the garbage?

**CAPTAIN:**
No. I think they like me.

**ZEPS:**
Well, my respect for you is growing by the minute, Captain. Come along and I'll show you those guest quarters.

*(Enter the **PROFESSOR** stage right.)*

**PROFESSOR:**
Oh, Captain, I'm glad I found you.
*(Ah-choo!)*
I've been sneezing like crazy ever since you gave me back my casings.
*(Ah-choo!)*
I thought you might like to have them, since they seemed to have brought you luck and me nothing but misery.
*(Ah-choo!)*

**CAPTAIN:** *(Taking the casings.)*
Thank you, Professor. They *did* bring me luck, didn't they?

**PROFESSOR:**
Good. Take them and be happy—just so I can stop sneezing my head off.

*(The **PROFESSOR** exits sneezing stage right. **ZEPS** and the **CAPTAIN** cross a little to the right, after the **PROFESSOR**, then back to the Plaza/Guest Quarters Scene.)*

**NARRATOR:**
Zeps escorted the Captain around, ending up at the guest quarters.

**ZEPS:**
Here you go—the guest quarters. What did I tell you? Pretty nice, huh?

**CAPTAIN:**
Very nice. I'll take it. How much.

**ZEPS:**
Uhhhh—*three* rubies?

**CAPTAIN:** *(Taking a diamond out of his pocket.)*
How about a diamond?

**ZEPS:** *(Taking the diamond.)*
Better yet. Those Olaks *were* good to you, weren't they? Enjoy, Captain, enjoy.

*(**ZEPS** exits stage left.)*

**NARRATOR:**
The Captain spent the rest of the day around the People's Plaza spending his precious gemstones. He was beginning to enjoy his vacation and even attended a party in the Luna Lounge. That evening, when he returned to the guest quarters, he spotted the casings lying on the table and fondly remembered the Olaks.

**CAPTAIN:**
I miss those guys. I wish they were with me now. I'll have to go down there and see them. I'll do that tomorrow for sure.

*(The **OLAKS** enter stage right and cross to the Plaza/Guest Quarters Scene. **RUBY** pantomimes knocking on the **CAPTAIN'S** door.)*

**CAPTAIN:**
Come in.

*(**EMERALDO** pantomimes opening the door and the three poke their heads in smiling. The **CAPTAIN** rises upon seeing them.)*

**CAPTAIN:**
Hey, guys—I was just thinking of you.

**DIAMONDO:**
We know.

**CAPTAIN:**
Gosh, it's good to see you—come in.

*(The **OLAKS** gather around the table.)*

**CAPTAIN:**
How did you know I was thinking of you?

**DIAMONDO:**
Oh, we have our ways.

**EMERALDO:**
Yes. We're exceptional Olaks.

**CAPTAIN:**
I'm finding that out. You certainly helped me out by giving me some of your precious gems. I was able to get these luxury quarters with a diamond.

**EMERALDO:**
Our rubies and emeralds and diamonds can get things like this?

**CAPTAIN:**
Just about anything you want.

**RUBY:**
Huh—what do you know about that?

**CAPTAIN:**
Except all the dazzling jewels in the universe can't get me the one thing I'd really like.

**EMERALDO:**
Really? What would that be?

**CAPTAIN:**
I'd really like to meet the Commander's daughter, Shalon.

**DIAMONDO:**
Oh, right—Shalon—hot.

**EMERALDO:**
Beyond hot—extreme.

**DIAMONDO:**
Extreme.

**RUBY:**
And nice.

**CAPTAIN:**
Do you know her?

**EMERALDO:**
Oh, sure. We like Shalon a lot. She's the only other human besides yourself who's ventured down to the caverns to visit us without trying to steal our emeralds . . .

**RUBY:**
. . . and rubies . . .

**DIAMONDO:**
. . . and diamonds.

**CAPTAIN:**
Do you think. . . ? No, I suppose not.

**DIAMONDO:**
Suppose not, get not. What's on your mind?

**CAPTAIN:**
Well, do you think you might introduce me to her?

**RUBY:**
Sure. No sweat.

**EMERALDO:**
We'll go get her right now.

**CAPTAIN:**
Fantastic! You three are going to stay up top for a while, aren't you? You can stay with me if you like.

**DIAMONDO:**
We like.

**EMERALDO:**
Definitely. We were beginning to mold down there in the caverns. You stay put, and we'll bring Shalon to you *el pronto.*

*(The **OLAKS** cross over as **SHALON** enters stage left, stepping into the Commander's Quarters Scene. **SHALON** is a nice, modern young woman who knows her mind but isn't entirely turned off by the fairy tale/knight-on-a-white-horse dream.)*

**EMERALDO:**
Hey, Shalon. How you been, sweetie?

**SHALON:**
What are you three doing above ground?

**RUBY:**
Not happy to see us, Sha?

**SHALON:**
Of course I'm happy to see you—just a little surprised.

**DIAMONDO:**
Well, we have another surprise for you. A special package wrapped in the form of a Star Fighter captain.

**RUBY:**
Right. He's a great guy and wants to meet you big time.

**SHALON:**
You know what my father thinks of fliers.

**EMERALDO:**
Yeah, bummer. But this man is the dream of your life, Shalon. You'll have to trust us on this.

**DIAMONDO:**
Do you want to risk your father's disapproval, or risk missing out on a chance of a lifetime?

**SHALON:**
He's that special?

**RUBY:**
Specialer than special.

**SHALON:**
All right, let's go.

*(**SHALON** follows the **OLAKS** back to center stage where the **CAPTAIN** is.)*

**NARRATOR:**
The Olaks took Shalon to meet the Captain. And, although they say it never happens, it was love at first sight.

**EMERALDO:**
Shalon, the dashing Captain. Captain, the fabulous Shalon.

**CAPTAIN:** *(Taking SHALON'S hand.)*
Very nice to meet you.

**SHALON:**
Nice to meet you, too.

**CAPTAIN:**
Would you like to sit down and talk? It would be nice to get to know you.

**SHALON:**
Yes, we can talk for a while.

*(The CAPTAIN and SHALON sit at the table.)*

**DIAMONDO:**
Come on, Ruby, let's get out of here.

**RUBY:**
Get out of here? We just got here.

**EMERALDO:**
I know, but there are times when humans like to be alone with each other. And I can tell that this is one of those times, so let us depart.

**DIAMONDO:** *(Leading RUBY away.)*
Right, we'll go play on the quasar slide.

**RUBY:**
Ooo, I like the quasar slide.

**DIAMONDO and EMERALDO:**
We know.

*(The OLAKS exit stage right.)*

**NARRATOR:**
The Captain and Shalon talked for hours on end. The more they talked, the more they found they had in common, and the more they fell in love. The time flew by before Shalon realized how late it was and that she should be getting back to her quarters.

**SHALON:** *(Standing.)*
I should be getting back. My parents will be wondering what's happened to me.

**CAPTAIN:**
Of course. I apologize for keeping you so long. I just had such a wonderful time, I didn't want it to end. May I see you again tomorrow?

**SHALON:**
Yes, I'd like that. Well, good night.

*(The CAPTAIN smiles and warmly holds her hand. SHALON smiles back.)*

**NARRATOR:**
Yes, Shalon was smitten with the Captain. Actually, she was crazy about him.

*(SHALON crosses to the Commander's Quarters Scene where the COMMANDER and DE MORA, SHALON'S mother, enter and wait. DE MORA is a good mother and loving wife but probably has a high-paying, responsible job as well. The COMMANDER is stern but fair.)*

**COMMANDER:**
Where have you been, young lady?

**DE MORA:**
Shalon, we were worried.

**SHALON:**
I'm sorry, Mother. I should have let you know where I was. I was with a captain of the Star Fighters.

**COMMANDER:**
A Star Fighter? Shalon, you know how I feel about those fly-boys.

**SHALON:**
Yes, Father, I know. But this one is really quite different from the others. He's so very nice and considerate. Even the Olaks like him.

**DE MORA:**
The Olaks? Perhaps he is different from the others, darling.

**COMMANDER:**
Still, in time he'll fly off and leave Shalon with a broken heart. It's in their blood.

**SHALON:**
Daddy, I know you don't want to see me hurt, and I love you for it. But I'm a grown woman now, and you can't protect me forever. If I'm going to get hurt, I guess I'll just have to be hurt. I honestly think the Captain is too gentle a man to ever hurt me, or do so purposely.

**DE MORA:**
So, does this captain have a name?

**SHALON:**
I'm sure he does. I just forgot to ask it.

**DE MORA:**
Well, how are you going to introduce us to him if you don't know his name?

**SHALON:**
I'll find out his name.
*(Embracing her mother.)*
Thank you for understanding, Mother. I do love him, you know.

*(SHALON exits stage left.)*

**COMMANDER:**
This is unbelievable. How can she be in love with this man when she doesn't even know him?

**DE MORA:**
Please don't be too hard on her, darling.
*(Putting her arm around him.)*
We barely knew one another when we fell in love.

**COMMANDER:**
Well . . .

*(The* **COMMANDER** *escorts* **DE MORA** *out stage left then crosses to the Plaza/Guest Quarters Scene on the* **NARRATOR'S** *cue. Also on cue, the* **OLAKS** *return to mill around the table setting with the* **CAPTAIN** *and* **ZEPS**.*)*

**NARRATOR:**
The next morning the Commander went looking for the Captain and found him sitting in a restaurant with Zeps and the Olaks.

**RUBY:** *(Holding her head.)*
Ow.

**DIAMONDO:**
I told you not to go down the quasar slide headfirst.

**EMERALDO:**
It's a good thing Ruby went down headfirst. That way she landed on her head and didn't hurt anything real important.

**RUBY:**
Ha, ha, very funny.

**COMMANDER:**
Are you the Captain who spent yesterday with my Shalon?

**CAPTAIN:** *(Standing.)*
Yes, sir, Commander. She's a lovely young woman.

**COMMANDER:**
I know that. Sit down.

*(The* **CAPTAIN** *sits down quickly as* **ZEPS**, *who was sitting in the other chair, stands.)*

**ZEPS:**
Would you like a chair yourself, Commander?

*(The* **COMMANDER** *stares at* **ZEPS**, *who gets out of the way.)*

**ZEPS:** *(Continued.)*
I guess you do.

*(**ZEPS** stands with the* **OLAKS** *while the* **COMMANDER** *sits down.)*

**COMMANDER:**
So what do you want with my Shalon?

**CAPTAIN:**
Well, I know this may sound a little rushed, but to be honest, I hope to marry your daughter . . . after a reasonable courtship . . . under your supervision . . . I love Shalon very much.

**COMMANDER:**
Yes? And when you're ready to go fly off again, you'll leave her alone and brokenhearted, correct?

**CAPTAIN:**
No, sir. How could I ever leave such a wonderful woman? I couldn't bear to be away from her ever. I'll never leave this station if this is where she wants to stay.

**COMMANDER:**
Mmmmm. I'll think about it. But if you hurt her, I'll put you in the ejector portal and eject you into space myself.

**CAPTAIN:**
Yes, sir—I mean, no, sir.

*(The **COMMANDER** exits stage left as the **OLAKS** look on.)*

**DIAMONDO:**
Man, kind of a heavy dude, isn't he?

**ZEPS:**
Oh, he's all right. He's just being a daddy.

**RUBY:**
Must be a pretty heavy trip, this being a daddy.

**EMERALDO:**
Heavy, man. Heavy.

*(**VIC** enters stage right and crosses to the **CAPTAIN**.)*

**VIC:**
Hey, Captain, I worked overtime and got your Star Fighter up and running good as new. It's a good thing, too. Word is your squadron can really use your help in fighting those Devil Fighters.

**CAPTAIN:**
But I just promised I would stay here.

**DIAMONDO:**
Man, deserting your squadron in time of war—radical.

*(**SHALON** enters stage left and crosses to the **CAPTAIN**.)*

**SHALON:**
Captain . . .

**CAPTAIN:** *(Taking **SHALON'S** hand.)*
Shalon, I'm so glad to see you.

**SHALON:**
Captain, I need to know your name to introduce you to my parents.

**VIC:**
No time for that, I'm afraid. The Captain needs to get back to his squadron. They're in big trouble out there.

**SHALON:**
You're leaving me?

*(The **COMMANDER** and **DE MORA** enter stage left and join the others.)*

**COMMANDER:**
You see, De Mora? I told you he would end up hurting our Shalon.

**DE MORA:**
Well, there *is* something to be said in having a sense of duty and responsibility, darling. He can't very well abandon his squadron in their time of need.

**CAPTAIN:**
I don't know what to do. I love you so much, Shalon, but I have to go back to my squadron. I'll return, I promise.

**SHALON:** *(Near tears.)*
What if you're killed out there?

**COMMANDER:**
There you go. He's breaking her heart. I told you!

*(The **COMMANDER** grabs the **CAPTAIN** and moves him over onto the ejector portal.)*

**COMMANDER:** *(Continued.)*
You want to join your squadron so badly? I'll help you join your squadron. I'll eject you out of here myself!

**SHALON:**
Father, no!

*(Everyone protests. And just as the **COMMANDER** puts his hands on the ejector lever to pull it, the **PROFESSOR** hurries in from stage right waving a piece of paper before her.)*

**PROFESSOR:**
Commander! Commander, I have an urgent message for you.

*(The **PROFESSOR** gives the **COMMANDER** the piece of paper and steps back to where the **OLAKS** are. The **COMMANDER** reads the message.)*

**DE MORA:**
What is it, darling?

**COMMANDER:**
Listen to this, De Mora. It's from the Northern Hemisphere. I've been appointed to the High Council.

**DE MORA:** *(Taking the **COMMANDER'S** arm.)*
Oh, my, what an honor.

*(The others applaud.)*

**CAPTAIN:**
Congratulations, sir.

**COMMANDER:**
Thank you.

*(Helping the **CAPTAIN** off the ejector portal.)*

**COMMANDER:** *(Continued.)*
Oh, come down off there, son. I lost my head there for a moment. I wasn't really going to eject you—just scare you a little. I hope you can forgive me.

**CAPTAIN:**
Understood, sir.

**ZEPS:**
If you're going to be a member of the High Council, who's going to take over the position of commander to this space station?

**COMMANDER:** *(Reading the message.)*
It says here a Captain Hershel. Who's Captain Hershel?

**CAPTAIN:**
*I'm* Captain Hershel, sir.

**COMMANDER:**
You are? Well, if the High Council thinks enough to appoint you commander of this space station, I guess I'll have to change my mind about you.

**DE MORA:**
Does that mean you'll give these young people your permission to marry, darling?

**COMMANDER:**
With the Captain commanding this space station, he isn't as likely to be in a position to get killed—and he'll be around to keep my little girl happy. Yes, I give my blessing most willingly.

*(**SHALON** steps over to kiss her father on the cheek.)*

**SHALON:**
Thank you, Father.

**CAPTAIN:**
Thank you, sir.

**COMMANDER:**
Sir? What's this *sir* business? Come along, son, I'll show you the operation. Later, we'll discuss wedding plans.

*(**SHALON** embraces the **CAPTAIN** as **DE MORA** embraces the **COMMANDER** and all four exit stage left. At the same time, **ZEPS**, **VIC**, and the **PROFESSOR** exit stage right, leaving the **OLAKS** alone at center stage.)*

**DIAMONDO:**
Well, isn't that nice, the way it all worked out.

**RUBY:**
And just in the nick of time, too.

**DIAMONDO:**
I especially liked the part about promoting the Commander to the High Council.

**EMERALDO:**
Why, thank you. That was my idea, you know.

**DIAMONDO:**
Brilliant.

**RUBY:**
I arranged to have the Captain put in charge of the space station.

**DIAMONDO:**
Yes, that was exceptionally clever, too.

**EMERALDO:**
Well, we Olaks *do* have our ways.

(*The **OLAKS** exchange high-fives and low-fives, congratulating one another, as the **NARRATOR** speaks.*)

**NARRATOR:**
And so Captain Hershel became commander of the space station and married a very happy Shalon. The Commander became an important leader of the High Council of the Northern Hemisphere and helped in winning the war against the Devil Fighters of the Southern Hemisphere. And the Olaks? Well, the Captain and Shalon became very good friends of the Olaks and kept them close by, because, although they were a strange-looking trio, those Olaks *do have their ways.*

(*Curtain.*)

END OF CASINGS

the
pied piper of
Hamelin

# The Pied Piper of Hamelin

*A Little Comedy by Joan Garner*
*Based on the German legend*

## CAST OF CHARACTERS (m=male   f=female)

NARRATOR (m/f)         FELIX (m)                          PIED PIPER (m)
MARTA (f)              BURGHERMEISTER HAAS (m)            HANSEL (m)
TOWN CRIER (m)         FRAU BURGHERMEISTER HAAS (f)       GRETEL (f)
HEIDI (f)

## CHARACTER AND COSTUME DESCRIPTIONS

**MARTA:** Marta is a loving but probably dull mother. Marta is a simple peasant with drab dress (circa 1284) consisting of undergown with tight-fitting sleeves, a sleeveless surcoat, and a porkpie coif (hat). Neutral hose and soft slippers.

**TOWN CRIER:** The Town Crier is a loving but probably dull father. The Town Crier is dressed in a tattered short tunic and hose (circa 1284). He might have a small sign hanging about his neck reading "Town Crier." Soft felt shoes and tall round hat.

**HEIDI:** Heidi is a very high-class lemming. She wears the lastest in fashion (circa 1990s). Later, when sunbathing, the best effect would be to have her wear a brightly colored bathing suit of dress with bloomers (circa 1900s). Her makeup is a fashion model's, and to indicate that she is a lemming, a lemming nose and ear piece are attached or tied on.

**FELIX:** Felix is a very yuppie rat. He wears the lastest in fashion (circa 1990s). Later on, when sunbathing, the best effect would be to have him wear a brightly colored bathing suit of trunks and top (circa 1900s). To indicate that he is a rat, a rat nose and ear piece are attached or tied on.

**BURGHERMEISTER HAAS:** Haas acts like a leader, strong and demanding. He can be an average person, perhaps a little on the round side, and should be better dressed than the Town Crier. He wears a parti-colored dress with tall hat, and sword belt with sword. Hose and felt boots and tall round hat.

**FRAU BURGHERMEISTER HAAS:** Frau Haas is very nice, but she is also strong enough to make us believe she can stand up to her husband. She can be an average person, perhaps a little on the round side, and should be better dressed than Marta. Her undergown with tight-fitting sleeves, a sleeveless surcoat, and a porkpie coif (hat) should be of better and richer material.

**PIED PIPER:** The Pied Piper is an honest guy with a hustler's heart. He is very charming and can probably get you to do something you wouldn't do otherwise. The Pied Piper wears a pied coat (multicolored) and hose (circa 1284). Soft shoes and tall round hat.

**HANSEL:** Hansel is a cute little kid, but sickeningly so. He should act very cardboardish and fake. Hansel should wear the ethnic costume of Germany—the gray lederhosen with embroidered flowers on them, a white short-sleeved shirt, white knee socks, shoes, and alpine hat.

**GRETEL:** Gretel is just like Hansel—sickeningly sweet. She should wear the ethnic costume of Germany—a gray jumper dress with embroidered flowers on it, a short puffy-sleeved blouse, white knee socks, and shoes. Her hair should be braided into two pigtails, preferably sticking out from the sides of her head.

**Scene Design for** *The Pied Piper of Hamelin*

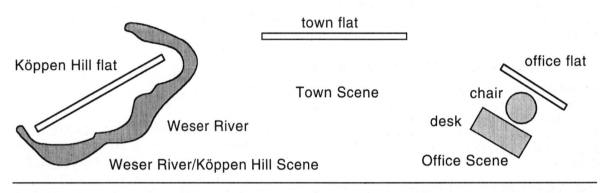

Blue Sky Drop

town flat

Köppen Hill flat

office flat

Town Scene

chair

desk

Weser River

Weser River/Köppen Hill Scene

Office Scene

Apron

## PROPS

horn, luggage, cooler, magazines, beach chairs, drinking glasses, pipe, sign, sunglasses, bell, Mickey Mouse hats, shopping bags.

## AS A STUDY LESSON

*The Pied Piper of Hamelin* incorporates and can teach all the comedy aspects required to perform this fun and highly entertaining vehicle. This play will help students learn comic timing, double takes, pausing for laughs, and physical movement to enhance humor.

## AS PERFORMANCE

Comedy generally plays well in most venues and to most age groups. The humor in this play is geared to both adults and youngsters to provide a good time for all.

## CONSIDERATIONS, EFFECTS, AND AFFECTS

Sets and costumes can be cartoonish. Designers can have just as much fun with this play as the actors.

Although this play takes place in 1284, the presence and attitude of the Pied Piper, Heidi, and Felix should be ultramodern. Only the people in the town of Hamelin should appear appropriate to their time period.

# The Pied Piper of Hamelin

**SET:** The town of Hamelin. It consists of three primary scenes (sets):
1) The Weser River Scene wraps around the Köppen Hill flat and flows offstage right. Köppen Hill is behind the river—stage right. The river can be painted on the floor or can be a cloth draped to look like ripples in the water. The river should be wide enough that the rats can jump into it and swim off stage.
2) The Town Scene—center stage. This can be a simple flat with exterior buildings painted on it.
3) The Office Scene—stage left. There should be a desk and chair, but the back flat can be a simple interior wall.

**AT RISE:**
Morning, July 24, 1284. A sunny day in the town of Hamelin, Germany.

**NARRATOR:**
Once upon a time—actually, it was July 24, 1284—there was a small burg nestled in the countryside of Westphalia, Germany, called Hamelin. Not that you'll be tested on any of this afterwards, but we thought you'd like to know that we have researched the story in-depth beforehand to bring these facts to you. . . . To proceed, Hamelin was a little village with shopkeepers and farmers, rich people and poor people, big people and little people, tall people and short people, fancy people and down-to-earth people, mothers, fathers, and children—the usual array of folk that make up a town. There was nothing especially unusual about Hamelin; it was like any other quaint little hamlet of that time. But then something extraordinary happened. An event that put Hamelin on the map; an occurrence that had people talking throughout the land; a happenstance that will forever be recorded in the annals of history; a day that will live in infamy—this day, July 24, 1284.

*(MARTA enters the Town Scene stage left and the TOWN CRIER enters stage right. MARTA is a loving but probably dull mother. The TOWN CRIER is a loving but probably dull father.)*

**MARTA:**
Good morning, Town Crier. How are you this morning?

**TOWN CRIER:**
Oh, so-so. And you, Marta?

**MARTA:**
Oh, so-so. Have you any news today?

**TOWN CRIER:**
Oh, same old, same old. And you?

**MARTA:**
Oh, you know—same old, same old.

**TOWN CRIER:**
And your daughter? How is Gretel?

**MARTA:**
Oh, she's fine.

**TOWN CRIER:**
That's nice.

**MARTA:**
And your son, Hansel? How is he?

**TOWN CRIER:**
Oh, he's fine.

**MARTA:**
That's nice.

**NARRATOR:**
Yes, it was a nice and fine little town until . . .

*(Enter **FELIX** and **HEIDI**, the **RATS**, stage right carrying matching designer luggage. **HEIDI** is a very high-class lemming. **FELIX** is a very yuppie rat.)*

**MARTA:** *(Looking over the **TOWN CRIER'S** shoulder to see the **RATS** who have entered. She speaks in a monotone voice.)*
Oh, rats.

**TOWN CRIER:**
Why? What's the matter?

**MARTA:**
No, I mean—
*(pointing)*
RATS!

*(**MARTA** screams, picks up her skirts, and runs offstage left.)*

**TOWN CRIER:** *(Turning to see the **RATS**.)*
Oh, my. Oh, dear. Go away, you. Go away now—shoo. Be off with you, you pesky little vermin.
*(Trying to sweep them away with a wave of his hand.)*
Shoo, shoo.

*(The **RATS** look at one another a little saddened, then back to the **TOWN CRIER**.)*

**TOWN CRIER:** *(Continued.)*
Go on now. No one wants you around here—begone!

*(The **RATS** simply stare deadpan at the **TOWN CRIER**.)*

**TOWN CRIER:** *(Continued.)*
Oh, my. I have to tell someone of this. After all, I *am* the Town Crier. It's my job to tell of events like this. I must tell everyone. I have to tell the Burghermeister.
*(He calls offstage as he exits stage left.)*
Burghermeister! Burghermeister!

**HEIDI:** *(Watching the **TOWN CRIER** scurry offstage. She sighs.)*
Everywhere I go, it's the same thing. Never do I get, "Hello, how are you? Welcome to the neighborhood." No, it's always shriek, scream, run away. There are never introductions. I never have the opportunity to ask if there are any four-star restaurants in town. It's always shriek, scream, run away.

**FELIX:**
So true. Sad to say—so true. I'm received the same way wherever I go. No respect. Not even mild curiosity as to who I am or what I'm doing there. It's always shriek, scream, run away.

**HEIDI:** *(Placing her bag on the ground and extending a hand to FELIX.)*
My name is Heidi.

**FELIX:** *(Placing his bag on the ground to shake HEIDI'S hand.)*
Charmed . . . Heidi—Heidi—that name is very familiar. Should I know you? We haven't met before, have we? Like at a mountain cottage or an orphanage or something?

**HEIDI:**
No, I don't believe so.

**FELIX:**
Mmmm. My name is Felix. Felix the Rat, Esquire.

**HEIDI:**
Felix the Rat. Now, see, your name seems very familiar to *me*.

**FELIX:**
Extraordinary, isn't it?

**HEIDI:**
Quite.

**FELIX:**
In any event, it would appear that we rats will be treated here with the same disrespect we receive wherever we journey.

**HEIDI:**
Oh, no, no, no. Excuse me, but I am not a rat.

**FELIX:**
You're not? You look like a rat.

**HEIDI:**
Well, I most assuredly am not.

**FELIX:**
What are you, then?

**HEIDI:**
I'm a lemming.

**FELIX:**
Lemming, rat—same thing.

**HEIDI:**
I beg to differ. When all of my brothers, sisters, aunts, uncles, and cousins arrive, I'm sure you'll notice the difference.

**FELIX:**
Oh? Where is your family now?

**HEIDI:**
Just up the road a piece. We lemmings are migratory vermin, you know. Periodically we mass together and move from one region to another.

**FELIX:**
Why do you do that?

**HEIDI:**
It's just something we do. It's something we've always done. Sometimes our migrations end in drowning in a sea or lake or river.

**FELIX:**
Why?

**HEIDI:**
It's just something we do.

**FELIX:**
Well, if that isn't the most idiotic thing I've ever heard.

**HEIDI:**
Yes, I agree.

**FELIX:**
Why do you do it, then?

**HEIDI:** *(Thinking.)*
Protocol.

**FELIX:**
Stupid.
*(He picks up his bag and exits stage right.)*
Stupid, stupid, stupid.

**HEIDI:** *(Picking up her bag and following **FELIX**.)*
Wait up, Felix. You know, you're rather attractive for a rat. Are you married or presently involved?

*(**BURGHERMEISTER HAAS** and **FRAU BURGHERMEISTER HAAS** enter stage left and cross into the Office Scene. **BURGHERMEISTER HAAS** acts like a leader, strong and demanding. **FRAU BURGHERMEISTER HAAS** is very nice, but she is also strong enough to make us believe she can stand up to her husband. The **TOWN CRIER** and **MARTA** enter behind the **HAASES** stage left and step into the Office Scene. **BURGHERMEISTER HAAS** sits at his desk, and the others huddle around him.)*

**BURGHERMEISTER HAAS:** *(As they enter.)*
Just how many rats did you see?

**TOWN CRIER:**
Hundreds.

**MARTA:**
Thousands.

**FRAU BURGHERMEISTER HAAS:** *(Alarmed.)*
Hundreds and thousands?

**TOWN CRIER:**
Well, maybe not quite that many.

**BURGHERMEISTER HAAS:**
How many is "not quite that many"?

**TOWN CRIER:**
Actually—uh—two.

**BURGHERMEISTER HAAS:**
Two? You've worked yourselves into a panic over two rats?

**MARTA:**
But they were big rats, Herr Burghermeister Haas.

**TOWN CRIER:**
And you know what they say: "Where there are two rats, more are soon to follow." You have to do something now before the place is crawling with them.
*(He shudders at the thought.)*
Oooo.

**BURGHERMEISTER HAAS:**
Very well. I'll look into it.

**TOWN CRIER:**
You'll look into it? I know what it means when public officials say they'll look into something. It means you'll bury the matter under a stack of papers, and there it will lie until it's too late to do anything about it.

**MARTA:**
Hey, that sounded very impressive, Town Crier. Have you ever thought of getting into politics?

**TOWN CRIER:**
Why, no. Do you think I'd be any good at it?

**MARTA:**
Yes, I do.

*(**BURGHERMEISTER HAAS** stands and hustles **MARTA** and the **TOWN CRIER** out of his office.)*

**BURGHERMEISTER HAAS:**
Please, the Town Crier in politics? This town can only handle one calamity at a time. I promise you, I will do something about the rats.

*(**MARTA** and the **TOWN CRIER** exit stage right as **BURGHERMEISTER HAAS** sits back down at his desk.)*

**FRAU BURGHERMEISTER HAAS:**
So, what are you going to do about the rats, dear husband?

**BURGHERMEISTER HAAS:**
I'll look into it.

**FRAU BURGHERMEISTER HAAS:**
Which means?

**BURGHERMEISTER HAAS:**
Which means I'll look into it. Don't you start with me too, dear wife.

**FRAU BURGHERMEISTER HAAS:**
Sorry . . . What would you like for lunch?

**BURGHERMEISTER HAAS:**
How about some sauerkraut and those little wieners?

*(**BURGHERMEISTER HAAS** and **FRAU BURGHERMEISTER HAAS** exit stage left.)*

**NARRATOR:**
Two days later, while Burghermeister Haas was "looking into the matter," the town of Hamelin became infested with rats. They were everywhere.

*(**MARTA** enters stage right screaming and waving her arms in the air. She quickly exits stage left.)*

**NARRATOR:** *(Continued.)*
They were in the streets, in the gutters, down the drains. The . . .

*(**MARTA** enters stage left screaming and waving her arms in the air. She quickly exits stage right.)*

**NARRATOR:** *(Continued.)*
The rats were on the sidewalks, on the windowsills, on the gables, and on the rain spouts. They . . .

*(**MARTA** enters stage right screaming and waving her arms in the air. She quickly exits stage left.)*

**NARRATOR:** *(Continued.)*
They were on Fräulein Duhurst's new Persian rug. They were on Herr Kemp's kitchen table. They . . .

*(**MARTA** enters stage left screaming and waving her arms in the air. She quickly exits stage right.)*

**NARRATOR:** *(Continued.)*
They were in the sinks and cupboards, in the food and drink . . .

*(**HEIDI** and **FELIX** enter stage right. They're wearing old-fashioned swimsuits and sunglasses. They carry beach chairs, a cooler, and magazines [probably* Vanity Fair *and the* New Yorker*]. While the **NARRATOR** continues to speak, they set up the chairs and sit down as if to spend an afternoon at the beach.)*

**NARRATOR:** *(Continued.)*
They were in Frau Bruker's fine linens and Herr Putzey's shaving mug.

*(**MARTA** enters stage right screaming and waving her arms in the air. She almost stumbles over **HEIDI** and **FELIX**, stops, screams even louder, and exits stage left.)*

**FELIX:** *(Watching after **MARTA**.)*
What's her problem?

**HEIDI:**
I haven't the faintest idea. Have you noticed the people around here seem to be utterly . . .

**FELIX:**
. . . flipped out?

**HEIDI:**
To the max.

**FELIX:** *(Changing the subject.)*
Isn't this great? I love it here. And your family—your relatives are party animals. I like them a lot.

**HEIDI:**
Thank you. I like your family, too.

**FELIX:**
When your Uncle Herman jumped off the flour bin right into the potato salad, it just cracked me up.

**HEIDI:**
Yes, Uncle Herman is a wild and crazy lemming, all right.

*(BURGHERMEISTER HAAS, FRAU BURGHERMEISTER HAAS, and the TOWN CRIER enter stage left and cross into the Office Scene.)*

**TOWN CRIER:**
What are you going to do? You said you were going to do something, but you didn't do something, so now you've got to do something. What are you going to do?

**BURGHERMEISTER HAAS:**
I don't know. . . . Something.

*(FRAU BURGHERMEISTER HAAS lifts up her skirt and screams. The men look over, and FRAU BURGHERMEISTER HAAS drops her skirt, embarrassed.)*

**FRAU BURGHERMEISTER HAAS:**
Sorry—rat.

**TOWN CRIER:**
Last night I caught them gnawing away at my apple fritters.

**BURGHERMEISTER HAAS:**
Oh, I like apple fritters.

**TOWN CRIER:**
You wouldn't like these apple fritters. They had rat droppings in them.

**FRAU BURGHERMEISTER HAAS:**
I think I'm going to be sick.

**TOWN CRIER:**
Burghermeister Haas, you've just got to do something about these rats. They're everywhere! What are you going to do?

**BURGHERMEISTER HAAS:**
I'm going to take affirmative action, that's what I'm going to do. We'll send out word that this town needs a rat exterminator.

**TOWN CRIER:**
Say, that's a good idea.

**BURGHERMEISTER HAAS:**
I thought you'd like it. So send out the word.

**TOWN CRIER:**
Oh, yes. I *am* the Town Crier, aren't I? Yes, send out the word.

*(The **TOWN CRIER** steps to center stage, in between **HEIDI** and **FELIX**.)*

**TOWN CRIER:** *(Continued.)*
Pardon me.

**FELIX:**
No problem. Say, ol' man, would you mind taking a step forward, you're blocking my rays.

**TOWN CRIER:**
Oh, yes, of course. Sorry.

*(The **TOWN CRIER** steps forward, takes the horn from his belt, blows it [not very well], and then cries out.)*

**TOWN CRIER:** *(Continued.)*
Hear ye! Hear ye! The town of Hamelin is now accepting applications for a rat exterminator. We offer a competitive salary with comprehensive benefits. Interested parties may inquire within.

**FELIX:** *(Not especially upset.)*
Now, that's not very friendly.

**HEIDI:**
It's rather rude, if you ask me.

*(Enter the **PIED PIPER** stage right. The **PIED PIPER** is an honest guy with a hustler's heart. The **PIED PIPER** steps up to the **TOWN CRIER**.)*

**PIED PIPER:**
I hear you're looking for a rat exterminator.

**TOWN CRIER:**
Wow, that was fast. I don't know the power of my own horn.

**PIED PIPER:**
Actually, I heard of your problem three towns down the road. They've already employed me to get rid of their rats.
*(Pulling out several papers.)*
My references.

**TOWN CRIER:**
Oh, yes. Right this way.

*(The **TOWN CRIER** takes the **PIED PIPER** into the Office Scene.)*

**TOWN CRIER:** *(Continued.)*
Herr Burghermeister Haas, this fancy gent says he can get rid of our vermin infestation.

**BURGHERMEISTER HAAS:** *(To the **PIED PIPER**.)*
Look at you, boy. That's hardly the proper attire to wear for a job interview.

**PIED PIPER:**
But it's the rage in Berlin. Soon everyone will be wearing one. You wait and see.

**FRAU BURGHERMEISTER HAAS:**
Do you think you can rid us of all these rats, young man?

**PIED PIPER:**
I know I can. It's a relatively simple procedure.

**TOWN CRIER:**
How do you do it?

**PIED PIPER:** *(Pulling his pipe out of a pocket.)*
With this.

**BURGHERMEISTER HAAS:**
You're going to rid our town of rats with a flute?

**PIED PIPER:** *(Peeved.)*
It's not a flute. It's a pipe.

**BURGHERMEISTER HAAS:**
Of course. How silly of me. You're going to exterminate the rats with a pipe.
*(Standing angrily.)*
Do you think I'm an idiot? Get out of here, you and your pipe. You're a flimflam man, that's what you are.

**PIED PIPER:**
Now, there's no need for name calling. I've come to you in good faith to offer you my services, and you treat me like a common swindler.

**BURGHERMEISTER HAAS:**
If the turned-up shoe fits . . .

**FRAU BURGHERMEISTER HAAS:**
How does the pipe work, Herr . . . ?

**PIED PIPER:**
Orkin, ma'am. My name is Orkin, but most folks just call me the Pied Piper because of my colorful pied coat here and my magic pipe that plays enchanting music.

**FRAU BURGHERMEISTER HAAS:**
It's a magic pipe?

**PIED PIPER:**
Of course it's a magic pipe. How did you think I used it? Bopped every single rat over the head with it? That would take forever. No, what I do is dance up and down the streets playing a little tune on my magic pipe.

**BURGHERMEISTER HAAS:**
You dance up and down the streets?

**PIED PIPER:**
It's part of the package deal. Anyway, I play my pipe and the music mesmerizes the little vermin, and they follow the music and me. So what I'll do for you is play my pipe, and the rats will follow, and I'll take them down to the Weser River, where they'll jump in and drown. Rat problem solved.

**BURGHERMEISTER HAAS:**
That's the most absurd thing I've ever heard.

**FRAU BURGHERMEISTER HAAS:**
Dear, why don't you let the Pied Piper try? We have nothing to lose.

**TOWN CRIER:**
Except our rats.

**BURGHERMEISTER HAAS:** *(To the PIED PIPER.)*
And how much are you expecting to get paid for this mumbo jumbo?

**PIED PIPER:**
Oh, let's say 100 deutsche marks.

**BURGHERMEISTER HAAS:** *(Exploding.)*
100 deutsche marks! Are you . . .

**NARRATOR:** *(To the ACTORS.)*
Pardon me, everyone. Pardon me. Could you pause a moment, please . . .
*(To the audience.)*
For those who don't know how much a deutsche mark is worth, it's approximately $2 in U.S. currency. Therefore, the Pied Piper's asking price for ridding the town of Hamelin of its rat population is about $200.
*(To the ACTORS.)*
You may proceed.

**BURGHERMEISTER HAAS:** *(Exploding again.)*
100 deutsche marks! Are you out of your ever-loving mind?

**PIED PIPER:**
Do you want my services or not? If you don't want to pay me, I can always go elsewhere. Rats are found wherever you go, you know.

**BURGHERMEISTER HAAS:**
All right. If you can rid this town of all the rats—that's every last one of them—I'll pay you your 100 deutsche marks.

**PIED PIPER:** *(Shaking BURGHERMEISTER HAAS'S hand.)*
Deal.

*(BURGHERMEISTER HAAS, FRAU BURGHERMEISTER HAAS, and the TOWN CRIER exit stage left, while the PIED PIPER steps over and in between HEIDI and FELIX.)*

**PIED PIPER:**
Good morning. And how are you this fine day?

**HEIDI:**
Why, we're excellent. Thank you so much for asking.

**FELIX:**
Say, I like your threads.

**PIED PIPER:**
It does catch the eye, doesn't it? Listen, you two appear to be intelligent rats . . .

**FELIX:**
Oh, we are. We've just been slandered for hundreds of years, that's all. It's a big conspiracy created by the squirrels and chipmunks to make us appear more unseemly and objectionable and make them look more adorable and precious.

**HEIDI:**
It's terrible. And the poor mice have been caught in the fallout as well.

**PIED PIPER:**
Yes, well, I have a proposition for you.

**HEIDI:**
A proposition? Interesting. Go on.

**PIED PIPER:**
You see, I've been hired to rid this town of all its vermin, i. e., you.

**FELIX:**
Well, what if we don't want to go?

**PIED PIPER:**
But why wouldn't you? You've about tapped out all the foodstuffs around here.

**HEIDI:**
He's right there, Felix. The only things left are a few horsehair ropes and a couple of wine corks. And it's about time we lemmings continued our migration. You and your family are welcome to come with us if you like.

**FELIX:**
No thank you. For some odd reason, the idea of jumping into a river and drowning doesn't appeal to me.

**PIED PIPER:**
Now, I think I can help you out there. Here's how the plan works . . .
(*He pulls out his pipe.*)
. . . I play my pipe here . . .

**FELIX:**
It looks like a flute to me.

**PIED PIPER:** (*Peeved.*)
It's a *pipe*. I play my pipe and you act as if the music mesmerizes you, and then you follow me off to the Weser River and jump in.

**HEIDI:**
Well, Felix has almost talked me out of drowning myself.

**FELIX:**
It's a stupid thing to do.

**PIED PIPER:**
You know that and I know that, but the townspeople of Hamelin are expecting you to jump into the river and drown. But what they won't know is that you don't drown.

**HEIDI:**
We don't?

**PIED PIPER:**
It isn't necessary. Besides, the animal rights activists would get all over my case if you drowned. No, what you do is swim across the river to a boat that'll take you deep into the Black Forest. You'll like it there. There's plenty to eat, and the scenery is spectacular. And I have some very nice time-sharing units that would be perfect for you.

**FELIX:**
Mmmm, it's something to consider. What do you get out of all this?

**PIED PIPER:**
100 deutsche marks.

**HEIDI:**
Deutsche marks? I tried those once—not very tasty.

**FELIX:**
Very well, we'll do it. I'll tell my family, and Heidi will inform her clan. When did you want to do this?

**PIED PIPER:**
As soon as possible.

**FELIX:** *(Standing and gathering his things.)*
Then I guess we'll go now.

**HEIDI:** *(Standing and gathering her things.)*
We can't go right now. I have to have time to pack.

**FELIX:**
In that case, we better make it this afternoon. Tomorrow would be better.

**HEIDI:**
You're making fun of me, Felix. I'm going to call off our engagement if you make fun of me.

*(***FELIX*** and ***HEIDI*** exit stage left as the ***PIED PIPER*** stands tall and prepares to play his pipe. ***MARTA*** enters stage right and scurries across.)*

**MARTA:**
Have they gone yet?

**PIED PIPER:**
Not yet.

*(***MARTA*** exits stage left while the ***TOWN CRIER*** enters stage right ringing a bell.)*

**TOWN CRIER:**
Hear ye! Hear ye! Playing today in the town of Hamelin for one show only is the Pied Piper and his magic flute.

**PIED PIPER:**
Pipe! Wrong instrument—wrong story!

**TOWN CRIER:**
Oh, sorry.
*(Calling out again.)*
And his magic pipe!
*(To the **PIED PIPER**.)*
Say, do you know how to play "Jingle Bells"? I just love "Jingle Bells".

**PIED PIPER:**
It's July 24th.

**TOWN CRIER:**
Oh. Oh, well . . .
*(Calling out again as he crosses the stage and exits stage right.)*
Hear ye! Hear ye! Playing today in the town of Hamelin for one show only is the Pied Piper and his magic flute.

**PIED PIPER:**
It's a pipe, you dunce!

**NARRATOR:**
And so the Pied Piper stood in the middle of town and began to play his magic flute—uh, pipe.

*(The **PIED PIPER** begins playing his pipe [some recording of Kenny G or the like would go well here].)*

**NARRATOR:** *(Continued.)*
He danced up and down the streets playing his music, and, as agreed, the rats came out of their hiding places to follow him. The little vermin came out of house and home, barn and shed, sewer and field, and followed the brightly dressed Pied Piper through the town.

*(**HEIDI** and **FELIX** enter stage left and join the **PIED PIPER** as they form a conga line. [Here a recording of conga music would be appropriate.] Eventually, the dance leads them to stage right near the Weser River. **MARTA**, the **TOWN CRIER**, **BURGHERMEISTER HAAS**, and **FRAU BURGHERMEISTER HAAS** enter stage left, step across into the Town Scene, and watch, cheering and applauding.)*

**NARRATOR:** *(Continued.)*
The Pied Piper and rats made their way to the Weser River, where the Piper stood by the banks, still playing his music . . .
[Sousa's "Stars and Stripes Forever" would be great here.]

**NARRATOR:** *(Continued.)*
. . . and all watched the rats jump into the water.

*(**HEIDI** and **FELIX** hold their noses, jump into the river, and swim offstage right.)*

**NARRATOR:** *(Continued.)*
It was a wonderful day after all. The people of Hamelin were happy to have the rats gone, and the rats were on their way to a gorgeous mountain retreat. What could be better?

**PIED PIPER:** *(Stepping back to the **TOWNSPEOPLE**.)*
There you go. No more rats.

**MARTA:** *(Jumping up and down and clapping.)*
No more rats. Hurrah!

**BURGHERMEISTER HAAS:**
I never would have believed it if I hadn't seen it with my own eyes.

**PIED PIPER:**
So you're pleased with my services?

**BURGHERMEISTER HAAS:**
Yes, yes. Very pleased.

**PIED PIPER:**
Then I'll be taking my 100 deutsche marks, please.

**BURGHERMEISTER HAAS:**
100 deutsche marks! Are you insane? I don't have 100 deutsche marks.

**PIED PIPER:**
But you said . . . We had a deal. I got rid of the rats, so now you have to pay the Piper.

**BURGHERMEISTER HAAS:**
Read my lips, boy. We don't have 100 deutsche marks—never did. Too bad, ol' sport.

*(**BURGHERMEISTER HAAS, FRAU BURGHERMEISTER HAAS, MARTA,** and the **TOWN CRIER** exit stage left, laughing.)*

**PIED PIPER:** *(Calling after the **TOWNSPEOPLE**.)*
Who's shafting who here?
*(Under his breath.)*
The nerve of these people.
*(Calling after the **TOWNSPEOPLE** once again.)*
You'll be sorry! Just you wait and see what happens when you don't pay the Piper!
*(Under his breath.)*
I'll have my revenge, but how?

*(Enter **HANSEL** and **GRETEL** stage right. They skip in smiling brightly. **HANSEL** is a cute boy, shiny clean and revoltingly sweet. **GRETEL** is even more so.)*

**HANSEL:**
Hello. I'm Hansel, she's Gretel.

**GRETEL:**
We're cute little kids.

**PIED PIPER:**
Hansel and Gretel?

**NARRATOR:**
Not *that* Hansel and Gretel.

**PIED PIPER:**
Oh.

**HANSEL:**
Ja, ja. We are the cute and adorable children from the town of Hamelin.

**GRETEL:**
Ja, ja. Everyone loves us because we are so precious and sweet.

**HANSEL** and **GRETEL:**
Ja, ja.

**PIED PIPER:** *(Thinking out loud to himself.)*
Cute and adorable, huh? The rats said everyone hated them because they *weren't* cute and adorable.
*(To **HANSEL** and **GRETEL**.)*
You say everyone loves the children of Hamelin because you're so cute and adorable.

**GRETEL:**
Ja, ja. And precious and sweet.

**PIED PIPER:**
Then I suspect all the grown-ups would miss you terribly if you were to go away.

**HANSEL:**
Ja, ja. Because we're so cute and adorable and precious and sweet.

*(**HANSEL** and **GRETEL** giggle.)*

**PIED PIPER:**
Ja, ja, I get the picture. Say, kids, how would you like to go up to Köppen Hill with me?

**GRETEL:**
Why would we want to go up to Köppen Hill with you? All that is up there is a dark, scary cave.

**PIED PIPER:**
Oh, no, not anymore. Some land developers have gone up there and really changed things. You'll like it up there, I know you will.

**HANSEL:**
It would have to be something pretty special to take us away from all the people who love us.

**PIED PIPER:**
It is. It's very special.

**GRETEL:**
Well, what is up there? What is so special?

**PIED PIPER:** *(Thinking hard.)*
Uhhh—why, it's, uhhh—Disneyworld.

**HANSEL** and **GRETEL:**
Disneyworld! Oh, boy!

**HANSEL:**
Okey-dokey, we will go with you.

**GRETEL:**
May we bring some of our friends with us?

**PIED PIPER:**
Sure, sure. Bring all the children of the town if you want. But don't tell the grown-ups. I only have enough day passes to get the children in.

**GRETEL:**
Okey-dokey. We'll go tell all the children.

**PIED PIPER:**
When you hear me play my pipe, hurry back and follow me. We'll make a game of it.

**HANSEL** and **GRETEL:**
Ja, ja. We hurry.

(*HANSEL* and *GRETEL* scurry offstage left.)

**NARRATOR:**
And so Hansel and Gretel scurried off to tell all the children of Hamelin that the Pied Piper was going to take them to Disneyworld. All right, we realize that Disneyworld wasn't around in 1284, nor is it in Germany. But this is a comedy, after all, so we'll ask you to go with the flow here.

(*The **PIED PIPER** begins playing his pipe again [possibly real flute music this time], and **HANSEL** and **GRETEL** reenter stage left to join the **PIED PIPER** as they dance towards Köppen Hill.*)

**NARRATOR:** (*Continued.*)
The Pied Piper played his pipe and all the cute and adorable children from the town ran out of their homes to follow him up to Köppen Hill and into the cave, whereupon the cave opening closed in behind them.

(*HANSEL* and *GRETEL* dance behind Köppen Hill and offstage right. ***BURGHERMEISTER HAAS, FRAU BURGHERMEISTER HAAS, MARTA,*** and the ***TOWN CRIER*** enter stage left and cross to the Town Scene.)

**MARTA:**
Mrs. Burghermeister Haas, have you seen my daughter, Gretel?

**FRAU BURGHERMEISTER HAAS:**
Why no, I haven't.

**TOWN CRIER:**
And have you seen my son, Hansel?

**FRAU BURGHERMEISTER HAAS:**
No, I haven't seen your son either. As a matter of fact, all the children of the town seem to be missing.

**PIED PIPER:** (*Crossing over to the **TOWNSPEOPLE**.*)
I told you something terrible would happen if you didn't pay the Piper. I took your adorable children away.

**MARTA:**
Oh, no—how horrible. What do we do now? How do we get out precious children back?

**BURGHERMEISTER HAAS:**
All right. We're sorry. You were right and I was wrong. Here.
(*Pulling out some money from a pocket.*)
We'll pay you your 100 deutsche marks. Just bring our children back.

**PIED PIPER:**
Not so fast. The price has just gone up to 300 deutsche marks.

**FRAU BURGHERMEISTER HAAS:**
Why you scoundrel—you cad—playing on our misery and sorrow just so you can turn a profit!

**PIED PIPER:**
Hey, welcome to the world of big business.

**TOWN CRIER:**
What can we do, Burghermeister Haas? We have to pay him to get our children back.

**BURGHERMEISTER HAAS:**
Oh, all right. I'll pay him—anything so he'll move on and leave us alone.
*(He pays the PIED PIPER.)*
Now, what have you done with our children?

**PIED PIPER:**
You'll find them in the cave on Köppen Hill.

*(The TOWNSPEOPLE start towards Köppen Hill and exit stage right.)*

**PIED PIPER:** *(Continued.)*
Uh, you may want to take some extra cash with you. Getting out of those Mickey Mouse souvenir shops can cost a fortune.

*(The PIED PIPER pockets his money and plays his pipe as he dances offstage left [probably to the music of "Hi-Ho"]. Quickly the TOWNSPEOPLE reenter stage right with HANSEL and GRETEL, who are wearing Mickey Mouse ear hats and carrying Mickey Mouse and Donald Duck plastic bags full of trinkets.)*

**NARRATOR:**
So the townspeople of Hamelin got their children back—after promising to return to Disneyworld on their next vacation; the rats made their way to the Black Forest; Felix and Heidi married and had several little rats and lemmings running about; and the Pied Piper invested his money in an exterminating business that he named after himself: Orkin. And all lived happily ever after. You too can live happily ever after if you remember one thing: You must always pay the piper, or at least leave the flutist a big tip.

*(Curtain.)*

### END OF THE PIED PIPER OF HAMELIN

# The Quib Blaster from Zantar

### *A Space Farce by Joan Garner*

## CAST OF CHARACTERS (m=male   f=female)

| | | |
|---|---|---|
| NARRATOR (m/f) | MAMA (f) | HARRY (m) |
| HECTOR (m) | DEPEWY (m) | JADE (f) |
| MELANIE (f) | COLLINS (m) | STEPHANIE HODGES (f) |
| LANCE (m) | MAUDE (f) | |

## CHARACTER AND COSTUME DESCRIPTIONS

**HECTOR:** Planetarian Hector is something of a blowhard. He is egotistical and likes to boss people around. Hector wears an outfit that should look futuristic in style, and there should be an emblem or sash over a shoulder to indicate that he is a high official.

**MELANIE:** Melanie is a typical teenager, but bored with her life. She longs for excitement. She wears an outfit that should look futuristic in style, but with nice feminine touches.

**LANCE:** Lance is also a typical teenager who desires excitement and adventure. Lance wears an outfit that should look futuristic in style, but not sloppy.

**MAMA:** Mama is a dull sort who alarms easily. Mama wears an outfit that should look futuristic in style, but boring.

**DEPEWY:** Depewy is something of a yes-man and something of a weasel, but he knows he's smarter than Hector. Depewy wears an outfit similar to Hector's, but his emblems and such should not be as ornate as Hector's.

**COLLINS:** Collins is a dim-witted individual who is tolerated by the rest. He's just there. Collins wears an outfit that should look futuristic in style, but should also look like a janitor's jumpsuit.

**MAUDE:** Maude is preoccupied with food and would probably be fun to be around if it weren't for her minor obsession. Maude should be costumed to look like an insect. It is suggested that she wear some sort of bodysuit with one or two sets of wings. Antennae are a definite must. A long nose would help.

**HARRY:** Harry is just like Maude in obsession and costume, but wears glasses and is slightly nerdish.

**JADE:** Jade is a slick and confident salesperson. Would you buy a used car from this person? Probably. Jade should wear something dazzling, like a silver metallic, space-type suit.

**STEPHANIE HODGES:** Stephanie is a stereotypical newscaster—nice in a phony way. Stephanie should dress ultraconservatively, with perfect hair and makeup—plastic looking. Only when the Quibs arrive can she be allowed to look unraveled.

**Scene Design for *The Quib Blaster from Zantar***

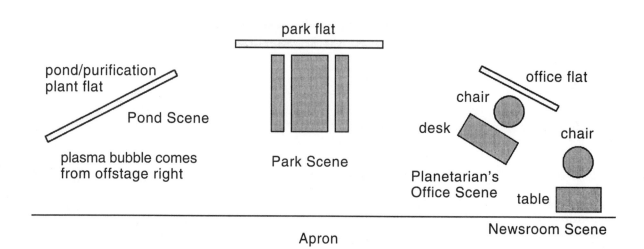

## PROPS

plates, glasses, food, oversized knives and forks, flyswatters, bicycle horns, earphones, Quib blaster gun, sign, papers, egg, potato chips.

## AS A STUDY LESSON

As a study in histrionics, *The Quib Blaster from Zantar* has been especially created for exaggeration. The characters and plot are broad enough to encourage overacting. As an overacting exercise, the play can help young actors find subtlety in delivery. (If not familiar with overacting exercises, the instructor encourages and works with the actor to bring forth a melodramatic and caricature-like performance. Once the extreme is accomplished, the instructor gradually brings down or tones down the performance until a more subtle and convincing presentation is created—showing the student the difference between mere exaltation and fine craft.)

## AS PERFORMANCE

*The Quib Blaster from Zantar* is perfect as a small, fun skit. It also travels well as a road show, requiring a minimum of props and a set that can easily be moved and set up. It can as easily and effectively be told with no set and very few props.

## CONSIDERATIONS, EFFECTS, AND AFFECTS

The plasma bubble can be a one-dimensional, roll-on flat with a circular frame and transparent material inside to see Lance and Melanie through (or nothing there at all). If a roll-on flat is not practical, a comical effect might be to have someone offstage throw in a large, clear beach ball while Jade shoots her blaster. One of the kids can catch the ball, then exit back out with it as they go on their way. Or the kids can merely exit as the *blasting* is acted out. Because the plasma bubble is described in the narrative, it need only be assumed.

The Quib blaster gun may be made, or may be a toy space gun or water gun.

# The Quib Blaster
# from Zantar

**SET:** There are four scene setups that can remain on stage throughout the play:
1) The Pond/Purification Plant Scene at stage right
2) The Park Scene at center stage
3) The Planetarian's Office Scene upstage left nearer to center stage
4) The Newsroom Scene downstage left

The plasma bubble should be transparent so that the kids can be seen when in it, and if the bubble is able to move onstage and offstage right, so much the better. There should be a picnic table in the Park Scene, a small desk and chair in the Planetarian's Office Scene, and a smaller table and chair off to the side for the Newsroom Scene. All can be very simple and cartoon-like if desired.

**AT RISE:**
Evening, July 24, present day. A pleasant night on the planet Picatell.

All but **HECTOR**, the Planetarian, sit around the picnic table. **HECTOR** is at the head of the table giving a speech. The others appear very bored. The others are **MELANIE** and **LANCE** at the end of the table downstage, then **MAMA**, **DEPEWY**, and **COLLINS**. **HECTOR** is something of a blowhard. He is egotistical and likes to boss people around. **MELANIE** is a typical teenager, but bored with her life. She longs for excitement. **LANCE** is also a typical teenager who desires excitement and adventure. **MAMA** is a dull sort who alarms easily. **DEPEWY** is something of a yes-man and something of a weasel, but he knows he's smarter than Hector. **COLLINS** is a dim-witted individual who is tolerated by the rest.

**NARRATOR:**
In the year _____ {present year}—give or take a billion years—the citizens of Picatell celebrated the twentieth anniversary of their planet being colonized. There was much joy throughout the land, and many celebrations and festivals were held to help mark this momentous occasion. In Colony 3.7, the community came together and held a picnic. Since the population of Colony 3.7 numbered only six, it wasn't terribly difficult to round everyone up. However, this didn't lessen the tiny population's great excitement and wild enthusiasm for the landmark day.

**HECTOR:**
And so, Picatell Citizens, as Planetarian, I would like to say that on this great day it gives me great pleasure to represent this great planet and its great people—especially the great citizens of Colony 3.7.

*(COLLINS falls asleep and drops his head in the plate of food before him. This doesn't seem to bother anyone, while the rest of HECTOR'S speech is said in the background [softer] of MELANIE and LANCE'S conversation.)*

**MELANIE:**
Is he going to be long?

**LANCE:**
Why should Planetarian Hector be any different from all the other Planetarians?

**MELANIE:**
Yawn . . .

**LANCE:**
Every year it's the same thing. We have a picnic, and the Planetarian gives this excruciatingly boring speech that no one listens to or cares about.

**MAMA:** (*Slapping* **LANCE** *on the arm.*)
Hush.

**LANCE:**
Ow.

**MELANIE:**
You'd think that one year we could do something different.

**LANCE:**
Boy, wouldn't that be *great*!

(**LANCE** *and* **HECTOR** *end their lines on "great" at the same time.*)

**HECTOR:** (*Eyeing* **LANCE** *with disapproval.*)
Ummm—and so, in conclusion . . .

(*Everyone cheers and applauds loudly and happily.*)

**HECTOR:** (*Continued.*)
Ummm . . . thank you.

(*Another round of applause as* **HECTOR** *sits and* **DEPEWY** *stands to address everyone.*)

**DEPEWY:**
And now, citizens of Colony 3.7, as your Assistant to the Undersecretary to the Deputy Director of the Assistant to the Under Planetarian, I would like to invite you all to the fireworks display down by the water purification facility.

**HECTOR:**
Lake, Depewy. It's a lake.

**DEPEWY:**
Lake? It's a big cement tank with a bunch of machinery hooked to it.

**HECTOR:**
We like to refer to it as a lake.

**DEPEWY:**
Well, excuse me. . . . We're going to have fireworks down by the *lake*.

**HECTOR:**
We are a small planet, but we are a great planet. We have forged a life out of the wilderness and have risked much and sacrificed a lot to create this great utopia we call Picatell. This was no small feat, no-sir-ee. We have worked hard and long, but now see the fruits of our labors. Now see how it was all worth the hard work and sacrifice. We have much to be proud of, citizens of Picatell. Yes, much to be proud of. And so here, on this great day, I would like to say how great everyone has been. You've been just *great*!

*(All begin to rise.)*

**MAMA:**
Maybe someone should wake up Collins. After all, he's the one in charge of the fireworks.

**HECTOR:** *(Pulling COLLINS'S head out of his plate of food.)*
Snap out of it, Collins—and wipe off your face, you look disgusting with that celery stalk sticking up your nose.

*(COLLINS wipes his face and joins the others who are starting to exit stage right.)*

**MELANIE:**
Shouldn't we clean up this mess first?

**HECTOR:**
No, leave it. We'll clean it up tomorrow. Meanwhile, if we're lucky, a wind will blow all this trash away.

*(The adults laugh. MELANIE and LANCE look at one another, not too sure about leaving things a mess, but exit stage right with the others. After a moment, MAUDE and HARRY, the QUIBS, enter stage left. They are two bug-like creatures with antennae who wear a large knife and fork in a holster buckled around their waists. MAUDE is preoccupied with food and would probably be fun to be around if it weren't for her obsession. HARRY is just like Maude in obsession and costume, but wears glasses and is slightly nerdish.)*

**MAUDE:**
My, my, my—I'm glad we buzzed this planet. Look what my multiprismed eyes are showing me here. Do you see this, Harry? Someone has foolishly left all their food and litter strewn about.

**HARRY:**
Yes, Maude, I see. It's a veritable smorgasbord of delectable treats.

**MAUDE:**
A veritable smorgasbord. Of course, none of this belongs to us, but since someone has just left it here . . .

**HARRY:**
Oh, I'd hate to see all of this go to waste, Maude.

**MAUDE:**
It would be criminal, Harry—just criminal. Besides, being the outstanding Quibs that we are, it's our duty to completely wipe out anything and everything that isn't nailed down.

**HARRY:**
So true.
*(Crossing closer to the picnic table, he dips his finger into a pie and licks it.)*
Mmmm, tasty. Cherry pie, with whipped cream no less.

**MAUDE:** *(Tasting the pie herself.)*
Exceptional. Truly exceptional.

**HARRY:** *(Drawing his knife and fork.)*
Shall we?

**MAUDE:** *(Drawing her knife and fork.)*
We shall.

*(They sit and begin to dig in.)*

**MAUDE:**
Wait, Harry.

**HARRY:**
What is it, Maude?

**MAUDE:**
I feel a little guilty about this. With such a find, shouldn't we share it with our friends and family?

**HARRY:**
Well, definitely family, but I believe including our friends might be too many.

**MAUDE:**
Let's see—between your family and my family, I estimate there would be about . . .

**HARRY:**
. . . about 100 to 200 million.

**MAUDE:**
Splendid. We'll have a party.

**HARRY:**
I'll send a message.

**(HARRY** *climbs up on the end of the picnic table. He then pulls his legs up to rub the bottom of his feet together.)*

**MAUDE:** *(Standing to join him.)*
What are you doing?

**HARRY:** *(Rubbing.)*
Sending a message.

**MAUDE:**
But that way is so archaic. No one rubs their feet together anymore. Don't you have Universal Fiber Optics calling, or at least direct dialing?

**HARRY:**
I didn't think of that. Of course I should use the UFO line.

**(HARRY** *pulls one of his antennae out a little further, removes a bicycle horn from his belt, and honks the horn into his mouth in some sort of code. He then reattaches the horn to his belt.)*

**HARRY:**
That should do it.

**MAUDE:**
Everyone should be here in an hour or so.

**HARRY:**
Do you think we ought to wait for them?

**MAUDE:**
It's the only polite thing to do.

**HARRY:**
The only polite thing . . .

*(The **QUIBS** look at one another for a beat, then seat themselves back at the table and begin eating.)*

**HARRY:**
Will you pass the sweet potatoes, please?

**MAUDE:** *(Passing the potatoes.)*
Why certainly. Butter?

**HARRY:** Yes, please.

*(The **QUIBS** eat away as the lights go down a bit. The **CITIZENS** of Colony 3.7 enter just to the far side of stage right, and ahh, ooo, and clap while looking upwards as **COLLINS** makes fireworks sounds.)*

**NARRATOR:**
So while the citizens of Colony 3.7 enjoyed the fireworks display, the Quibs sat down to dinner. While the citizens were oooing—

*(The **CITIZENS** ooo.)*

**NARRATOR:** *(Continued.)*
—and ahhing—

*(The **CITIZENS** ahh.)*

**NARRATOR:** *(Continued.)*
—the Quibs were mmming—

*(The **QUIBS** mmm.)*

**NARRATOR:** *(Continued.)*
—and making yummy sounds.

*(The **QUIBS** say "yummy" with a mouth full of food.)*

**NARRATOR:** *(Continued.)*
Oh, you probably don't know what a Quib is, do you? Well, a Quib is a tiny insect-like thing about the size of a microchip. Known to be able to adapt to any climate, Quibs fly throughout the universe looking for food. Scavengers at heart, Quibs prefer to eat whatever others leave behind rather then go out and grow or earn their own—

**HARRY:** *(Standing and addressing the **NARRATOR**.)*
Now wait a minute here. You make us sound like pesky little pests.

**NARRATOR:** *(To **HARRY**.)*
You *are* pesky little pests.

**MAUDE:** *(Standing.)*
Well, that may be true, but you don't have to announce it to the whole world.
*(She points toward the audience / into space.)*
By the way, what world is that?

**NARRATOR:** *(To the* **QUIBS***.)*
It's the planet Earth.

**MAUDE:**
The planet Earth, you say. Do they have people there that litter and don't pick up their trash?

**NARRATOR:**
More than I care to say.

**MAUDE** and **HARRY:** *(Very interested.)*
Really?

**NARRATOR:** *(To the audience.)*
Anyway, back to the story.

*(As the* **NARRATOR** *continues,* **HARRY** *and* **MAUDE** *exit stage left while* **MELANIE** *and* **LANCE** *exit stage right.* **MAMA, COLLINS, HECTOR,** *and* **DEPEWY** *cross over to the Planetarian's Office Scene. The lights come up to full.)*

**NARRATOR:** *(Continued.)*
Soon Harry and Maude were joined by their families, and Colony 3.7 became plagued with Quibs, much to the dismay of Planetarian Hector and the Assistant to the Undersecretary to the Deputy Director of the Assistant to the Under Planetarian Depewy.

*(***HECTOR** *sits at his desk, picks up a flyswatter, and swats the Quibs every now and then. The others swat at themselves and their fellow actors as they huddle around the desk discussing the situation.)*

**HECTOR:**
I don't know where they came from. One minute we're fine, and the next we have these pesky little pests all over the place.

**MAMA:**
What are they, Hector?

**HECTOR:**
I don't know.

**COLLINS:**
What are they, Depewy?

**DEPEWY:**
I don't know.

**COLLINS:**
What do we do?

**DEPEWY:**
I don't know.

**MAMA:**
Well, we simply have to get rid of them. They're ruining my hydrangeas.

**COLLINS:**
Not to mention what they're doing to my gladiolus.

**MAMA:**
They're not just eating our flowers.

**COLLINS:**
They're eating everything in sight!

**HECTOR:**
I know, I know.

**MAMA:**
Then what are you going to do, Hector?

**HECTOR:**
I don't know. I don't know.

**DEPEWY:**
I know.

**HECTOR:**
You know?

**DEPEWY:**
Yes, I know. We get help.

**HECTOR:**
Oh, brilliant.

**COLLINS:**
No, he's right.

**HECTOR:**
He is?

**DEPEWY:**
Don't you think I can be right?

**HECTOR:**
You've never been right before.

**MAMA:**
Right about what?

**COLLINS:**
Right about what we need to do.

**MAMA:**
What are we going to do?

**COLLINS** and **DEPEWY:**
Get help!

**MAMA:**
Who's going to get help?

**COLLINS** and **DEPEWY:**
Don't know.

**MAMA:**
Then what do we do?

**DEPEWY:**
We get ourselves a pest exterminator, that's what we do.

**MAMA:**
That sounds good.

**HECTOR:**
I should have thought of that myself.
*(To DEPEWY.)*
Know of any?

**DEPEWY:**
Of any pests? Why, yes, I know—

**HECTOR:**
Of any exterminators, you nitwit.

**DEPEWY:**
Well, no. But we could put out a Universal Fiber Optic call.

**COLLINS:**
Or we could just try the Yellow Pages.

**HECTOR:**
Do it, Depewy. Send out the call.

**DEPEWY:**
Me? I don't want to make the call.

**HECTOR:**
Why not?

**DEPEWY:**
Because everyone looks stupid making a UFO call.

**HECTOR:**
What—you want me to make the call and look stupid?

**DEPEWY:**
For you, looking stupid comes more naturally.

**HECTOR:** *(Standing and staring down DEPEWY.)*
Look here, you little pipsqueak, as Assistant to the Undersecretary to the Deputy Director of the Assistant to the Under Planetarian, it's your job to make all the Universal Fiber Optic calls.

**DEPEWY:** *(Staring back.)*
And it's your job as Planetarian, you big overstuffed blowhard, to address the situation!

*(The stare down continues until HECTOR swats a Quib on his neck.)*

**HECTOR:**
All right, I'll do it. It's my responsibility as Planetarian, so I'll do it.

*(**HECTOR** pulls a bicycle horn out of the desk drawer, puts on earphones with antennae on them, opens his mouth, and honks the horn into his mouth in code. Immediately a spaceship can be heard screeching across the sky, then slamming on its brakes [this can sound like car brakes]. In rushes **JADE** from stage right. She carries a large laser gun. **JADE** is a slick and confident salesperson.)*

**JADE:**
Greetings one and all. Jade's my name, Quib blasting's my game. I just happened to be in the neighborhood—only two million miles away—when I heard your UFO call. So I thought I'd pop in and help you out with your problem.

**MAMA:**
Thank goodness you're here. Suddenly the colony seems infested with these pesky little pests. They're eating us out of house and home.

**COLLINS:**
They especially like our hydrangeas and gladiolus.

**JADE:**
Mmmm. Sounds like Quibs to me.

**HECTOR:**
What's a Quib?

*(**JADE** takes **HECTOR'S** flyswatter, swats the desk, picks up the dead Quib on her finger, and puts the finger near **HECTOR'S** nose.)*

**JADE:**
That's a Quib.

**HECTOR:**
How do we get rid of them?

**JADE:**
Well, you're in luck.
*(Picking up her laser gun.)*
I just happen to have my superdeluxe, ultimate, high-powered Quib blaster with me. All I need to do is turn this baby on and powee, all the Quibs are blasted into outer space.

**MAMA:**
What happens to them after that?

**JADE:**
What do you care? They won't be around here anymore.

**HECTOR:** *(Slapping his neck again.)*
Fine. Do it.

**JADE:**
They seem particularly fond of you, don't they? Taken a bath lately?

**HECTOR:**
I don't have to stand here and be insulted. I have Depewy for that. Just get rid of these Quibs!

**JADE:**
Whoa . . . Hold on. We haven't discussed payment, General or Officer Whatzit. Just what are you, anyway?

**HECTOR:**
I'm Planetarian Hector.

**JADE:**
Don't you mean planetar*ium*?

**HECTOR:**
No. A planetar*ium* is a place to observe projections of planets and stars. A Planetar*ian* is one who—planets.

**DEPEWY:**
So how much do you want?

**JADE:**
Two kazillion bobos.

**HECTOR:**
Two kazillion bobos? Are you nuts? Nobody has two kazillion bobos. Make it one kazillion.

**JADE:**
Deal. Now, where would you say the heaviest concentration of Quibs is?

(As **MAMA, COLLINS, HECTOR,** and **DEPEWY** slap their necks and arms in unison.)

**MAMA** and **COLLINS** and **HECTOR** and **DEPEWY:**
Here!

**JADE:** (As she hoists her Quib blaster and cocks it.)
All right. Stand back.

(**JADE** steps to center stage while the **CITIZENS** huddle to the left of the Park Scene. **HARRY** and **MAUDE** enter stage right laughing. They don't notice **JADE** at first, but when they do, they stop dead in their tracks.)

**HARRY** and **MAUDE:**
Oh, no—JADE!

**JADE:**
There you are, you pesky little pests. Take that!

(**JADE** blasts the Quibs, who go tumbling offstage right. **JADE** will continue to blast away while the **NARRATOR** speaks.)

**NARRATOR:**
Jade proceeded to blast all of the Quibs off the planet, making Picatell a nice, but boring, place to live once again.

**JADE:** (Crossing back to the **CITIZENS**.)
There you go—every last Quib blasted into outer space. That will be one kazillion bobos, please.

**HECTOR:**
One kazillion bobos for a few seconds' work? Ridiculous.

**JADE:**
But you agreed . . .

*(Suddenly everyone in the scene freezes. Enter **STEPHANIE HODGES** stage left. She quickly crosses to the W.O.O.P.Y. Newsroom Scene. She places a sign on the desk that says "W.O.O.P.Y. Newsbreak," and sits with papers in hand. **STEPHANIE** is a stereotypical newscaster—nice and phony. While **STEPHANIE** enters, the **NARRATOR** will be saying this next line.)*

**NARRATOR:**
We interrupt this program to bring you a special news bulletin. Here now in the W.O.O.P.Y. Newsroom is anchorperson Stephanie Hodges.

**STEPHANIE:**
This just in to the W.O.O.P.Y. Newsroom. Scientists have discovered an unidentified swarming—something in space. All readings indicate this swarm is headed directly towards Earth. . . .
*(She stops and drops her papers on the desk while looking offstage.)*
This isn't another story like spotting Santa Claus and his reindeer over City Hall on Christmas Eve, is it? I mean, it was pretty cute the first time, but year after year after year . . . What? Oh—the W.O.O.P.Y. Newsroom will keep you posted on this story as it develops.

*(**STEPHANIE** exits with her sign while the **NARRATOR** speaks.)*

**NARRATOR:**
And now back to our regularly scheduled program.

*(The **CITIZENS** and **JADE** continue where they left off.)*

**JADE:**
You owe me one kazillion bobos.

**HECTOR:**
Well, I don't have one kazillion bobos. What do you think of that?

**JADE:**
This isn't fair. I'll sue. I'll . . .

**HECTOR:**
You'll do what? You know how things are these days. You should have gotten a signed contract. We're not legally bound to anything.
*(Laughing.)*
What a sucker.

*(**HECTOR** exits stage left with the other **CITIZENS**. They laugh at **HECTOR'S** name-calling.)*

**JADE:** *(Calling off to them.)*
You'll be sorry. You just wait and see. You'll live to regret this!
*(To herself.)*
It's so hard to make a decent living these days.

*(**STEPHANIE** enters once again downstage left to resume her spot at the news desk while **JADE** sits on top of the picnic table, dejected. After replacing her newsroom sign, **STEPHANIE** speaks.)*

**STEPHANIE:**
This is Stephanie Hodges with a W.O.O.P.Y. update. Scientists have now identified the unknown swarm that is traveling to Earth from outer space. Although specifics are not known yet, the team of scientists has been able to detect several itty-bitty metal objects

within the swarm. These objects are apparently made of silver or aluminum and are shaped like teensy-weensy knives and forks . . .
*(Looking offstage again.)*
All right, what is this? Is this some kind of joke? Marty, are you playing one of your practical jokes on me again?
*(She stands to exit.)*
Journalism is a serious business, you know. Stop horsing around.

*(**STEPHANIE** exits stage left, leaving the sign on the table this time.)*

**JADE:**
I ought to do something terrible to those cheapskates—teach them a lesson—that's what I ought to do.

*(Enter **MELANIE** and **LANCE** stage right.)*

**MELANIE:**
Hello.

**JADE:**
What? Yeah, hi.

**LANCE:**
A stranger in town, how exciting.

**MELANIE:**
We haven't had a visitor here in three years.

**JADE:**
Real stagnant place, huh?

**MELANIE:**
The worst.

**LANCE:** *(Pointing to **JADE'S** Quib blaster.)*
What's that?

**JADE:**
It's a blaster.

**MELANIE:**
What do you blast with it?

**JADE:**
Just about anything.

**LANCE:**
Boy, I wish you could blast us out of here.

**MELANIE:**
Yeah, to somewhere more exciting. Well, maybe to somewhere where the people are actually breathing—just a little bit.

**JADE:**
Well, now—you know—that could be arranged.

**MELANIE:**
Really? You're not teasing us, are you?

**JADE:**
Why should I tease you? If you want to get off this pathetically dull planet, I could blast you to, say, Zantar, where I come from. It's a thriving, hustling metropolis of over 20 million people. The planet never sleeps, and there are more things to see and do there than on any other planet for light years away.

**LANCE:**
Man, that sounds cool.

**JADE:**
It is cool. It's the best.

**MELANIE:**
Could you blast us there, please?

**JADE:**
Sure, why not?

**LANCE:**
Well, how much will it cost?

**JADE:**
For you two, not one bobo.

**LANCE:**
For nothing? What's the catch? Everything costs something.

**JADE:**
I see you young people are certainly more mature and intelligent than your adult counterparts here.

**MELANIE:**
What do we do? How is it done?

**JADE:**
It's all very scientific. I create a plasma bubble around you, then blast you into space. I can set the coordinates as I create the bubble so it will head towards Zantar and deposit you on my Uncle Tad's front lawn. If you explain things to him, I'm sure he'll take you in and show you a good time until I can return to Zantar myself.

**LANCE:**
What if, after a while, we want to come back here?

**JADE:**
Then I blast you back. But I don't suspect you'll be wanting to leave Zantar any time soon—maybe in one or two millennia. You just say the word and it's done.

*(MELANIE and LANCE look at one another and smile.)*

**MELANIE:**
All right. Let's do it.

**JADE:**
Good.
(***JADE*** *hoists her Quib blaster again and cocks it.*)
Okay, stand over there.

(***MELANIE*** *and* ***LANCE*** *stand near the picnic table.* ***JADE*** *stands extreme stage right. As she shoots the blaster, a plasma bubble rolls onstage in front of the* ***KIDS***, *or a ball is tossed to them. [****LANCE*** *or* ***MELANIE*** *can simply hold out a hand to stop the bubble once it reaches them, then stand behind it so it appears they are now inside, or they can catch the ball.]*)

**JADE:** (*Continued.*)
Say hello to Uncle Tad for me. I just know he'll be a nice and gracious host, especially if you gently remind him that I caught him peeking into that girlie show and promised not to tell Aunt Lu about it. Have a great time.

(***JADE*** *blasts away again, and the plasma bubble rolls back offstage right with* ***MELANIE*** *and* ***LANCE*** *inside. They wave good-bye. As the* ***KIDS*** *exit,* ***STEPHANIE*** *enters the Newsroom Scene from downstage left with papers in one hand and a flyswatter in the other. She doesn't look as put-together now and swats Quibs as she speaks.*)

**STEPHANIE:**
News flash! The swarm is here—all over—everywhere!
(*She slaps the desk as if to kill one of the pesky little pests.*)
President of the United States _____ {the name of the current president}, as well as Governor _____ {the name of your state's governor}, and Mayor _____ {the name of the city's mayor} have just come out of an emergency meeting to discuss what to do about the situation. It was agreed to call out the National Guard to help in the matter, and all assure us that these pesky little pests will be exterminated as soon as we know exactly what they are and how to get rid of them. In the meantime, you are asked to stay indoors. Keep all foodstuffs and edible items tightly wrapped and stored, and the Surgeon General suggests that you yawn as little as possible to avoid swallowing the insects en masse. This is Stephanie Hodges reporting from the W.O.O.P.Y. Newsroom.

(***STEPHANIE*** *exits downstage left as* ***HECTOR***, ***MAMA***, ***COLLINS***, *and* ***DEPEWY*** *enter upstage left and cross over to* ***JADE***.*)

**MAMA:**
Has anyone seen Lance? I haven't seen him all day.

**COLLINS:**
Melanie is missing too.

**JADE:**
They went exploring.

**MAMA:**
Exploring? Where?

**JADE:**
Oh, this big wide universe via Zantar.

**MAMA:**
Zantar? How?

**JADE:**
I blasted them away, just like I blasted the Quibs away.

**COLLINS:**
But why?

**JADE:**
You didn't pay me for my services—I got even.

**HECTOR:**
How long will they be gone?

**JADE:**
Well now, that's hard to say—probably not until you grown-ups learn to keep your word, so it may be a very long time.

**MAMA:**
This is terrible. What are you going to do about this, Hector?

**HECTOR:**
I don't know.

**COLLINS:**
But we have to do something.

**HECTOR:**
I know. I know.

**DEPEWY:**
So what are you going to do?

**HECTOR:**
I don't know. I don't know.

*(**HECTOR, DEPEWY, MAMA,** and **COLLINS** exit stage left, squabbling. **JADE** shakes her head in disbelief, hoists her Quib blaster over a shoulder, and exits stage right.)*

**NARRATOR:**
And so what have we learned here today? One, don't litter. Two, keep your word and promises. And three, no matter where you go in this universe, you will always find pests.

*(**MAUDE** and **HARRY** enter stage right and walk across until they exit stage left.)*

**MAUDE:**
I take exception to that.

**HARRY:** *(Eating from a bag of potato chips.)*
You *are* the exception, Maude.

**MAUDE:**
Thank you.

**HARRY:** *(Taking an egg from his pocket and offering it to **MAUDE**.)*
My, how I love this planet Earth. I may stick around for a very long time. With the amount of trash these people make, our entire species could live here for years. Spoiled egg?

**MAUDE:** *(Taking the egg.)*
Mmmm, yummy. I love spoiled eggs.

**HARRY:**
Moldy cheese is the best, though.

**MAUDE:**
Oh, without a doubt, unless we're talking serious best, and then we're talking rotten hot dogs.

**HARRY** and **MAUDE:**
Mmmmmmmmmmmmmmm.

*(Curtain.)*

END OF THE QUIB BLASTER FROM ZANTAR

# Beauty and the Beast

# Beauty and the Beast

*A Romantic Tale of Enchantment by Joan Garner*
*Based on the French fairy tale*

## CAST OF CHARACTERS (m=male   f=female)

CAVETTE (f)  BEAUTY (f)  PAPA (m)
CHANTELL (f)  CHARLES (m)  BEAST (m)

## CHARACTER AND COSTUME DESCRIPTIONS

(The following costume suggestions are for a realistic production. Because there is very little set and scenery involved, realistic and elaborate costumes of the era will add to the play.)

**CAVETTE:** Cavette is physically attractive, but unpleasant in personality. She wears a simple dress of the late eighteenth century in neutral colors, white stockings, and soft slippers. After receiving her new dress, she wears a much fancier dress with frilly collar, sleeves, and underskirt. It should probably be made of bright yellow or green satin. Cavette will also wear more jewelry and a white lace cap. Her hair should be long and done up with several ringlets. White stockings and embroidered shoes.

**CHANTELL:** Chantell is physically attractive, but unpleasant in personality. She wears a simple dress of the late eighteenth century in neutral colors, white stockings, and soft slippers. After receiving her new dress, she wears a much fancier dress with frilly collar, sleeves, and underskirt. It should probably be made of bright purple or peach satin. Chantell will also wear more jewelry and a white lace cap. Her hair should be long and done up with several ringlets. White stockings and embroidered shoes.

**BEAUTY:** Beauty is generous and loving. Although stubborn in opinion, she is kind and learns to be more open-minded. Beauty wears a simple country dress of the period with lace around the collar and half sleeves. The dress should be cream or light yellow, nothing loud, but not drab either. Neutral stockings and soft slippers.

**CHARLES:** Charles is in his mid-teens. He is unsure of himself but always eager to please. Charles wears a tattered brown long coat and tan waistcoat. His shirt should be simple with no frills, and his buckskin breeches should come down to just below his knees. Tall brown boots. Black tricorne hat.

**PAPA:** Papa is an honest man of his word. He loves his children and worries about them. Papa wears a red hunting coat with a yellow waistcoat. His shirt is moderately frilly and his breeches are gray. Black riding boots. Black tricorne hat.

**BEAST:** The Beast is sullen but tender of heart. His beastly presence should be shown in his size and features, but his gentle nature should be shown in his manner. The Beast is the best dressed of all. He wears a loose, frilly shirt with lace at the collar and sleeves. The waistcoat should be multicolored, sparkling satin, and his coat should be dark burgundy or royal blue velvet with elaborate gilded buttons and bric-a-brac. His breeches should be white and his boots black. Makeup for the Beast might consist of a full head appliance and hoofed gloves for his hands. However the Beast is made up, it is important that his eyes remain relatively human so that expression may be seen. The Beast may also have animal feet of fur and claws if desired.

Scene Design for *Beauty and the Beast*

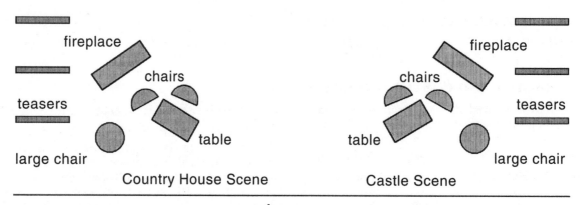

SET

It is suggested that this set be as simple as possible. Although the furniture and fireplaces should look real, there shouldn't be any walls behind them. A single white drop that lighting may be applied to may serve as the background, or you may choose to drape the set with light curtains that will reflect the lighting.

PROPS

basket of potatoes, basket of clothing, smoked bacon, plates and glasses, vase with rose, coat, mirror, blanket, bottle, spoon, note, comb, knife, handkerchief, blindfold, Papa's hat, Papa's scarf, papers, stick, Beauty's cape, flagon, Charles' gloves.

AS A STUDY LESSON

Although *Beauty and the Beast* is a tale of enchantment, this play does not employ magic effects to communicate a special aura. Instead, it depends on the actors to convey charm and magic. The play is more of an acting challenge than the previous plays in this series inasmuch as it relies solely on the actors to convey the story. Although it is a familiar story, it is also an abbreviated telling, requiring the actors to work harder in creating convincing and sympathetic characters in a limited amount of time.

AS PERFORMANCE

This play will be excellent to perform before parents, other classes, or the general public. It is a bit longer than other plays in this series (with the exception of *Winds of Silk*) and can be very effective with the proper lighting, costuming, and makeup.

CONSIDERATIONS, EFFECTS, AND AFFECTS

In all probability, the Beast can be two actors; the Beast and the Beast as a man. This will eliminate the concern of not having enough time to get out of the Beast makeup, as the time lapse is only a few seconds. However, if the Beast's costume is created with a hood and gloves, these should be relatively simple to get out of in time.

Thunder may be achieved using a recording. Lightning may be achieved using lighting.

If moderate theatre lighting is available, soft amber gels can be used to create a more fanciful atmosphere. Colors of costumes and set should be deep, rich, and vibrant.

# Beauty and the Beast

**SET:** The play has two settings that mirror one another.
1) At stage right is the Country House Scene. A table and chairs sit in front of a fireplace, and a larger, more comfortable chair sits down right from the table.
2) At stage left is the Castle Scene. A table and chairs sit in front of a grand fireplace, and a larger, more comfortable chair sits down left from the table. Where the Country House Scene is light and airy, the Castle Scene is dark and heavy.

**AT RISE:**
Winter: France, 1765.

Lights are up over the Country House Scene. Sisters **CAVETTE** and **CHANTELL** enter from stage right. Both are physically attractive but unpleasant in personality. They are moping and sad.

**CAVETTE:**
Oh, look, my pitiful hands are so plain and naked. I once had six diamond and ruby rings on my fingers.

**CHANTELL:**
Remember the gorgeous diamond necklace I wore around my neck?

**CAVETTE:**
And we wore such lovely dresses—blue and pink and green silks with delicate laces and gold braiding. We weren't forced to don these awful rags.

**CHANTELL:**
Oh, why did Papa have to lose all his money? It was so irresponsible of him to put us in this state of poverty.

*(Enter **BEAUTY** stage right carrying a basket of potatoes. **BEAUTY** is generous and loving. Although stubborn in opinion, she is kind and learns to be more open-minded.)*

**BEAUTY:**
You're not wearing rags, dear sisters; they are respectable, simple dresses. And as for jewelry, well, gems and jewels are nice to have, but nothing we can't live without. Perhaps if you helped with the cooking and house chores a little more, you wouldn't have all this time on your hands to whine and complain.

**CHANTELL:**
Listen to Beauty. It sounds as if she enjoys our plight. You can't tell me you don't miss all the fine things we once had, the many servants waiting on us hand and foot, and all the rich gentleman callers who appeared at our doorstep?

**BEAUTY:**
Of course I miss the servants and the finery *and* the attentive men. But it's all gone now. All we can do is make the best of our present situation.

*(**BEAUTY** places the potatoes by **CAVETTE**.)*

**BEAUTY:** *(Continued.)*
Here, Cavette. I'm certain peeling these potatoes will help get your mind off your misery.

*(**BEAUTY** reaches over and takes a coat that has been hanging over the large chair.)*

**BEAUTY:** *(Continued.)*
And Chantell, I'm quite confident all your worries will vanish once you begin mending Papa's coat. Now if you'll excuse me, I have laundry to do.

*(**BEAUTY** exits stage right.)*

**CAVETTE:** *(Mocking.)*
"Here, Cavette. I'm certain peeling these potatoes will help get your mind off your misery." I hate her.

**CHANTELL:** *(Disgusted.)*
She's so good and beautiful.

**CAVETTE:**
Our precious Beauty.
*(Under her breath.)*
I know what I'd like to do to our precious Beauty.

*(**CHANTELL** smiles at **CAVETTE**, then they break out in a wicked laugh. **BEAUTY** enters from stage right with a basket of clothes.)*

**BEAUTY:**
The mending basket is in my room, Chantell.

**CHANTELL:**
I know. You're not our mother, Beauty. Stop acting like you are.

*(Enter **CHARLES** stage right with a slab of bacon. **CHARLES** is in his mid-teens. He is unsure of himself but always eager to please.)*

**CHARLES:**
I hope this bacon tastes good. It's the first piece of meat I've ever smoked. It seems to have kept all right in the cellar.

**BEAUTY:**
I'm sure it will taste delicious, Charles. We'll have it as a special treat tonight for supper.

**CAVETTE:**
Special treat? It's only bacon.

**BEAUTY:**
It's not only bacon. It's meat that Charles has cured with his own two hands. At least he's helping this family through these hard times. What are you doing?

*(**PAPA LaMARR** enters stage right holding a piece of paper high in the air. **PAPA** is an honest man of his word. He loves his children and worries about them. **PAPA** is excited.)*

**PAPA:**
Children! Children, I have wonderful news! I just received word that one of my ships thought lost at sea has reached port!

**CHANTELL:**
Will we be rich again, Papa?

**PAPA:**
No, no, dear Chantell. I'm afraid we'll never be as rich as we once were, but the profit from the cargo on this ship should help pay all my debts. I may even have enough to bring home a few presents.

**CAVETTE:**
Presents! Oh, Papa, I'd like a new silk dress—lots of silk dresses!

**CHANTELL:**
And I want a big bottle of perfume—the biggest bottle you can find.

**PAPA:**
Yes, we'll see. And you, Charles? What would you like?

**CHARLES:**
Perhaps new gloves to work in the stable with.

**PAPA:**
They're yours, son. . . . And you, Beauty? What can I bring home to my Beauty?

**BEAUTY:**
I don't need anything, Papa—just bring yourself back to us safe and well. That's all I want.

**PAPA:**
Bless you. But surely there must be some small token or trinket I might get for you.

**BEAUTY:**
Well, if you happen upon one, I'd like one perfect rose.

**PAPA:**
A rose may be hard to find in the middle of winter, but I shall try. Goodness, I must pack and leave for the harbor city as soon as I can. Come help me, children.

*(BEAUTY, CHARLES, CAVETTE, and CHANTELL follow PAPA offstage right. The lights slowly go down on the Country House Scene. There is a crack of thunder, and the lights flash as if it were lightning. The sound of a fierce storm with wind and rain is heard over the stage, and there are one or two more thunder cracks and lightning bolts. When the sound of the storm dies down, the lights in the Castle Scene come up. But the lighting over the Castle Scene is not as bright as it was over the Country House Scene. After a beat, PAPA enters stage left. He has put on a scarf and hat for his trip.)*

**PAPA:** *(Looks about the place; then he speaks out, hoping the proprietor will hear him.)*
Hello? Hello? It was storming outside and your door was unlocked, so I let myself in. I hope it's all right. I've lost my way in this wood. Hello? You have a beautiful castle here. Have I happened upon a duke or lord? My name is LaMarr, I . . .

*(PAPA stops at the table as he sees a note placed there with a plate of food and a flagon of drink. At the center of the table is a vase of roses. PAPA picks up the note and reads it out loud.)*

**PAPA:** *(Continued.)*
"Share my food and drink and warm yourself by the fire, but take nothing from here upon leaving." *(Calling out to whomever.)*
You're most gracious. Thank you, whoever you are.

*(PAPA sits down and begins to eat. The lights on the Castle Scene fade to black as the lights on the Country House Scene come back up to full. CAVETTE, CHANTELL, BEAUTY, and CHARLES enter stage right. BEAUTY and CHARLES seem very worried, CAVETTE and CHANTELL not quite as much.)*

**CHARLES:**
Where could Papa be? He should have been home long before now.

**BEAUTY:**
You mustn't worry yourself so, Charles. I'm sure there's a simple explanation. Maybe Papa's business has taken him longer than he expected, or he decided to wait out the storm in a roadside tavern.

**CHARLES:**
I hope that's all it is. I'm going to wait in the stable. You can see the road better from there.

*(CHARLES exits stage right.)*

**CHANTELL:**
Admit it, Beauty. You're just as worried about Papa as Charles is.

**BEAUTY:**
Yes, I'm very worried, but I couldn't show poor little Charles how concerned I am. I only hope Papa has found his way out of this terrible storm.

**CAVETTE:**
Me too.

**BEAUTY:**
Why, Cavette, you're worried for Papa too? I'm touched.

**CHANTELL:**
Well, of course we're worried for Papa. What do you take us for? Uncaring, selfish pigs?

**BEAUTY:**
I'm sorry. My remark was cruel and unwarranted. I apologize.

**CAVETTE:**
That's better.

**BEAUTY:**
I think I'll join Charles and wait for Papa in the stable.

*(BEAUTY exits stage right.)*

**CAVETTE:**
Besides, if Papa is out in this horrible rain, it probably means our new dresses are getting all wet.

*(CAVETTE and CHANTELL exit out stage right as the lights to the Country House Scene go down and lights to the Castle Scene come up. PAPA stands and calls out once more.)*

**PAPA:**
That was a splendid dinner. Thank you, wherever you are. As it sounds like the storm may have died down a bit, I will take my leave. Thank you again.

*(**PAPA** begins to leave but notices the vase of roses on the table. He steps over to them.)*

**PAPA:** *(Continued.)*
Roses. How wonderful. However did he come upon roses this time of year? Since they're already cut, I'm sure he wouldn't mind if I took one home to Beauty.

*(**PAPA** lifts a rose from the vase and turns to leave when the **BEAST** enters stage left roaring and towering over **PAPA**. The **BEAST** is sullen but tender of heart. His beastly presence should be shown in his size and features, but his gentle nature should be shown in his manner.)*

**BEAST:**
What are you doing?!

*(Startled and scared to death, **PAPA** stumbles away and huddles behind the large chair.)*

**PAPA:**
Dear God in Heaven.

**BEAST:**
I share my food and shelter, and this is how you repay me—by taking one of my precious roses?!

**PAPA:**
No, I—please. I thought you wouldn't mind. I would have asked for the rose if I had only known you were within these walls.

**BEAST:** *(Calming down.)*
The roses are from my garden. They are the only true beauty in this entire estate. To lose even one is like losing a child.

**PAPA:** *(Cautiously stepping out from behind the chair.)*
Then I know you'll understand why I wanted it, your majesty.

**BEAST:**
I was a king once and the title "majesty" fit quite well, but as you can see, I am no longer a king. What am I now?

**PAPA:** *(Afraid to answer.)*
What are you now?

**BEAST:**
You have eyes, man. You can see what I am. Who stands before you?

**PAPA:**
Well, with all due respect, sire, you are a beast.

**BEAST:**
Then call me Beast!

**PAPA:**
Yes, sire—yes, Beast. I am LaMarr, a simple merchant.

**BEAST:**
You said I would understand. Understand what?

**PAPA:**
Why I took the rose. You see, it wasn't for me, but for my child, my Beauty. Dresses were plentiful enough to buy one for Cavette, and the bottle of perfume easily found for Chantell, but I was having a most difficult time finding a rose for my dear Beauty.

**BEAST:**
You have a daughter named Beauty?

**PAPA:**
Yes, sire. She was the most beautiful gift her mother and I had ever received, so we named her Beauty. And true to her name, she grows more lovely and beautiful with every passing day. Might you allow me to take home this perfect rose for my Beauty?

**BEAST:**
Quite impossible. You disobeyed me, and by law you must die for it.

**PAPA:**
Die? But surely . . .

*(The **BEAST** grabs **PAPA'S** neck.)*

**BEAST:**
Say no more. Pleading will not help you here. This court condemns you to death.

**PAPA:** *(Choking.)*
It's a most unjust law.

*(The **BEAST** releases **PAPA** from the stranglehold.)*

**BEAST:**
But law is law.

**PAPA:**
Yes, I broke your law and I will pay the punishment for it. But before I die, might I be granted one final request?

**BEAST:**
And that request?

**PAPA:**
Allow me to go home one more time to say good-bye to my family. If I can see them and say farewell, I will gladly return and face my sentence.

**BEAST:**
Very well, but mark my words: If you do not return to this castle, I will kill everyone in your family. Do you understand?

**PAPA:**
Yes, Beast, I understand. I can see you are a very powerful monarch and a person of your word. I am a man of my word as well. I promise to return.

**BEAST:**
Be back by nightfall tomorrow night.

**PAPA:**
By tomorrow night? That barely gives me enough time to travel there and back.

**BEAST:**
By nightfall tomorrow night, or your family will die.

**PAPA:**
I will be back by then.

*(PAPA begins to exit stage left.)*

**BEAST:**
Old man.

*(PAPA stops and turns back to the BEAST.)*

**PAPA:**
Yes, sire?

**BEAST:** *(Picking up the rose.)*
Since you are to pay the ultimate price for stealing the rose, you might as well take it to your Beauty.

**PAPA:** *(Taking the rose.)*
Yes, sire. Thank you, sire.

*(Sadly, PAPA exits stage left.)*

**BEAST:**
As my name is Beast, her name is Beauty. She must be a lovely vision to behold to have such a name.

*(The BEAST roars in anguish as he exits stage left. The lights dim on the Castle Scene and come up on the Country House Scene. CAVETTE enters behind CHANTELL stage right. They are both yawning and stretching.)*

**CAVETTE:**
Good morning, Chantell.

**CHANTELL:** *(Yawn.)*
Mmmm, good morning Cavette.

**CAVETTE:**
Sleep well?

**CHANTELL:**
Not so well. The thunder and lightning kept waking me up.

*(BEAUTY enters, helping a very tired Charles to the large chair.)*

**BEAUTY:**
Here, Charles, this chair will be more comfortable than the wooden stools in the stable.

**CAVETTE:**
Were you two out in the stable all night?

**BEAUTY:**
Yes, we stayed awake all night thinking we would see Papa coming down the road, but we didn't.

*(**PAPA** enters with open arms.)*

**PAPA:**
My dear children! I've missed you so.

*(All go to **PAPA**. **BEAUTY** hugs **PAPA**.)*

**BEAUTY:**
Papa, we were so worried.

**PAPA:**
But I'm fine. Charles, my boy, you look tired.

**CHARLES:**
I stayed up all night waiting for you.

**PAPA:**
I'm sorry. My trip home took an unexpected turn.

**CAVETTE:**
Were you caught in the storm, Papa?

**PAPA:**
Yes, I was. But I was able to find shelter in the woods.

**CHANTELL:**
In the woods?

**PAPA:**
If you two young ladies want to take the trunk off the mule outside, I think you might find some pretty dresses and perfume in it.

*(**CAVETTE** and **CHANTELL** scream in delight and rush out stage right. **PAPA** sits in the large chair after pulling out a pair of gloves from his pocket.)*

**PAPA:** *(Continued.)*
Your gloves, Charles.

**CHARLES:** *(Taking the gloves.)*
Thank you, Papa. They're very fine. Thank you.

**PAPA:**
You're very welcome. And for you, Beauty.
*(He carefully pulls the rose out of his coat.)*
Your rose.

**BEAUTY:**
It is a beautiful rose, Papa, but you didn't have to.

**PAPA:**
Please take it. It cost me dearly.

**BEAUTY:**
What do you mean? What's wrong, Papa?

*(CAVETTE and CHANTELL come waltzing in, swishing their new dresses in the air and dancing about with them.)*

**CAVETTE:**
Isn't it divine? And the lace. Look at this fine lace. It just has to be imported.

**CHANTELL:**
See how nicely the color matches my eyes? Oh, Papa, you're the best papa in the whole world.

**CAVETTE:**
Thank you, Papa. I love you so much.

**CHANTELL:**
Me too.

*(CAVETTE and CHANTELL kiss PAPA on the cheek and dance and sing around the room again with their dresses.)*

**BEAUTY:**
Sisters, please, something is wrong.

**CAVETTE:** *(Sniffing the bottle of perfume in her hand.)*
Wrong? What could be wrong?

**CHARLES:**
Papa was about to tell us.

**CHANTELL:**
Did your business not fare as well as you had hoped, Papa? Are they going to take away our dresses again?

**PAPA:**
No, you may keep your dresses. I promise.

**BEAUTY:** *(Looking at her rose.)*
There is something about this rose. It's strange in a way, but I couldn't say how. Papa, where did you find a rose in bloom this time of year, it being out of season and all. Did you get it from a greenhouse or conservatory?

**PAPA:**
Last night on my way home, a big storm came up. I was in the middle of the woods, and with the light of the moon disappearing behind the rain clouds, I lost my way. However, I managed to find refuge in a castle. It was a magnificent castle, yet peculiar and foreboding at the same time. I had not known it was there before.

**CHARLES:**
What castle? Where?

**PAPA:**
Out there. It was very hard to find. I hope I'm able to find it again.

**CHANTELL:**
Why again?

**PAPA:**
Because I must go back.

**CAVETTE:**
Why?

**PAPA:**
I made a promise to the Beast.

**CAVETTE** and **CHANTELL:**
Beast!

**CHARLES:**
An animal?

**PAPA:**
Yes, but not like any animal we are accustomed to. He stood tall like a man, but fur was all over his face. He talked eloquently like a man, and his eyes were that of a man's, but the rest were animal parts—horns, claws, fangs. Horrible.

**BEAUTY:**
Whatever must have happened to him?

**PAPA:**
I don't know.

**CHANTELL:**
It sounds as if he was cursed by an evil witch or wizard. If this is so, Papa, you best stay away from the Beast.

**CAVETTE:**
Chantell is right, Papa. If you go back there, you might be turned into a beast as well.

**PAPA:**
But I must go back.

**CHARLES:**
Why?

**PAPA:**
I gave my word. The Beast allowed me into his castle and shared his food with me, but warned me not to take anything from there. But when I saw the vase of roses on the table, I thought of Beauty and took one to bring home to her.

**BEAUTY:**
This rose?

**PAPA:**
Yes, that rose. The Beast was very angry. I had broken the law, so now I must return to face my punishment.

**CHARLES:**
What is the punishment, Papa?

**PAPA:**
My dear children, I have been sentenced to death.

**CAVETTE:**
No! It can't be!

**CHANTELL:**
Just for taking a rose? Say it isn't so.

**CHARLES:**
We won't allow it. I'll go kill the Beast myself.

**PAPA:**
No, no, son. Just as the Beast must be enchanted and cursed, so can he enchant and place spells on us. If I don't return, he will kill us all.

**BEAUTY:**
Can't we talk to him? If we reason . . .

**PAPA:**
I tried to reason with him, but the law is the law. He has permitted me to return home and say good-bye, but now I must go if I plan to make it back to the castle by nightfall.

**BEAUTY:** *(Crying.)*
Oh, Papa, no. This can't be happening.

**PAPA:** *(Standing and placing an arm around **CHARLES**.)*
You will be the man of the house now, Charles. Be good to your sisters.

**CHARLES:**
Yes, Papa.

**PAPA:**
Cavette, Chantell, my pretty young ladies, you must put your new dresses and perfume to good use and find yourselves two handsome and rich husbands.

**CAVETTE** and **CHANTELL:** *(Weeping.)*
Yes, Papa.

**PAPA:**
Beauty, you must be strong for your brother and sisters.

*(**BEAUTY** embraces **PAPA**.)*

**BEAUTY:**
I will try, Papa.

*(**PAPA** gently pushes **BEAUTY** away and steps back.)*

**PAPA:**
Good-bye, children. Know how much I love you.

*(All say good-bye; then **PAPA** turns and exits stage right. **BEAUTY** falls into the large chair crying.)*

**CAVETTE:**
This dress doesn't seem as pretty anymore.

**CHANTELL:**
Poor Papa. What are we going to do without him?

**BEAUTY:** *(Raising her head in determination.)*
We're *not* going to do without him.

**CHARLES:**
What?

**BEAUTY:**
I've got to do something. I can't let Papa die.
*(Reaching for her cape.)*
He took the rose for me. It's my fault Papa's in this terrible trouble.

**CHARLES:**
But Beauty, what can you do?

**BEAUTY:**
I'm going to follow Papa to the castle and meet with this Beast. If he let Papa return to us to say good-bye, there must be some good in him. Perhaps I can find this decency and change the Beast's mind about Papa.

**CAVETTE:**
But he may change you into a beast as well.

**BEAUTY:**
He may. I'll just have to take that chance. Come, Charles, and help me saddle my horse. If we hurry, I can catch up to Papa and follow him.

*(**CHARLES** and **BEAUTY** exit stage right.)*

**CAVETTE:**
Wait for us!

*(**CAVETTE** and **CHANTELL** scurry out stage right as the lights dim over the Country House Scene and come up over the Castle Scene. **PAPA** enters stage left.)*

**PAPA:**
Beast? Beast, I have returned like I promised, and before nightfall. I trust you will keep your word and let my family live.

**BEAST:**
Your family will live.

*(Startled, **PAPA** swings around to find the **BEAST** sitting in the large chair.)*

**PAPA:**
Oh! I didn't see you there.

**BEAST:**
Then your eyesight must be failing you, for I am one that is hard to miss.

**PAPA:**
Well . . . Do with me what you will, Beast.

**BEAST:** *(Standing.)*
Did you give your Beauty the rose?

**PAPA:**
Yes, but she would rather not have the rose than to have me pay for it with my death.

**BEAST:** *(Wrapping a hand around **PAPA'S** neck.)*
The law is the law.

**PAPA:**
Beast, Beast, a moment, please. If you will, as long as I'm going to die, may I ask what will happen to me after my heart stops beating?

**BEAST:**
After?

**PAPA:**
Yes. As you are a beast, is it your intent to eat me?

**BEAST:** *(Releasing **PAPA**.)*
Eat you? I kill animals to eat. Do you not do the same?

**PAPA:**
Yes, I suppose I do. But like you say, they are animals.

**BEAST:**
I will not eat a man.

**PAPA:**
Ah. This is a comforting thought at such a time. Thank you.

*(The **BEAST** takes **PAPA** in a stranglehold once again and begins choking **PAPA** until **BEAUTY** rushes in from stage left.)*

**BEAUTY:**
No, don't! Please, you mustn't! I beg of you, please spare my father!

*(The **BEAST** releases **PAPA** and quickly turns his back while **BEAUTY** hurries to embrace **PAPA**.)*

**BEAUTY:**
Papa, are you all right?

**PAPA:**
Beauty, what are you doing here? It's much too dangerous. Run away before it's too late.

**BEAUTY:**
No. I won't leave you, Papa. This is all my fault. If I hadn't asked for the rose, you wouldn't be in such trouble.

**PAPA:**
It doesn't matter.

**BEAUTY:**
It matters to me.

*(**BEAUTY** steps towards the **BEAST**.)*

**BEAUTY:**
Beast—sire, may I speak to you, please? I must speak to you on behalf of my father. Please, sire.

*(The **BEAST** turns to **BEAUTY**. **BEAUTY** steps back with a slight gasp upon seeing the **BEAST**, but quickly regains her composure and goes on.)*

**BEAUTY:** *(Continued.)*
Sire, surely there must be some other way to resolve this situation.

**BEAST:**
Your father broke the law here.

**BEAUTY:**
Yes, I know. I'm not saying that my father shouldn't pay for his crime, but to be put to death . . . Is there not another choice?

**BEAST:**
I might consider . . .

**BEAUTY:**
Yes, whatever it is. Anything.

**BEAST:**
I will let your father return to his family, but you must stay here with me.

**PAPA:**
That is out of the question, Beast!

**BEAUTY:**
Papa, please.
*(To the **BEAST**.)*
How long would I have to stay here?

**BEAST:**
Forever.

**PAPA:**
No. Take me. Kill me.

**BEAUTY:**
No, I'll stay. If it will stop you from killing Papa, I will stay with you, Beast.

**BEAST:**
Agreed.

*(The **BEAST** quickly grabs **PAPA** and carries him out of the room stage left under **PAPA'S** protest.)*

**BEAUTY:**
Papa! Wait!

**PAPA:** *(On his way off.)*
Beauty, I love you!

*(**BEAUTY** sobs as the **BEAST** returns.)*

**BEAUTY:**
You didn't even let me say good-bye.

**BEAST:**
I wanted to spare you the pain of a long good-bye.

**BEAUTY:**
Spare me the pain? You wanted to see me cry, that's all. You're a horrid beast, and I can't stand the sight of you. If I must spend the rest of my days here, let it be alone. I do not wish to be with anyone so cruel as to keep a family apart.

**BEAST:**
I am not cruel. But there are rules that must be obeyed within this enchantment, or all is lost.

**BEAUTY:**
Is one of the rules to kill? For if it is, this is not an enchanted place, but a wicked and evil one.

**BEAST:**
There is enchantment, and there is survival. Until the one is broken, the other cannot be changed.

*(Pause.)*

**BEAUTY:**
What would you have of me, then?

**BEAST:**
I want nothing of you but perhaps your friendship.

**BEAUTY:**
How can I be your friend if I am your prisoner?

**BEAST:**
You're not a prisoner here. You may go in any room you wish and explore the castle grounds whenever you like.

**BEAUTY:**
But I cannot go beyond the castle gates.

**BEAST:**
This was the deal you made. Are you hungry? Food is plentiful here. Some fresh fruit, perhaps?

**BEAUTY:**
Don't be silly. It's the middle of winter. There is no fresh fruit this time of year.

**BEAST:**
How can you look at this bedeviled face before you and not believe there can be fresh fruit here?

**BEAUTY:**
What happened to you? How did you become a beast?

**BEAST:**
You mustn't ask such questions of me, for I cannot answer them. But we may speak of other things. Whatever you want.

**BEAUTY:**
Do you know of the world? Have you knowledge of all the faraway and wonderful places I've heard people tell of?

**BEAST:**
Yes. Not to boast, but I am quite a learned individual. I have been to many exotic places and have met many a fascinating soul on my travels.

**BEAUTY:**
Would you tell me of these?

**BEAST:**
Nothing would give me greater joy, sweet Beauty. And after you dine each evening, there will be entertainment.

**BEAUTY:**
What kind of entertainment?

**BEAST:**
Music, stories. Do you like stories, Beauty?

**BEAUTY:**
Very much.

**BEAST:**
Then one evening I will tell you a story, and the next evening you may tell one to me. Does this appeal to you?

**BEAUTY:**
And what do we do when we run out of stories?

**BEAST:**
I will read to you. There are many libraries in this castle, with thousands of books. You will never be bored, dear Beauty. I promise you that.

**BEAUTY:** *(Thinking it over.)*
Will you tell me a story now?

*(Pleased, the **BEAST** cups his hands behind his back and begins telling **BEAUTY** a story as they exit stage left.)*

**BEAST:**
Once upon a time, long, long ago, in a land of green grass and honeysuckle, there roamed a valorous knight and his squire . . .

*(The lights dim on the Castle Scene and come up on the Country House Scene. **PAPA** enters stage right and sits in the large chair to review some business papers he has. **CHARLES**, **CAVETTE**, and **CHANTELL** enter stage right. **CHARLES** crosses over to sit on the floor by **PAPA**. He is whittling on a stick. **CAVETTE** enters holding a mirror, and **CHANTELL** comes in with a comb. They will say their lines while entering. [**CAVETTE** and **CHANTELL** are wearing their new dresses.])*

**CAVETTE:**
Do you think this blush is too heavy, Chantell?

**CHANTELL:**
Heavy? No, not if you're a clown.

**CAVETTE:**
You're so amusing, Chantell.

*(CAVETTE sits at the table and uses a handkerchief to remove some of the blush. CHANTELL also sits.)*

**CHANTELL:**
What do you think of my hair up like this? Does it make me look more sophisticated?

**CAVETTE:**
It makes you look old.

*(Displeased, CHANTELL takes her hair down.)*

**CHANTELL:**
How did your business dealings go this month, Papa?

**PAPA:**
Very well, Chantell. I dare say the company brought in a greater profit this month than the month before and the month before that, though I thought it quite impossible.

**CAVETTE:**
Will we soon have enough money to move back to the city?

**PAPA:**
We have enough money for that now, but we can never move from here.

**CHANTELL:**
Why not?

**CHARLES:**
What if Beauty were to return? We can't have her coming home to an empty house. How would she know where to find us?

**PAPA:**
Charles is right. We must stay and be here for when Beauty comes home.

**CAVETTE:** *(Crossing over to PAPA.)*
Papa, I know how much you miss Beauty. We miss her too, but it's been three months. I don't think she's coming back.

**CHARLES:**
Yes she is! She'll be here as soon as she can escape from the Beast.

**CHANTELL:** *(Crossing over to CHARLES.)*
Charles, there's no escaping the Beast. You've heard Papa tell of this horrid monster. He is powerful and magical. How can Beauty ever hope to win against the Beast?

**PAPA:**
Still, we will stay here, for a while at least. But I don't want to deprive you girls of your happiness. If you want, why not plan a vacation to the city? I will sponsor the trip.

**CAVETTE:**
Oh, thank you, Papa. That would be grand.

**CHANTELL:**
We'll go tomorrow.

**CAVETTE:**
Tomorrow? There's too much to do—too much to plan to go tomorrow.

**CHANTELL:**
All right. But we'll leave as soon as we can. Will you be coming with us, Charles?

**CHARLES:**
I don't know.

**CAVETTE:**
Oh, you must. You must see the sights of the city.

*(CAVETTE and CHANTELL drag CHARLES offstage right. PAPA chuckles at the girls' excitement and follows them off. The lights dim on the Country House Scene and come up on the Castle Scene. The BEAST enters. He has a blindfold over his eyes, and his arms are extended out that he may find his way.)*

**BEAST:** *(Calling out.)*
Beauty? Where are you, Beauty? You can't hide from me.
*(He swipes at the air.)*
She's really very good at this.
*(The BEAST lifts up the corner of the blindfold as if to peek out, then puts it back and returns to swiping at the air.)*
Come now, I'm beginning to feel ridiculous.

*(BEAUTY enters stage left and hides behind the large chair. The BEAST fumbles his way to the table and grabs a chair.)*

**BEAST:** *(Continued.)*
Aha! I've got you!
*(Feeling the chair.)*
Oh. A thousand pardons.

*(The BEAST replaces the chair and continues feeling his way through the room. It's difficult for BEAUTY to keep herself from laughing out loud. Mischievously, she sneaks up behind the BEAST and taps him on the back of his shoulder. When the BEAST swings around, BEAUTY moves to the other side.)*

**BEAST:** *(Continued.)*
There you are—drat! There you *were*. I think I like the hide-and-go-seek game better than this one . . . Mercy, Beauty, take pity on this tired old beast.

*(BEAUTY taps him on the back of his shoulder again. The BEAST swings around, but just as BEAUTY begins to move away, the BEAST grabs her, and they tumble to the ground laughing.)*

**BEAUTY:** *(Playfully rapping on his chest.)*
It took you forever to catch me that time.

**BEAST:** *(Removing his blindfold.)*
Oh, my. I'm quite out of breath. What a perfectly absurd game.

**BEAUTY:**
Oh, you liked playing it.
*(She tickles him.)*
Come on, confess. You liked playing my game.

**BEAST:**
All right. All right. I liked playing the game. Stop now.

*(The **BEAST** holds **BEAUTY** to keep her from tickling him. Once they both stop laughing, they stay in the embrace for a moment, both looking at the other with an endearing glance. But this bothers **BEAUTY**, and she breaks from the **BEAST** to stand and step away.)*

**BEAUTY:**
This was a most strenuous game. I'm all flushed.

**BEAST:** *(Also rising.)*
Beauty . . .

**BEAUTY:**
You were right, Beast. We'll do much better if we just play hide-and-go-seek.

**BEAST:**
Beauty, I love you.

**BEAUTY:**
Love me? Oh, dear, now who is speaking of the ludicrous?

**BEAST:**
From the moment I met you—all of these days that you have been with me—I have loved you. Will you marry me?

**BEAUTY:**
You want me to marry you? No, that is impossible.

**BEAST:**
Why? Have you not come to care for me a little? If you are to remain here with me for the rest of our lives, why not have it be as husband and wife?

**BEAUTY:**
We could never be husband and wife.

**BEAST:**
Never? Does my touch offend you so?

**BEAUTY:**
Oh, no—to the contrary. I have come to like your touch, and I hate myself for liking it. I *have* become very fond of you, Beast. You are kind and wise and fun to be with, but . . .

**BEAST:**
. . . but I am a beast.

**BEAUTY:**
Yes.

**BEAST:** *(Hurt and dejected.)*
Well, it's getting late. I will say good night.

**BEAUTY:**
Beast . . .

*(The **BEAST** exits stage left.)*

**BEAUTY:**
Beast, please . . . Oh, why must things be the way they are? Poor Beast.

*(**BEAUTY** sits in the large chair, frustrated. She ponders a moment, then looks strangely. She looks about the room and becomes frightened.)*

**BEAUTY:** *(Continued.)*
Beast! Beast!

*(The **BEAST** reenters and **BEAUTY** goes to him.)*

**BEAST:**
What is it?

**BEAUTY:**
Oh, Beast, something is wrong. It's Papa. Something is very wrong. I can feel it.

**BEAST:**
But, Beauty . . .

**BEAUTY:**
He's hurt, or sick. Yes, that's what it is. My Papa is sick. Beast, he's dying. I know he's dying!

*(**BEAUTY** weeps in the **BEAST'S** arms.)*

**BEAST:**
There, there, my love.

**BEAUTY:**
My Papa is dying, and I can't go to him. I can't be there to tend and comfort him. Now he'll never know how much I think of him and how much I love him.

**BEAST:**
Don't cry now, Beauty. Your Papa will know how much you love him.

**BEAUTY:**
But how will he know this if I must stay here?

**BEAST:**
Because I release you of your promise. You may go to your father.

**BEAUTY:**
Beast, you would do this for me?

**BEAST:**
I cannot bear to see you sad and crying. Go home to your family. These castle gates will never close on you again.

**BEAUTY:**
Thank you, Beast. Thank you for letting me go. I must hurry before it's too late.

*(BEAUTY begins to leave, but turns back to see the BEAST one more time before rushing out stage left. The BEAST looks lost. When he approaches the table, he is overcome with rage and slams his fists down on the table top. Then the BEAST slumps to his knees and buries his head in his arms. An agonizing roar comes from deep inside him as he rises and stumbles out stage left.)*

*(The lights dim on the Castle Scene and come up on the Country Home Scene. CAVETTE and CHARLES enter stage right helping PAPA come in. They ease him into the large chair and place a blanket over his lap. CHANTELL follows from behind with a bottle and spoon.)*

**CAVETTE:**
There, Papa. Are you comfortable here?

**PAPA:**
Yes. It feels nice to be sitting.

**CHANTELL:**
Please take your medicine, Papa. The doctor said . . .

**PAPA:**
. . . I know what the doctor said. The medicine will do little good.

**CAVETTE:**
If you won't take your medicine, at least have something to eat. I could make a soothing broth for you.

**PAPA:**
Bless you, Cavette. You children have been so good to me. But I know of only one thing that could make me well again.

**CHARLES:**
I know, Papa. But we can't bring Beauty home to you. No matter how much we wish for it, or how much we pray . . .

*(BEAUTY joyfully rushes in stage right.)*

**BEAUTY:**
Papa! Dear Papa!

*(BEAUTY goes to PAPA and they embrace.)*

**PAPA:**
Beauty, is it really you?

**BEAUTY:**
It's really me, Papa.

**PAPA:**
Oh, my Beauty. Now I can get well knowing you'll be here with me.

**CAVETTE:**
How ever did you escape from the Beast?

**BEAUTY:**
I didn't escape. The Beast released me from my promise.

**CHANTELL:**
Why?

**BEAUTY:**
I knew there was something wrong. I felt in my heart that Papa was sick. So the Beast released me from my promise so I could come home to see Papa.

**PAPA:**
The Beast must be of a kindlier nature than he was before.

**BEAUTY:**
He is, Papa. He's very kind and good to me.

**CAVETTE:**
A beast? Kind?

**BEAUTY:**
He's more than just kind. He's smart and gentle. He lets me win all the games we play. He reads to me, and we talk of faraway lands and magical kingdoms. He's become my best friend.

**CHANTELL:**
Gosh, Beauty, to hear you talk, it sounds like you're in love with this beast.

**BEAST:**
Love him? No, I . . .

**PAPA:**
Beauty, come here.

*(**BEAUTY** sits on the floor next to **PAPA**.)*

**PAPA:** *(Continued.)*
Love is the most precious gift anyone can receive. You must hold on to it as tightly as you possibly can and cherish it, because true love doesn't come to all. You must accept it and embrace it no matter where it comes from. If you love this beast and he loves you, then your place is with him.

**BEAUTY:**
But Papa, you are ill.

**PAPA:**
My illness came from my thinking you were miserable and unhappy, having to stay in the castle with a terrible beast. But I see by the shine of your eyes that this creature has made you happy. And you have told us that he is good to you. I worried that he was not. As long as I know you are happy, I will be well.

**BEAUTY:**
Oh, I do love him. I don't know how this can be, but I do.

**CAVETTE:**
You're crazy, Beauty, to love a beast.

**BEAUTY:**
Yes, to love my lovely, handsome beast.

**PAPA:**
Then it is settled. Our Beauty will visit with us for a day or two, then return to the castle and her beast.

**BEAUTY:** *(Hugging **PAPA**.)*
Thank you for understanding, Papa.

**CHARLES:**
Beauty, come see my garden. I planted it myself.

**BEAUTY:**
Charles, you're becoming quite the farmer.

*(**BEAUTY**, **PAPA**, **CAVETTE**, **CHANTELL**, and **CHARLES** all exit stage right. The lights go down over the County House Scene and come up on the Castle Scene. After a moment the **BEAST** enters slowly. He appears sick and weak. He leans on the table and coughs, then sits in the large chair and holds onto his heart. His eyes close. Soon you hear **BEAUTY** approaching. She calls out to him.)*

**BEAUTY:**
Beast! Beast, where are you?

*(**BEAUTY** enters stage left and looks about the room.)*

**BEAUTY:** *(Continued.)*
There you are. Thank Heaven. I've missed you so much.

*(**BEAUTY** goes to the **BEAST'S** side as he opens his eyes.)*

**BEAST:** *(Very weak.)*
Beauty, you came back to me.

**BEAUTY:**
I couldn't stay away. Papa made me realize that this is where I belong now.

**BEAST:**
How is your father?

**BEAUTY:**
He's well again, thank you. Oh, Beast, can you ever forgive me?

**BEAST:**
Forgive you for what?

**BEAUTY:**
For being so foolish. For denying my feelings for you. Beast, you are my life. You are my heart.

**BEAST:**
Sweet Beauty, how I've longed to hear you speak these words. You have made me very happy.

**BEAUTY:**
But Beast, what's wrong? Why do you feel so cold and weak?

**BEAST:**
I'm dying, Beauty.

**BEAUTY:**
No. You can't. I won't let you.

**BEAST:**
When you went away there was nothing left for me. I didn't want to go on.

**BEAUTY:** *(Crying.)*
You must go on. I'm here, Beast, and I'll never leave you again.

**BEAST:**
It will be better this way. How could I have ever believed you would want to be the wife of a beast?

**BEAUTY:**
But I do want to be your wife. I love you.

**BEAST:**
It's too late.

**BEAUTY:**
No. I won't believe that.

**BEAST:**
Please, turn away. I don't want your memories of me to be of my death.

**BEAUTY:** *(Holding on to him.)*
No, I want to stay with you.

**BEAST:**
Please!

*(The **BEAST** rises and stumbles out of the room stage left. **BEAUTY** falls into the large chair sobbing. She buries her head in the armrest and doesn't notice that the lights over the Castle Scene come up fuller, making the scene brighter and more alive. After a moment, a handsome gentleman, the **BEAST**, enters. He goes to **BEAUTY** and kneels by her side.)*

**BEAST:**
Beauty? Beauty, my love, you mustn't cry. Beauty, look up and see me.

**BEAUTY:** *(Looking up.)*
Who are you?

**BEAST:**
Don't you recognize me? Don't I seem familiar?

**BEAUTY:**
No. Where did you come from? What have you done with Beast?

**BEAST:**
Beast is gone, Beauty. He disappeared when you said "I love you." I have taken his place.

**BEAUTY:**
You?

**BEAST:**
When I was a young man, I was arrogant and mean. When I refused shelter to an old woman, she turned me into a beast. And so I was to stay a beast until I could learn to love unselfishly and I might earn another's love in return. I thought it impossible for someone to love a beast. But then you came to my castle and I began to hope that maybe . . . And here you have professed your love, and I am a man again.

**BEAUTY:**
I don't know what to make of this. I love the Beast because of who he is. You're like a stranger.

**BEAST:**
But I haven't changed inside. You'll see. We'll start over. We can play games like we did before. Beauty, do you think you might learn to love me like you learned to love the Beast?

**BEAUTY:**
The eyes are the same. Still . . .

**BEAST:** *(Taking **BEAUTY'S** hand.)*
And my touch? Isn't the touch the same? Could the Beast do this?

*(He kisses her tenderly.)*

**BEAUTY:** *(Thinking about it.)*
Perhaps—if you told me a story.

*(He takes her arm in his and escorts her offstage left.)*

**BEAST:**
Once upon a time, there was a young prince who lived in a splendid castle . . .

*(Curtain.)*

### END OF BEAUTY AND THE BEAST

# OPPOSING
# FORCES

# Opposing Forces

*A Space Drama by Joan Garner*

**CAST OF CHARACTERS (m=male   f=female)**

NARRATOR (m/f)          COLLAN (f)          BORREL (m)          BRIGHTON (m)
JENNY (f)

## CHARACTER AND COSTUME DESCRIPTIONS

(The following costume suggestions are for a surrealistic production.)

**JENNY:** Jenny is strong and confident, smart and decisive, but being hurt, she shows a certain vulnerability. Jenny wears a futuristic uniform, probably of stretch material and plastic-looking armor accessories. There should be insignia on the outfit to signify the Nova Patrol, and another nondescript emblem to distinguish the rank of Lieutenant. High-top boots (over the knee would be nice).

**COLLAN:** Collan is a gentle character, caring, compassionate, and almost childlike. She is highly embarrassed and shy about her appearance, and although she may be timid about accepting kindness at first—not expecting such—she gratefully warms to offerings of friendship. Collan basically wears rags. The white, long-sleeved blouse has patches sewn on the elbows, and the jumper and long dress has patches sewn here and there. The only thing of quality will be the red velvet cloak with hood that should cover her completely when required. The hands and feet are exposed and should look like those of a lizard-type creature. Foam rubber appliances may be added to achieve this effect, though modified boots and gloves would be easier for the actress to discard when the time comes. The head should also be lizard-like and look very alien. This can be accomplished by creating a hood-like or close-fitting, wimple-like appliance where the forehead is extended and the ears are hidden. The same color of makeup may be added to the creature's eyes, nose, mouth, and face, but it is recommended that these features not be modified greatly to allow the actress to be expressive. There isn't a lot of time provided for the actress to change from creature to human, but this can be accomplished if some thought and care are given to the construction of her costume.

**BORREL:** Borrel is definitely preoccupied with his experiments and, when disturbed, is angry and gruff. He radiates a presence of power and physical strength. Borrel wears a pieced-together outfit that can probably look similar to that worn by the Mad Max character from the movie. He wears an eye patch, and, to symbolize nonconformity, long, lush hair.

**BRIGHTON:** Brighton is the most simplistic character of the four. He is a nice fellow and genuinely concerned with and affected by Collan's predicament. He's no pushover, but is willing to see situations in their proper perspective without jumping to conclusions. Brighton wears the same Nova Patrol uniform as Jenny's, with the possible exception of the tall boots.

**Scene Design for *Opposing Forces***

White Drop

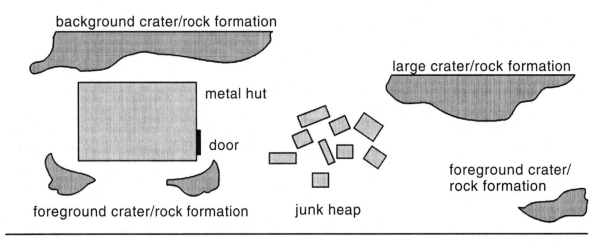

background crater/rock formation

large crater/rock formation

metal hut

door

foreground crater/
rock formation

foreground crater/rock formation    junk heap

Apron

## SET

The set as suggested consists of three-dimensional structures. A surrealistic feel to this set is also suggested.

## PROPS

plate/food, cup, bottles, cotton puffs, bandages, pitcher, knife, shackles and chains, wet cloth, key, pot, box, container.

## AS A STUDY LESSON

*Opposing Forces* is a pure acting vehicle full of symbolism, representations, and undercurrents. Whereas in *Beauty and the Beast*, the characters Beauty and Beast are the focal performers, in *Opposing Forces*, Brighton (Beauty) and Collan (the Beast) become secondary personifications of goodness and the ideal. The magnetic friction of Borrel's experiments spill over with the unwanted but strong attraction Jenny and Borrel feel for one another. It will be a good acting exercise in projecting these aesthetic qualities and appropriate pathos quickly and convincingly.

## AS PERFORMANCE

*Opposing Forces* is perfect from which to select a scene for classroom presentation, or for a group effort in production and performance. It is also worth considering as material for district and regional acting contests because of its completeness and brevity.

## CONSIDERATIONS, EFFECTS, AND AFFECTS

The explosion can be created inside the hut with lighting and sound effects. If smoke were to come out of the door and cracks in the structure, so much the better.

The crash of the spaceship can also be done with sound effects and lighting.

This is a very visual play. Dialogue almost takes second place, as most of the play is acted out in gesture, movement, and reaction.

# Opposing Forces

**SET:** The exterior of a distant ashen planet. There are oddly shaped stalagmites and small mounds rising from the ground. At stage left is a large mound/rock formation that is strong enough to sit on. This mound should stretch a good length across the stage from center stage to stage left. At stage right opposite this large mound is a small hut crudely constructed of thin, flat squares of tin and other metals. A door into the hut should face left and have a curtain over it. Nothing should be seen of the inside of the hut. The horizon casts a strange greenish-yellow color; fog rolling on the ground at the beginning and end of the play would add an extra eerie effect. All should appear barren and severe.

**AT RISE:**
Dusk: Before Earth.

The stage should be dark at first, except for the stars in the sky; then the lights will gradually come up as the **NARRATOR** speaks.

**NOTE:**
It is suggested that the **NARRATOR** not be seen during this play and that his or her voice either be a recording or come from an offstage microphone. An echoing effect is desirable to help give the overall illusion of distance and alienation.

**NARRATOR:**
Once upon a time, long before our sun did blaze, long before a fiery tempest formed the earth, before the warm light of day, before the inviting colors of spring flowers first caught the eye and the welcome feel of a cool autumn breeze first touched the cheek, a planet called Starcrest whirled around its fiery sun—a thousand light years away—in another time before time . . .

*(Lights come up to full on the planet Starcrest. Shuffling and busywork are heard in the hut. The curtain opens, and a pot is tossed out onto the ground. You can't see who tosses the pot out, just the flying pot. Then, after more noise, a box comes out and tumbles to the ground, and then another container of some sort. In the area of the newly resting pot, box, and container are other unrecognizable yet familiar-looking objects. All the objects seem to be badly worn, beat up, and spent. It's a scrap heap.*

*When a little more time passes, a louder sound is heard screeching across the sky, first from the right, then high above the stage, then to the left. It is the sound of a spaceship. Once the sound is on the left, offstage a horrible crash and explosion is heard. Red and orange colors, as if from a fire, flare up from offstage left to illuminate the hut and stage.*

*A cloaked head peeks out from the curtain on the door of the hut. It looks over to where the explosion is, then cautiously steps out and over stage left to get a better look. However, whoever or whatever the thing is can't be seen entirely—a large sweeping cloak covers most of the body. It's only on occasion that the cloak flips aside and a foot or hand may be seen, and when these extremities are visible, it is clear that some kind of creature wears the bright red cloak. The creature, **COLLAN**, watches the flames for a moment, then hurries back inside the hut. **COLLAN** is a gentle character, caring, compassionate, and almost childlike. She is highly embarrassed and shy about her appearance, and although she may be afraid to accept kindness at first—not expecting such—she gratefully warms to offerings of friendship. A loud human roar of anger is heard inside the hut, and more objects are heard being tossed and toppled about inside.*

*Soon, **JENNY** enters stage left. Her face is charred, and her uniform is badly torn and has multiple burn spots. Where there is exposed flesh, a few cuts and bruises can be seen. She appears shaken as well as physically hurt. **JENNY** is strong and confident, smart and decisive, but, being hurt, she shows a certain vulnerability.)*

**JENNY:**
Hello? Is there anyone here?

*(**JENNY** hears a rustling inside the hut and steps towards it.)*

**JENNY:** *(Continued.)*
Hello?

*(Feeling weak and light-headed, **JENNY** sits on the edge of the mound. After a beat, an ominous, deep voice comes from the hut.)*

**VOICE:**
Who are you?

**JENNY:** *(Standing and speaking towards the hut.)*
I'm Lieutenant Jennifer Lo of the Nova Patrol. The fuel system malfunctioned, and I had to crash-land my ship in the ravine.

**VOICE:**
Are you hurt?

**JENNY:**
No, not badly . . .
*(Pause.)*
Would you happen to have a communications device that I might use to send a distress signal to the Patrol?

*(Pause.)*

**VOICE:**
We have no such device here.

**JENNY:**
Oh. Well, thank you anyway.

*(**JENNY** sits back down on the mound, not knowing what to do. **COLLAN** comes out of the hut and cautiously steps towards **JENNY**, holding out a cup of water to the young woman.)*

**JENNY:** *(Taking the cup.)*
Thank you.

*(**COLLAN** stretches her hand out and gently pats **JENNY** on the shoulder.)*

**COLLAN:**
There, there.

**VOICE:**
Collan!

*(**COLLAN** darts back into the hut. **JENNY** drinks the water while watching the hut, then stands and steps to the door. When she gets very close, another roar comes from inside the hut.)*

**VOICE:**
Stay back!

*(Startled, JENNY stumbles back, tripping on the scrap heap and falling to the ground. BORREL comes out of the hut. He is magnificent, strong and handsome, and wears a patch over one eye. BORREL is definitely preoccupied with his experiments and, when disturbed, is angry and gruff. He radiates a presence of power and physical strength. When BORREL speaks, you realize his was the ominous VOICE.)*

**BORREL:**
Never approach the castle! It's forbidden.

**JENNY:** *(Attempting to stand.)*
Castle?

**BORREL:**
You're not welcome here.

**JENNY:**
It wasn't my idea. I didn't have a choice.

*(BORREL turns to go back into the hut, and JENNY quickly steps towards him.)*

**JENNY:**
Wait, I . . .

**BORREL:** *(Turning / lashing back at JENNY.)*
I told you!

*(Frightened, JENNY jumps back, trips over the edge of the large mound, and tumbles back behind it. BORREL watches a moment, then crosses back behind the mound, bends down, and carries an unconscious JENNY around to in front of the mound. He props her up against it, then steps back, watching her carefully. BORREL hurries into the hut and returns quickly with shackles and chains. He attaches a shackle around JENNY'S ankle and attaches the other end of the chain to a large piece of equipment that sits near the mound. As JENNY awakens, BORREL stands over her once again.)*

**BORREL:**
You were told not to go where you're not welcome.

**JENNY:** *(Moving her leg, then noticing the shackles.)*
What is this? Why are you doing this?

**BORREL:**
Silence! You will keep quiet and not bother us.

*(BORREL exits back into the hut.)*

**JENNY:**
What is this horrible place?
*(She holds her head in pain.)*
What have I done wrong?

*(COLLAN comes out of the hut with a wet cloth. She steps towards JENNY, offering it like she had offered the cup of water.)*

**COLLAN:**
Here—for your face.

**JENNY:** *(Taking the cloth.)*
Thank you—again.
*(She wipes her face.)*
Who are you?

**COLLAN:**
Oh, I'm no one really.

**JENNY:**
Who's the one who likes to bark?

**COLLAN:**
That's Borrel. He's my friend.

**JENNY:**
Friend? How can you stand him?

**COLLAN:**
The point is, how can he stand me?

**JENNY:**
What do you mean?

*(Timidly, **COLLAN** removes her hood and smiles. It is an endearing smile—a smile so engaging that one can almost forget it's on the face of an alien. **JENNY** just stares until **BORREL** roars for **COLLAN** to come inside. At that, **COLLAN** repositions the hood over her face and hurries back into the hut. **JENNY** continues to use the wet cloth on her cuts and bruises while watching the hut. As the lights dim, **JENNY** will tug at her shackles, sit on the ground and use the mound as a back support, then finally huddle on the ground next to the mound. Also, as the lights dim, the sound of wind will pick up. The **NARRATOR** will speak over it.)*

**NARRATOR:**
As darkness fell over the bleak and miserable planet, Jenny was left alone to bear the stinging touch of the fierce winds and the biting snap of the cold night. Without food or shelter, the young lieutenant suffered through the hours huddling near the rocks, sleeping little, shivering, and praying for morning.

*(Slowly the wind dies down as the lights come back up to full. **JENNY** is curled in a ball near the mound. In time, **COLLAN** comes out of the hut and carries a plate of food to **JENNY**. **COLLAN** places the plate on the ground and gently taps **JENNY** on the shoulder.)*

**COLLAN:**
Jenny. Pretty Jenny.

*(**JENNY** awakens and quickly moves back as far as she can go, thinking it is **BORREL**. **COLLAN** jumps, startled by **JENNY'S** swift and violent movement, then tries to comfort the frightened **JENNY** by gesturing that all is well. **COLLAN** picks up the plate of food and offers it to **JENNY**. Cautiously, **JENNY** takes the plate.)*

**JENNY:**
Thank you. I *am* hungry.

*(**JENNY** eats while they talk.)*

**COLLAN:**
Are you feeling better this morning, Miss Jenny?

**JENNY:**
I guess. It depends on what that madman plans to do with me.

**COLLAN:**
I don't think Borrel quite knows what to do with you. You were not expected.

**JENNY:**
Then why doesn't he let me go find help? Why does he keep me shackled here like a common criminal?

**COLLAN:**
I never question Borrel's actions or intent.

**JENNY:**
You should.

*(BORREL comes out of the hut and stands near the door staring at COLLAN and JENNY. JENNY looks up and stops eating, and COLLAN looks over her shoulder to see BORREL. Quickly COLLAN rises and darts back into the hut. BORREL continues to stare at JENNY.)*

**JENNY:** *(Holding the plate close to her.)*
Would you deny me food, too?

**BORREL:**
I will go to the wreckage tomorrow and see if there is anything salvageable or if there might still be a way to communicate your location to the Nova Patrol.

**JENNY:**
Tomorrow? Why not go now?

**BORREL:**
I'm too busy. Your rescue is not a high priority for me.

**JENNY:**
Well, it is for me. Heaven forbid that I should inconvenience you. Let me go back to my ship and see if anything can be done.

**BORREL:**
No.

**JENNY:**
Why not?

**BORREL:**
You might not go to your ship. You might try to go into the castle.

**JENNY:**
I'm not going into your precious castle. I couldn't care less what you're doing in there. Just unchain me.

*(BORREL stares at JENNY for a moment more, then turns and reenters the hut. Frustrated, JENNY tugs on her shackles again and tries to free herself. After a beat, a young man in a similar uniform to JENNY'S sneaks in from stage left. He slips in behind the large mound, then*

*pokes his head up over it. This is* **BRIGHTON**. *He is the most simplistic character of the four. He is a nice fellow and genuinely concerned with and affected by Collan's predicament. He's no pushover, but is willing to see situations in their proper perspective without jumping to conclusions.)*

**BRIGHTON:** *(Whispering.)*
Jenny. Psst! Jenny!

**JENNY:** *(She quickly spins around and calls out in excitement.)*
Brighton!

**BRIGHTON:**
Shhhh . . . Are you all right?

**JENNY:** *(Speaking in a hush, as will* **BRIGHTON***.)*
How did you find me?

**BRIGHTON:**
The homing device in your spacecraft alerted us.

**JENNY:**
I thought it was destroyed in the crash. It wasn't working when I left it to come here.

**BRIGHTON:**
What is this place, anyway?

**JENNY:**
A refuge for the freakish and demented.

**BRIGHTON:**
What?

**JENNY:**
An obsessed man lives in that hut over there. He calls it a castle.

**BRIGHTON:**
A castle?

**JENNY:**
I told you—demented. And Brighton, there's some kind of creature here as well.

**BRIGHTON:**
Creature? A creature like an animal?

**JENNY:**
No, she's like nothing I've ever seen. She's—it's difficult to describe her—but she speaks well and has been very kind to me when that maniac lets her.

**BRIGHTON:**
Was this man the one who chained you up?

**JENNY:**
Who else? He's afraid I'm going to go into the hut.

**BRIGHTON:**
Why? What's in there?

**JENNY:**
I don't know.

(**BRIGHTON** *looks intently at the hut, then slips around the mound to join* **JENNY**.)

**BRIGHTON:**
Come on, let's get you out of here.

(**BRIGHTON** *and* **JENNY** *both tug on the shackles.* **BRIGHTON** *tries to move the machine where the shackles are attached but can't, so the two go back to tugging and looking at other ways to release her. Both have their backs to the hut and don't notice* **BORREL** *coming out the door.* **BORREL** *rushes over to* **BRIGHTON** *and shoves him down and away, then draws a knife.* **JENNY** *screams and throws herself on* **BRIGHTON** *to protect him.*)

**JENNY:**
No, don't! He's my brother!

(*Upon hearing this,* **BORREL** *steps back but keeps the knife ready. In the meantime,* **BRIGHTON** *scrambles to right himself, but stays on the ground, not wanting to provoke* **BORREL** *into attacking.*)

**BORREL:**
Who are you?

**BRIGHTON:**
Lieutenant Brighton Lo of the Nova Patrol. I'm also Jenny's brother. Who are you?

**BORREL:**
Borrel.

**BRIGHTON:**
What are you doing here on Starcrest? This is an uninhabited planet.

**BORREL:**
We're here because it *is* an uninhabited planet where I may do my work in peace.

**BRIGHTON:**
What work?

**BORREL:**
Collan!

(**COLLAN** *pokes her head out of the curtains.*)

**BORREL:** (*Continued.*)
Another set of shackles.

(**COLLAN** *pops her head back inside, then quickly emerges carrying another pair of shackles that she obediently gives to* **BORREL**. **BORREL** *tosses the shackles over to* **BRIGHTON**.)

**BORREL:** (*Continued.*)
Put them on.

**BRIGHTON:**
I'm not going to . . .

**BORREL:** *(Making a threatening gesture with his knife.)*
Put them on!

*(Reluctantly **BRIGHTON** puts on the shackles and chains himself up to the same heavy piece of machinery that **JENNY** is chained to.)*

**JENNY:**
My brother is here now. We have a way to get off this planet. If you let us go, we won't bother you any more. You'll be free to do whatever it is you're doing.

**BORREL:**
You're of the Nova Patrol. You'll tell the others and they'll come to get Collan.

**JENNY:**
No, we won't tell anyone you're here. We promise, don't we, Brighton?

**BRIGHTON:**
I don't care if I ever see or hear of you again.

**BORREL:**
The risk is too great.

*(**BORREL** turns and retreats back into the hut. **COLLAN** stays near the door, content to look at **BRIGHTON**, until . . .)*

**BORREL:** *(Continued.)*
Collan!

*(**COLLAN** hurries back into the hut.)*

**BRIGHTON:** *(Shouting towards the hut.)*
My sister's hurt. She needs medical attention!

**JENNY:** *(Sitting on the mound.)*
Please, Brighton, don't provoke him.

**BRIGHTON:** *(Sitting next to **JENNY** on the mound.)*
Provoke him? I'd like to wring his neck.

*(**COLLAN** comes out with a tray of bottles, cotton puffs, bandages, and a pitcher. She crosses over to the two young people.)*

**COLLAN:** *(Showing the tray as she places it on the mound by **JENNY'S** side.)*
Medicine for your cuts.

**JENNY:**
Thank you.

*(**COLLAN** nurses **JENNY'S** cuts while **BRIGHTON** questions her.)*

**BRIGHTON:**
He called you Collan. Is that your name?

**COLLAN:**
Yes.

**BRIGHTON:**
What are you doing here, Collan?

**COLLAN:** *(Offering the pitcher from the tray to **BRIGHTON**.)*
Water?

**BRIGHTON:**
Why are we chained up like animals?

**COLLAN:**
Borrel is afraid you'll go into the castle. It's dangerous. If you're chained here, you can't go inside.

**JENNY:**
Well, if he's so concerned about our well-being, why did he leave me outside all night? It was cold and the wind was awful.

**COLLAN:**
Borrel has much on his mind. You're very attractive, Jenny. I'm afraid you pose quite a distraction.

**BRIGHTON:**
Collan, will you take off your hood and let me see you?

**COLLAN:**
Has Jenny told you of my ugliness? Does cruel curiosity make you ask this of me?

**BRIGHTON:**
No, I . . . I'd like to see the person who has been so kind to us. Please, it's unpleasant talking to just a hood.

**COLLAN:**
My grotesqueness will repulse you.

**BRIGHTON:**
I promise, it won't.

*(Shyly, **COLLAN** removes her hood, then looks away until **BRIGHTON** puts a gentle hand on her shoulder. She turns back to him.)*

**BRIGHTON:** *(Taking her hand and shaking it.)*
Hello, Collan. It's very nice to meet you.

*(**COLLAN** coyly returns **BRIGHTON'S** smile.)*

**BRIGHTON:** *(Continued.)*
Are you Borrel's servant or slave?

**COLLAN:**
Oh, no. I am neither a servant or slave. Borrel is helping me.

**JENNY:**
Helping you? How?

**COLLAN:**
You would not believe me if I told you.

**BRIGHTON:**
Of course we would. This is all so strange, Collan. Please help us understand it.

*(Reluctantly **COLLAN** sits on the mound beside **BRIGHTON** and tells her story.)*

**COLLAN:** *(To **JENNY**.)*
I was once like you. I was pretty, or so everyone said. A long time ago I traveled with my family to the planet Hollaper. During our journey, a peculiar phenomena moved over our spacecraft. It was later referred to as a space anomaly, but whatever it was, it killed many passengers on board, and it left me like this. They wanted to lock me away for further study, but I would have none of that, and I escaped to Fortarri.

**BRIGHTON:**
Fortarri? That's where we're from.

**COLLAN:** *(She smiles and continues with her story.)*
One night Borrel found me in a small outpost there. I was hiding in the alley behind a tavern. On occasion the tavern owner took pity on me and gave me scraps of food when I came to the back door. Once Borrel was able to get a good look at me, I thought he would turn and go away like all the rest, but he stayed. He even sat down and struck up a conversation. He seemed very curious as to how I came to be this way. I suspected this curiosity was encouraged by the large quantity of alcohol he had just consumed, but I welcomed the exchange. It had been so long since anyone looked at me like I was something other than a freak. He looked at me the way you're looking at me now—full of wonderment, but kindly and friendly . . .

*(There is a loud rustling in the hut and **BORREL** shouts out disgustedly, but then all is quiet again.)*

**JENNY:** *(Looking back.)*
He's certainly an angry man.

**COLLAN:**
You hear his frustration. I haven't knowledge of Borrel's past, and it would be impolite to ask, but I have a feeling his has been a sad life. . . . Borrel knew of a very wise man. He said this old man knew more about the universe than all the great professors and philosophers of our time, and if anyone would know how to reverse the phenomenon that affected me, it would be him. Truthfully, I thought Borrel would be rid of me once he had sobered and taken a healthy look at this unnatural creature in the light of day, but he collected me the next morning, and we went forth to seek the wise man.

**JENNY:**
Were you able to find this man?

**COLLAN:**
Yes. He was a magnificent old man who lived in a tiny room behind the conservatory near the crater gardens.

**BRIGHTON:**
What did he say?

**COLLAN:**
He told us a riddle, no more than that.

**JENNY:**
What was the riddle?

**COLLAN:**
"A creature you will be forever
Unless opposing forces come together."

**JENNY:**
Opposing forces?

**COLLAN:**
Borrel believes the space anomaly that changed me into this creature was some kind of energy displacement—a reaction of sorts to a cosmic force that had gone awry. Taking this theory in relation to the wise man's riddle of opposing forces coming together, Borrel thinks if he can somehow create two strong magnetic force fields and join them at their negative or positive poles—negative on negative or positive on positive—it will create a counterforce that will reassemble the displaced energy mass of my physical being.

**JENNY:**
By bringing opposing forces together. It's an intriguing hypothesis. Borrel must be a physicist or something.

**COLLAN:**
Yes. Borrel is very smart, but stays within himself. We came here that he might conduct his experiments without interference.

**JENNY:**
Have you had any success at all?

**COLLAN:**
A little. But whenever Borrel tries forcing like magnetic poles together, a violent recoil occurs, dispensing random electric charges. There have been many explosions. It's how Borrel lost his eye. I keep pleading for him to stop before we're both blown up—that if I must spend the rest of my days like this, then so be it—but Borrel refuses to give up.

**BORREL:** *(From inside the hut.)*
Collan, I need you!

**COLLAN:** *(Standing.)*
I must go.

**BRIGHTON:** *(Holding her back.)*
Wait. Thank you for telling us your story.

**JENNY:**
Collan, do you think you might turn us loose? We promise we'll not go near the castle or tell anyone what goes on here. Please.

**COLLAN:**
It's too dangerous.

**BRIGHTON:**
We promise to stay right here. Please, Collan—for me?

*(**COLLAN** hesitates, then reaches into her pocket and pulls out a key that she gives to **BRIGHTON**.)*

**BRIGHTON:**
Thank you.

*(BRIGHTON touches COLLAN'S cheek warmly. She willingly accepts the affection with a smile, but turns and hurries into the hut. BRIGHTON watches COLLAN go inside the hut as JENNY takes the key away from him and busies herself unlocking their shackles.)*

**JENNY:**
God bless Collan. Now we can get out of here.

**BRIGHTON:**
We can't leave them.

**JENNY:**
What? Are you joking?

**BRIGHTON:**
Maybe we can help.

**JENNY:**
Help? You saw her, Brighton. There's no hope for that poor creature. Borrel's theory may be a solution to the old man's riddle, but it isn't going to change Collan back. Collan said it herself. All Borrel is going to accomplish with these experiments is to blow up the place.

**BRIGHTON:**
Still, I can't leave her here.

**JENNY:**
Brighton, I know you have a good heart. You were always bringing home stray and starving animals when we were children. But we're not children anymore. We have a responsibility to the Patrol. I'm going back. Are you coming?

**BRIGHTON:**
No, I'm staying here.

**JENNY:**
Brighton . . . Fine. Have it your way.

*(JENNY begins to exit stage left.)*

**JENNY:** *(Continued.)*
I'm going now.

**BRIGHTON:**
I see that.

**JENNY:**
I'm not coming back after you.

**BRIGHTON:**
Fine.

*(JENNY exits in a huff. BRIGHTON watches her leave but remains sitting on the mound. COLLAN comes out of the hut and crosses to BRIGHTON.)*

**COLLAN:**
You should go with her.

**BRIGHTON:**
I don't want to.

**COLLAN:**
Jenny is right. Nothing can be done to change me back. Borrel's scientific mind will only allow him to believe that there must be an answer if he just looks hard and long enough. But I'm afraid the answers are beyond us.

**BRIGHTON:**
There must be something we can do.

**COLLAN:**
Please, go home with Jenny.

**BRIGHTON:**
No, I'm not leaving you.

**COLLAN:**
I don't want your pity, Brighton.

**BRIGHTON:**
I don't pity you. I don't think of you that way at all. It's just that—well, you don't deserve what's happened to you.

(**BRIGHTON** *wipes a tear from* **COLLAN'S** *eye.*)

**BRIGHTON:** *(Continued.)*
Oh, don't cry, Collan. Everything will be all right, I promise.

(**BRIGHTON** *holds* **COLLAN** *in his arms until* **BORREL** *calls for her.*)

**BORREL:** *(From inside the hut.)*
Collan, hurry, I almost have it.

(*The sides of the hut begin to shake.* **COLLAN** *breaks from* **BRIGHTON** *and hurries to the hut. She turns back to see him.* **BRIGHTON** *stands and almost follows her, but remembers his promise and sits back down on the mound.* **COLLAN** *goes into the hut. The sides of the hut stop shaking when* **JENNY** *returns from stage left after a moment.*)

**JENNY:**
You drive me crazy, Brighton. Do you know that?

**BRIGHTON:**
What is it?

**JENNY:**
You were supposed to come to your senses and follow me to the ship.

**BRIGHTON:**
I told you I wasn't going to.

**JENNY:**
I know, but I thought you would.
*(She sits next to him.)*
What's going on?

**BRIGHTON:**
I think Borrel is reinitiating his scientific experiments.

**JENNY:**
Scientific experiments. He's not a scientist. He looks more like a bum to me. Although I must admit, he *is* very handsome, even with only one eye.

**BRIGHTON:**
Uh-huh. Did you come back after me or Borrel?

**JENNY:** (*Jabbing **BRIGHTON** in the ribs.*)
Stop it.

(***BRIGHTON** and **JENNY** share a chuckle until the sides of the hut begin to shake again, and a tremendous humming sound like that of an engine is heard inside. There is a flash, then an explosion inside the hut. **BRIGHTON** runs into the hut.*)

**JENNY:**
Brighton, no! Borrel!

(*After a beat, **BRIGHTON** helps a singed and injured **BORREL** out. He sits **BORREL** on the mound and darts back into the hut.*)

**BORREL:** (*Dazed.*)
I almost had it. I was so close.

(***JENNY** grabs a bandage from the tray and goes to **BORREL**, administering aid to a bleeding gash on his arm.*)

**JENNY:** (*Angrily.*)
You idiot, you could have gotten yourself killed. What happened?

**BORREL:**
Just like always. I'm able to move the force fields together, but just when the poles are about to touch, they discharge, sending energy currents all over the place.

**JENNY:**
It's an insane theory. What are you thinking of, forcing magnetic poles together like that? Do you want to die?

**BORREL:**
If so, what of it?

**JENNY:**
 It would be a tremendous waste.

**BORREL:**
So? No one cares.

**JENNY:**
I do—

(***JENNY** catches herself. Obviously she prefers to keep her feelings to herself, but now that her concern for **BORREL** has been revealed, the two just stare at one another until **BRIGHTON** comes out of the hut carrying **COLLAN**. She is completely shrouded by her cloak so that nothing can be seen of her. **COLLAN** is limp as **BRIGHTON** sits her on the ground and holds her.*)

**JENNY:**
Oh, no.

**BRIGHTON:**
She isn't moving.

**BORREL:**
She got too close. I told her not to get too close. It's all my fault.

**BRIGHTON:**
She can't be dead. She just can't.

**BORREL:**
It's over. I thought I could do something, but all I've managed to do is kill the very person I tried to help.

*(**JENNY** comforts **BORREL** by placing an arm around his shoulders.)*

**BRIGHTON:**
I never did think she was ugly and repulsive. She was sweet and kind. To me she was beautiful.

*(After a beat, there is movement inside the cloak and **BRIGHTON** happily removes the hood to see a frail but alive **COLLAN** smiling up at him. But this isn't the alien **COLLAN**; she has been transformed into a pretty young woman.)*

**BRIGHTON:** *(Continued.)*
Collan, look!

*(**BORREL** and **JENNY** cross to join **BRIGHTON** and **COLLAN**. **BRIGHTON** takes **COLLAN'S** hand and holds it up for her to see.)*

**BRIGHTON:** *(Continued.)*
It worked! You're back to normal again!

*(A stunned **COLLAN** looks at her hand, then touches her face, disbelieving.)*

**COLLAN:** *(Excited.)*
It worked. It worked!

**BRIGHTON:**
You're beautiful.

*(Joyfully, **COLLAN** and **BRIGHTON** embrace.)*

**JENNY:**
It's a miracle.

**COLLAN:** *(Reaching out and taking **BORREL'S** hand.)*
You did it, Borrel. You changed me back. How can I ever thank you?

**BORREL:**
I didn't do it. I'm happy you're no longer a creature, but I didn't do it. The poles never touched. I can't take credit for this.

**COLLAN:** *(Moving to him.)*
You are a success to me.
*(She kisses him on the cheek.)*
I'm grateful to you.

**BRIGHTON:** *(Standing and taking **COLLAN** by the hands.)*
Come, Collan. We'll go to my ship and send a message to the Patrol. We'll need a larger transport to take all of us off this forsaken planet.

*(Happily, **BRIGHTON** and **COLLAN** exit stage left.)*

**BORREL:**
But I didn't do it. The experiment failed. All my experiments fail. I'm a failure. I've always been.

**JENNY:**
Are you? You came here to change Collan back into a human, and that's what happened. No matter how it happened, you're still a hero in her eyes. Does that make you a failure?

**BORREL:**
What do *you* think? I know you hate me.

**JENNY:**
I hated you, yes. But that was before I understood what it was you were trying to do, and why you treated me like you did.

**BORREL:**
I shouldn't have left you out in the cold like that. I'm sorry. I don't know what I was thinking.

**JENNY:**
You were thinking of your experiments.

**BORREL:**
It's no excuse. And I wasn't thinking of just my experiments. If you had been hurt as well, I wouldn't have been able to live with myself. I . . . never mind.

*(**BORREL** sits back on the mound, and **JENNY** crosses to continue bandaging his arm.)*

**JENNY:**
Maybe the magnetic poles weren't the opposing forces the wise man referred to in his riddle.

**BORREL:**
What else could it have been?

**JENNY:**
Perhaps the opposing forces were a handsome Brighton looking beyond Collan's ugly creature to find beauty in her heart. Perhaps the opposing forces were your denying me shelter and warmth, then allowing Collan to bring me water and tend to my injuries. Perhaps they were my hating you and believing you to be a cruel and unfeeling monster, only to find out you're truly a caring and compassionate man. I believe your theory was right in thinking the opposing forces were energy-related, but maybe your error came in working with the wrong energy force. What if the riddle "until opposing forces come together" means differences of opinion changing so an understanding can be reached? The "coming together" is both sides having enough insight to see the situation from the other's point of view. By not judging too harshly or unfairly, harmony can come to all.

**BORREL:**
Your words are very pretty, but they're painted in romantic illusion.

**JENNY:**
And your world that can only see stark and cold facts is better? Have you no room in your heart for the poetic?

**BORREL:**
I have no room in my heart for anything.

**JENNY:**
Haven't you?

*(The two stare at each other until **JENNY** takes his hand and holds it gently.)*

**JENNY:** *(Continued.)*
I think you do.

*(**BORREL** sits surprised by **JENNY'S** understanding, but he doesn't quite know what to do.)*

**BORREL:**
If there is something left in this shadow of a man, you're the one to find it.

**JENNY:** *(Smiling.)*
Let's go home.

*(**BORREL** and **JENNY** exit stage left.)*

*(Curtain.)*

## END OF OPPOSING FORCES

# Koba and the Red Lion

# Koba and the Red Lion

*A Jungle Fable by Joan Garner*

## CAST OF CHARACTERS (m=male    f=female)

| | | | |
|---|---|---|---|
| TEM (f) | JACA (m) | ZEBRA (f) | MONKEY (f) |
| ATTAR (m) | KOBA (m) | VULTURE (m) | VORASEE (f) |
| RED LION (m) | SUTU (f) | COBRA (f) | |

## CHARACTER AND COSTUME DESCRIPTIONS

(The following costume suggestions are for a realistic production.)

**TEM:** Tem is a meek woman, warm and loving. She wears a simple smock and chamma (outer garment) of earth tones. She also wears handmade bracelets and necklaces. Barefoot.

**ATTAR:** Attar is a good provider and understanding father. He wears a brown leather breechcloth with a strip of material coming up and over his left shoulder. Barefoot.

**RED LION:** The Red Lion is the only animal who does not speak; therefore, he should act and sound as much like a real lion as possible. In this same vein, the Red Lion's costume should be as realistic-looking as possible, although the lion will be more of a rusty red than sand color.

**JACA:** Jaca is very much like Attar but should be physically smaller. Jaca wears a brown breechcloth with a strip of material coming up over his left shoulder. He also wears a bracelet on his upper right arm. Barefoot.

**KOBA:** Koba is an honest and caring young man. Koba wears a breechcloth of a brown color. His does not extend up over a shoulder like Attar's and Jaca's. He wears a necklace made of animal teeth. Barefoot.

**SUTU:** Sutu is often demure, but if encouraged, she could be a more forceful and confident young woman. Sutu wears a simple white smock and brightly colored bracelets and necklaces. Barefoot.

**ZEBRA:** The Zebra is quite nervous. Her movement should be jerky, responding to another's movement. The Zebra wears a white stretch bodysuit with stripes painted on it. A partial zebra head cap appliance is worn on top of the actor's head. Makeup on the face of the actor should be done to blend into the neck of the Zebra. Hands and feet are exposed.

**VULTURE:** The Vulture is an unsavory creature. His voice should project contempt, and his movements should be awkward, like those of a real vulture. The Vulture wears a black stretch bodysuit with trains of feathers draping over and down from the shoulders. A collar of fluffy white feathers encircle its neck. A partial vulture head and beak cap appliance is worn on top of the actor's head. Makeup on the face of the actor should be done to blend into the neck of the Vulture. Hands and feet are exposed.

**COBRA:** The Cobra slithers and hisses. She is a mean and coy snake. Her movement should be slow and graceful unless striking. The Cobra wears a brown stretch bodysuit. A complete cobra head (prepared to stike) cap appliance is worn on top of the actor's head. Makeup for the actor's face should be done to blend into the yellow and white throat of the Cobra. Hands and feet are exposed.

**MONKEY:** The Monkey is droll in character, being much wiser than anyone else. The Monkey may be any variety of African monkey, but not a baboon or chimpanzee. The Monkey wears a gray or tan stretch bodysuit, and fur may be painted on or applied if desired. There shouldn't be any appliances added to make the actor look more like a monkey. Instead, the natural colors of the Monkey's face should be mirrored for the actor's makeup. Hands and feet are exposed.

**VORASEE:** Vorasee is a wise woman with a superior attitude. Vorasee wears a colorful print smock and an even brighter and more colorful chamma. She also wears an abundance of bracelets and necklaces.

**Scene Design for *Koba and the Red Lion***

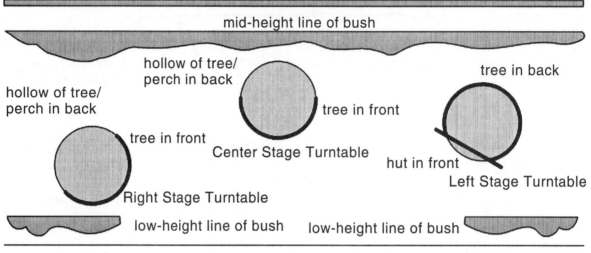

Blue Sky Drop

mid-height line of bush

hollow of tree/ perch in back

tree in back

hollow of tree/ perch in back

tree in front

tree in front

Center Stage Turntable

hut in front

Left Stage Turntable

Right Stage Turntable

low-height line of bush     low-height line of bush

Apron

### SET

The set as suggested consists of realistic scenery.

### PROPS

3 spears, baby, 2 lion cubs.

### AS A STUDY LESSON

As a fable with talking animals, this play gives young actors the opportunity to take on the characteristics of animals. Students need to observe the animals they are portraying in order to emulate the animals' movements and traits. This play will be a good lesson in learning grace and fluid movement on stage.

If this play is designed in a specific style (e.g., naturalism, realism, expressionism), it would prove a nice study of art and performance style and its part in the theatre.

### AS PERFORMANCE

As *Koba and the Red Lion* is a fable, the obvious target audience is children. However, if the costumes and sets are designed realistically and the play elevated to a more mature level, it can also prove very entertaining for peers and adults.

### CONSIDERATIONS, EFFECTS, AND AFFECTS

The baby can be a doll or a rolled-up towel with a blanket over it.

The cubs can be hand puppets where a hand is inside the head to manipulate mouth and head movement. The other arm and hand can hold the cub close to the body.

It is suggested that this play be performed and designed as realistically as possible. Even though the animals are actors in costume, the seriousness of their presentation will enhance the natural characteristics of the animals.

It is also suggested that no blood be shown through injury or killing.

# Koba and the Red Lion

**SET:** The stage is a combination of African bush and jungle. At stage left is a small turntable with a tree on the front and a tiny hut on the back. At stage right and center stage are two more turntables, each with a tree on the front and a hollowed-out area with a perch on the back. A line of bushes a little above waist height follow from stage left to stage right upstage. Vines hang down and intertwine at each end of the stage, and a blue sky drop hangs far back upstage.

**AT RISE:**
Old Africa. Evening.

*(TEM sits on a small stool outside the hut, stage left. She tenderly rocks a baby while speaking. TEM is a meek woman, warm and loving.)*

**TEM:**
It is a warm evening here. Many an evening for a long time now has been very warm and dry. In Old Africa, the honey bronze sun beats down on the windswept grasses of the valley and shimmers in the crest of our majestic waterfalls. Here, the white summer clouds ease up over the tall mountains and move above lush, dense jungles. Across the land the giraffe and impala roam from high plain to sandy desert, and the leopard and cheetah stalk the bush and vine. This is where the elephants wallow in the mud of the riverbanks, and all life is ruled by the seasons. The season of the rains is very important to us, for without the rains, the watering holes dry up to dust, and the plants and fruits wither and die. Without green leaves to eat, the small animals and the animals who roam in herds leave our land in search of food and water. Without these animals, there is nothing for the hunters to hunt—the hunters who are warriors . . .

*(ATTAR enters stage left. ATTAR is a good provider and understanding father. He stalks, watching carefully, spear ready to throw.)*

**TEM:** *(Continued.)*
. . . and the hunter who is beast.

*(At stage right, behind the line of bush, is seen the top of the head and mane of the huge **RED LION**. The **RED LION** is the only animal who does not speak; therefore, he should act and sound as much like a real lion as possible. You can hear his movement against the bush and the breaking branches beneath his feet, but it is difficult to clearly see him.)*

**ATTAR:**
Be still now, gentle Tem, I hear him stalking through the bush. He is near.

**TEM:**
The Red Lion?

**ATTAR:** *(Calmly and cautiously.)*
Shhh. Take the baby into the hut. He will go for the baby if he thinks he can.

**TEM:**
Please, dear husband, the family cannot afford to lose you to the Red Lion.

**ATTAR:**
I will do my best to keep myself from becoming the Red Lion's next meal. Now go quickly and keep the baby still.

*(TEM slips into the hut with the baby. ATTAR watches carefully when JACA enters from stage left. JACA is very much like ATTAR but should be physically smaller. His spear is also poised to throw.)*

**JACA:**
Is he here?

**ATTAR:**
It feels like he is here.

**JACA:**
Where is Tem?

**ATTAR:**
I sent her into the hut with the little one.

**JACA:**
The Red Lion has never come this close to our huts before.

**ATTAR:**
He is becoming more brazen every day.

**JACA:**
He is becoming more desperate. We must kill him before he eats our own. Once he has the taste of human blood in his mouth, we all are in great danger.

**ATTAR:**
Here—he is going off this way.
*(Calling out.)*
Mama Tem.

*(TEM comes back out of the hut with the baby.)*

**ATTAR:** *(Continued.)*
The Lion is headed for the river. Jaca and I will follow.

**JACA:**
If we can trap him in a hollow, we can best the king of beasts.

**TEM:**
Such a magnificent animal—a lion as big as the rising moon and as bright red as the setting sun. It seems a shame to have to kill him.

**JACA:**
If we do not kill him, sister Tem, he will surely kill us. He has already taken all our goats and pigs. Others of the village have left, fearing the Red Lion will come for them.

**TEM:**
If only the rains would come. For two seasons the rains have not beat upon our soil, and water and food have become scarce for all. If the rains would only come, all the animals would return, and this land would be plentiful and in balance again.

**JACA:**
There is a reason for all things, Tem. For now, we must do the best with what we are given.

**ATTAR:**
Hurry, Jaca, or we will lose the Lion's trail.

**TEM:**
Take care, Attar, and return safely.

**ATTAR:**
I will take great care, my wife.

*(**ATTAR** and **JACA** exit stage right. **TEM** watches them leave. A moment later, **KOBA** and **SUTU** enter from stage left. **KOBA** is an honest and caring young man. **SUTU** is often demure, but if encouraged, she could be a more forceful and confident young woman. **KOBA** carries a spear, but the weapon is smaller, and it isn't poised for attack.)*

**TEM:**
Koba, where have you been?

**KOBA:**
I was hunting for food, but all I could find were small lizards and ants.

**TEM:**
We may be feeding upon lizards and ants before long.

**SUTU:**
Where is my father and Uncle Attar?

**TEM:**
The Red Lion came very close to our home just now. The men have gone after it.

**KOBA:** *(Heading for the right.)*
I should help them.

**TEM:**
Koba, no!

**KOBA:**
But, Mother, three spears are better than two.

**TEM:**
It is too dangerous.

**KOBA:**
It is more dangerous for only two than it would be for three.

**TEM:**
No, you are but a boy.

**KOBA:**
I am a man, Mother. I am a warrior.

**TEM:**
You are a young warrior. You do very well hunting small animals, but you are not experienced enough to hunt a killer like the Red Lion. It is bad enough that your father and uncle must place their lives in peril. You stay here where it is safe.

**KOBA:**
But—

**TEM:** *(Firmly.)*
You will stay here. Promise me you will stay here.

**KOBA:** *(Reluctantly.)*
I promise.

**TEM:**
Thank you. Sutu, is there still water in the well?

**SUTU:**
I believe so—a little.

**TEM:**
I will take the baby there. She is thirsty.

*(**TEM** exits stage left.)*

**KOBA:**
I should be with my father. I am old enough. How can I prove I am a good warrior if I cannot go on a great hunt, like for the Red Lion? They say I am a man, but they treat me like a child.

*(**SUTU** takes **KOBA'S** spear and starts out stage right.)*

**SUTU:**
I am not a child.

**KOBA:**
Wait. What are you doing?

**SUTU:**
You may have promised your mother not to go after the Red Lion, but I did not.

**KOBA:**
But you cannot go. You are not a warrior. You are only a girl.

**SUTU:**
My father is out there, too. You can care about your father, but I am not allowed to care about mine?

**KOBA:**
You know nothing of the bush or the jungle.

**SUTU:**
This is not my fault. I was never taught the ways of the wild because I am a girl. It matters little. I am going to help my father.

*(**SUTU** exits stage right.)*

**KOBA:** *(Calling after her.)*
Sutu! Sutu!

*(**KOBA** looks back stage left.)*

**KOBA:** *(Continued.)*
But I promised . . . Oh—

*(**KOBA** hurries offstage right. The turntable at stage left turns around to show the tree—the hut disappears to the back. After a beat, the head of the **RED LION** is seen from behind/over the line of bush. He enters stage left and exits stage right. After another beat, **ATTAR** and **JACA** enter stage left. They are keen on the trail of the **RED LION**.)*

**ATTAR:** *(Patting **JACA** on the shoulder and pointing.)*
This way.

*(**ATTAR** and **JACA** swiftly exit stage right. A moment later, **SUTU** and **KOBA** cautiously enter stage left. **KOBA** has taken his spear back from her.)*

**SUTU:**
Maybe we should go back. I did not think we would have to go this deep into the jungle.

**KOBA:**
You are the one who wanted to do this. It is too late to cry about it now.
*(Seeing how concerned **SUTU** is.)*
There is nothing to be afraid of.

**SUTU:**
If I knew what to do, I would not be this frightened.

**KOBA:**
Do you hear something?

**SUTU:**
Yes—from over there.

*(There is a rustling sound beyond stage right.)*

**KOBA:**
Here, step back until we know what it is.

*(**KOBA** and **SUTU** step back against the line of bush. After a beat, the **ZEBRA** hurries in stage right. She is hurt and limps in. Out of breath, the **ZEBRA** stops while looking back offstage right. The **ZEBRA** is quite nervous. Her movements should be jerky, responding to another's movement. She is scared and hurt.)*

**KOBA:** *(Whispering.)*
It is a zebra. I have not seen a zebra in these parts for a long time.

**SUTU:**
She looks hurt, the poor thing.

*(**KOBA** and **SUTU** step out. The **ZEBRA** sees them and stumbles back terrified.)*

**KOBA:**
Shhh. Calm yourself. We mean you no harm.

**ZEBRA:**
Everyone means me harm. It is my fate. Once I could run fast and escape my enemies, but now the end is near.

**SUTU:**
How terrible for you. How did you hurt yourself?

**ZEBRA:**
I have been sick. When my family left for the higher plains, I could not keep up and I fell behind. The lion caught my leg.

**KOBA:**
The Red Lion?

**ZEBRA:**
Is there another?

**KOBA:**
Is he near?

**ZEBRA:**
He is always near.

*(The turntable at stage right turns around to show the **VULTURE** perched in the hollow. The **VULTURE** is an unsavory creature. His voice should project contempt, and his movements should be awkward, like those of a real vulture.)*

**VULTURE:**
And you always manage to free yourself from his jaws and teeth, Zebra.

**ZEBRA:**
You will just have to wait for me, Vulture. You will have to wait for a very long time.

**VULTURE:**
Waiting is what I do best.

**KOBA:**
Vulture, what are you doing here?

**VULTURE:** *(Chuckling.)*
Waiting. Perhaps I am waiting for you—or her. Wherever the Red Lion hunts, there will be someone I can wait for.

**KOBA:**
It isn't a very noble thing you do, Vulture—scavenge and pick at what the Lion leaves behind.

**VULTURE:**
I have a purpose, boy. Besides, why should I hunt for food when I can get it by simply waiting?

**ZEBRA:**
Wait and wait and wait for me, Vulture. I am not ready to be the Lion's prey.

*(The **ZEBRA** begins to stumble out.)*

**KOBA:**
No, don't go.

**ZEBRA:**
Why not? Do you want me for your supper pot?

**KOBA:**
No, I will not kill a defenseless animal. Honor comes in hunting a strong and healthy beast—one man and his spear pitted against a swift antelope or a cunning panther. This is how the true warrior hunts.

**ZEBRA:**
But your family is hungry. All the families here are hungry. Would I not make a tasty meal for all?

**KOBA:**
All right. Begone with you before I change my mind.

*(The **ZEBRA** hesitates.)*

**KOBA:** *(Continued.)*
Go on!

*(The **ZEBRA** stumbles out stage left.)*

**SUTU:**
But, Koba, you didn't ask her where the Red Lion was.

**KOBA:**
She made me angry.

**SUTU:**
She was hurt and frightened.

**VULTURE:**
She is dying. It is only a matter of time. I can wait.

**SUTU:**
Ooo, I hate you, Vulture.

**VULTURE:** *(Amused.)*
Yes, I am not well liked. I can live with this.

**KOBA:** *(Alerted.)*
Something else comes.

*(The center stage turntable turns around to show the **COBRA** slithering on her perch. The **COBRA** slithers and hisses. She is a mean and coy snake. Her movements should be slow and graceful unless striking.)*

**SUTU:**
Koba, hurry. Kill it! Kill it!

**KOBA:**
Stay still, Sutu.

**COBRA:**
Hello, children. What are you doing this deep in the jungle?

**KOBA:**
Stay away, Cobra, or I will take my spear to you.

**COBRA:**
You will? Are you fast enough, little man? Can you bury the tip of your spear into my heart before I dig my fangs into your flesh? Can you pull back in time and stab me again before I strike a second time, filling your blood with my deadly venom? No, no, little man. You keep your distance, and I will keep mine.

**SUTU:**
But is it not your nature to strike and kill us?

**COBRA:**
If I were to kill you, what would I do with you? You are much too large to swallow whole. You would go to waste.

**VULTURE:**
She would not go to waste. This is what I am here for.

**SUTU:** *(To the VULTURE.)*
You stay out of this.

*(Suddenly, the **COBRA** lunges towards **KOBA** and **SUTU**. **KOBA** bats at the **COBRA** with his spear. **SUTU** screams. Instantly the **MONKEY** runs in stage right screeching, running about, flailing her arms in the air, and distracting the **COBRA**. The **COBRA** tries to strike at the **MONKEY**, but the **MONKEY** is too fast and too annoying. Soon the **COBRA** slithers back to the center stage turntable and disappears as the turntable turns back around to show the tree. The **MONKEY** stands a moment, hands on hips, catching her breath, and looking peeved at **KOBA** and **SUTU**. The **MONKEY** is droll in character, being much wiser than anyone else.)*

**MONKEY:**
What on earth were you thinking of? Do you not know how to behave when facing a cobra?

**SUTU:**
No, I have never been taught this.

**MONKEY:**
Why not?

**SUTU:**
Because I am a girl.

**MONKEY:**
And girls will never come in the way of a deadly snake? Stupid people. Why are you two young people in the jungle by yourselves?

**KOBA:**
We have come to hunt the Red Lion.

**MONKEY:**
To hunt the Red Lion . . . ? Stupid people. They think humans are a higher life-form than apes, but who leaves their children the work of the adult? Which of us animals does not teach their young how to survive in the wild? It is not your fault, little girl. If you are not taught these things, how will you ever know? No, all humans feel they must separate the man from the woman in everything they do and everything they are, and live by it forever because it is tradition. It is the man's job—it is the woman's job. Stupid people. Stupid, stupid people.

*(The **MONKEY** begins to exit stage left.)*

**KOBA:**
Monkey, wait. Do you know where the Red Lion is?

**MONKEY:**
Do you have a death wish, boy? The Red Lion stands as tall as you. His mouth can consume an entire warthog. His claws can rip the arms off your body. Go home, young people, before it is too late.

**SUTU:**
Maybe the Monkey is right, Koba. Let us go home. This place frightens me.

**KOBA:**
You are the one who wanted to come here.

**SUTU:**
I know. I am sorry for making you break your promise to your mother. Please, may we just go?

**KOBA:**
All right, Sutu. We will go back.

**MONKEY:**
Smart boy. This is a smart thing you do. Go home. Be safe. Live long.

**KOBA:**
Thank you, Monkey, for saving us from the Cobra.

**MONKEY:**
You are welcome, human.

*(**KOBA** and **SUTU** exit stage left.)*

**MONKEY:** *(To the **VULTURE**.)*
What are you looking at?

**VULTURE:**
The mighty hero.

**MONKEY:**
It is better than sitting all day like you.

**VULTURE:**
You robbed me of a meal, Monkey. You owe me.

**MONKEY:**
Well, every animal on the face of the earth is accountable to all the other animals. Until each and every species realizes this, there will be no balance. . . . So, are you going to sit there for the rest of the day?

**VULTURE:**
I think I just may.

**MONKEY:**
Mmmmm. People are not the only stupid things of the world.

*(The **MONKEY** exits stage left. After a beat, the **RED LION'S** roar can be heard offstage right. Next, from offstage right, **JACA** is heard yelling, and **ATTAR** calls out for **JACA** to run. **JACA** then stumbles in stage right and falls to the ground. The **RED LION** is still heard offstage. The **VULTURE** looks offstage right, then slips off his perch and cautiously approaches **JACA**, who isn't moving. The **VULTURE** sniffs at **JACA**, then touches the downed man a few times with his wing. The **VULTURE** spreads his wings and bends over **JACA** as if ready to take a bite out of the fallen man. **ATTAR** hurries in, hollering and swinging his spear at the **VULTURE** to make the bird move off **JACA**.)*

**ATTAR:**
Get away! Begone, you vile creature. Go on!

*(The **VULTURE** flaps its wings and squawks at **ATTAR**, but also circles around **JACA** until he is behind the two men. The **VULTURE** then crawls up onto his perch, and the right stage turntable turns back around to hide him from sight. **ATTAR** kneels by **JACA'S** side.)*

**ATTAR:** *(Continued.)*
Jaca . . . Jaca . . .

*(**JACA** stirs, then lifts himself up to sit.)*

**JACA:**
I did not see him, Attar. I knew we were close, but I did not see him.

**ATTAR:**
Do not speak, Jaca. Save your strength. I need to get you back to the village.

**JACA:**
Attar . . .

**ATTAR:**
Yes, Jaca.

**JACA:**
Thank you for chasing Vulture away.

*(**ATTAR** helps **JACA** to his feet.)*

**ATTAR:**
You are welcome, Jaca.

*(**ATTAR** helps **JACA** exit stage left. Again, the head of the **RED LION** is seen at stage right behind the bush. After a moment the head disappears back stage right. The left stage turntable turns around to show the hut. **TEM** enters stage left carrying her baby as **KOBA** and **SUTU** enter stage right.)*

**TEM:**
Koba, where have you been?

**KOBA:**
Sutu went into the jungle, and I followed to protect her.

**TEM:**
And what were you doing in the jungle, Sutu?

**SUTU:**
I went to help my father.

**TEM:**
Children, I know you want to help, but sometimes you help more by doing what you are told.

(*ATTAR enters stage right with JACA. Both are out of breath. ATTAR helps JACA to the ground once they reach center stage. TEM, KOBA, and SUTU cross to them.*)

**SUTU:**
Father!

**TEM:**
Jaca. Oh no!

**JACA:**
I am sorry, my sister. I guess I got too close.

**ATTAR:**
We had tracked the Red Lion to the river. Then suddenly, he was behind us on the knoll.

**TEM:**
Sutu, go get Vorasee.

**SUTU:**
But—

**TEM:**
Hurry now. We need Vorasee.

(*SUTU dashes offstage left.*)

**KOBA:**
Mother, is my uncle badly hurt?

**TEM:**
Yes, Koba, he is. Please be quiet.

**KOBA:**
I should have stayed. I should have stayed in the jungle and hunted the Red Lion with you.

**ATTAR:**
You were in the jungle, Koba? I am happy you were able to come back out of the jungle unharmed, but you should not have gone in without me.

(*SUTU enters stage left with VORASEE, the village high priestess/medicine woman.*)

**VORASEE:**
Stand back. Stand back now and let Vorasee see this man.

(*VORASEE bends over JACA and studies the wounds.*)

**VORASEE:** (*Continued.*)
He will live. Take him to my hut where I may tend to him.

**ATTAR:**
Yes, Vorasee. Thank you.

*(ATTAR and TEM help JACA to his feet and assist him out stage left. SUTU follows them out. VORASEE also begins to follow until she hears KOBA.)*

**KOBA:** *(Angrily.)*
I am going to kill that Red Lion if it is the last thing I do!

**VORASEE:**
Do you want to smite the Lion to help your family, or to gain fame and glory, young Koba?

**KOBA:**
I do not understand.

**VORASEE:**
The one to kill the Red Lion will be highly regarded in this village. The people will speak of the great warrior Koba, who killed the mightiest foe this village has ever seen. Is this what you seek—to be thought of in this way?

**KOBA:**
The Red Lion has tasted the flesh of my uncle. He will want more now. I have a baby sister who is defenseless against anyone or any animal. I think of her, not myself.

**VORASEE:**
Then your purpose is honorable and pure. This alone may assist you in killing the Red Lion, but perhaps it is not enough. Perhaps you will need more.

**KOBA:**
What more will I need? I have my spear and the skill to use it. What else could there be?

**VORASEE:**
Yes, you are a skillful hunter, Koba, but you are no match for the Red Lion. To go up against such an impressive enemy, you must prepare and be sure that you use all you can to gain the advantage. If you were aided by magic, then perhaps you would have the advantage.

**KOBA:**
Magic? What kind of magic?

**VORASEE:**
Vorasee can weave her magic powers over your spear and turn it into a fierce weapon. With a magical spear in your hand, you will have no fear upon facing the Red Lion. As he too stands with no fear, the challenge will be equal.

**KOBA:**
Yes, then. Would you do this for me? Would you turn my spear into a powerful weapon that I might be victorious over my enemy?

*(VORASEE takes KOBA'S spear. The lights dim and a spotlight comes over VORASEE as she holds the spear over her head.)*

**VORASEE:**
Powers of the earth and sky, hear Vorasee. See this spear I hold before you? Take the wood of its shaft and make it strong that it might fly straight. Take the metal of the head and make it sharp that it might pierce easily through its target. Help this young man overpower the magnificent Red Lion and free his family and this village.

*(The spotlight should come to full [or a strobe may wash over **VORASEE** and the spear for a second or two]; then the lighting should return to normal. When this occurs, **VORASEE** will hold the spear out for **KOBA** to take. He carefully and reverently takes the spear.)*

**KOBA:**
Thank you.

**VORASEE:**
Be careful, Koba, and remember: No amount of magic can better a human's wit and cunning. Be wise, young Koba. Be smart.

**KOBA:**
Yes, Vorasee, I will be careful and try to keep my wits about me. Thank you, again.

*(**KOBA** exits stage right. **VORASEE** watches him leave as **TEM** reenters stage left.)*

**TEM:**
Vorasee, please come. Jaca is weakening.

**VORASEE:**
Yes, I will come.

**TEM:**
Where is Koba?

**VORASEE:**
He has gone to slay the Red Lion.

**TEM:**
He has what? No! How could you let him go?

**VORASEE:**
It is time Koba proves himself as a man. I know you are Koba's mother and you fear for him, but you must let him find his own way and face the dangers of the world alone, or he will never become one with life itself.

**TEM:**
What if he dies while becoming this man?

**VORASEE:**
What if he does not? Place your trust in the purposes of the earth. Place your trust in your son.

*(**VORASEE** leads **TEM** out stage left as the turntable at stage left turns around to show the tree. After a beat, the **MONKEY** enters stage left and looks around. She sneaks over and looks into the bush and beyond the tree stage right, then quietly crosses back to stage left and motions for someone to enter. **KOBA** enters stage left. He steps carefully with his spear poised for throwing.)*

**KOBA:** *(Whispering.)*
Is he here?

**MONKEY:**
He was. Be ready, human, he will come again.

**KOBA:**
Let him come. I am ready.

**MONKEY:**
Are you not afraid—not even a little?

**KOBA:**
No, why should I be?

**MONKEY:**
Well, for one thing, the Red Lion is bigger than the two of us put together.

**KOBA:**
You may be afraid because you are just a little monkey, but I am not because I am a warrior—and I have a magic spear.

**MONKEY:** *(Highly skeptical.)*
A magic spear. I see.

*(The **MONKEY** begins to exit stage left.)*

**KOBA:**
Where are you going?

**MONKEY:**
I am just a little monkey. I *am* afraid, magic spear or not.

*(The **MONKEY** exits stage left as the center stage turntable turns around to show the **COBRA** on her perch. **KOBA** stands at the ready.)*

**KOBA:**
Stay back, Cobra. I am in no mood to dance with you again.

**COBRA:**
So, the boy has returned. Where is the girl?

**KOBA:**
She did not come. You only have me to deal with this time, and I am not afraid of you.

**COBRA:**
Well, where is the fun of taunting you if you are not afraid of me?

*(The roar of the **RED LION** is heard again offstage right, and then the **ZEBRA** runs in and falls to the ground. **KOBA** goes to the **ZEBRA'S** side.)*

**ZEBRA:**
I cannot do this much longer. The next time, I will not be able to escape the Red Lion.

*(The right stage turntable turns around to show the **VULTURE** on his perch.)*

**VULTURE:**
Stop talking about it and just do it, Zebra. Do us all a favor and just die.

**ZEBRA:**
I will die, but not here. I want to die in peace.
*(To **KOBA**.)*
Let me die in peace.

**KOBA:**
I will keep the Red Lion from you, I promise.

**ZEBRA:**
Thank you. You have a good heart. Good-bye, man warrior.

**KOBA:**
Good-bye, Zebra.

*(The **ZEBRA** stumbles out stage left. The **VULTURE** gets down from his perch and begins to follow the **ZEBRA** until **KOBA** stops him by threatening the **VULTURE** with his spear.)*

**KOBA:** *(Continued.)*
No, you don't. You leave the Zebra be. She does not need you hovering overhead, waiting for her to die.

**VULTURE:**
Do not disturb the balance, boy. I am here to eat the dead. Let me do what I am here for.

**KOBA:**
You may go later, but not now. Let her die in peace.

**VULTURE:**
If I wait until later, there will be others.

*(The **COBRA** suddenly strikes at **KOBA**, and **KOBA** quickly turns to defend himself, allowing the **VULTURE** to slide by.)*

**VULTURE:** *(Continued.)*
Aha, a distractive maneuver. Thank you, Cobra. We unsavory types must stick together!

*(The **VULTURE** exits stage left while the **COBRA** continues to lunge towards **KOBA**, who bats at it and attempts to jab it with his spear. Finally, with a decisive jab, **KOBA** mortally wounds the **COBRA**, and she shrieks and hisses.)*

**COBRA:**
Aaugh! You have destroyed me!

**KOBA:**
I told you not to try me. This spear is too strong and powerful.

**COBRA:**
I will die now, cursed boy. I will die!

*(The **COBRA** slithers back up to her perch in the center stage turntable.)*

**COBRA:** *(Continued.)*
Say good-bye to the Cobra.

*(The center stage turntable turns around and the **COBRA** disappears. As this happens, the **RED LION** is heard again roaring offstage right. **KOBA** readies his spear.)*

**KOBA:**
I have come for you, Red Lion. Prepare to fight!

*(**KOBA** exits stage right. A fierce battle is heard offstage right, with the **RED LION** roaring viciously. In a moment, **KOBA** stumbles in backwards with the **RED LION** chasing him. The **RED LION** pounces on top of **KOBA**, and there is a struggle as they tumble over and over. Then **KOBA** is able to right himself, and standing over the **RED LION**, thrusts his spear deep into the belly of the animal. The **RED LION** roars in agony, moves a little, then dies.)*

**KOBA:** *(Continued.)*
Now you will no longer hunt my people, Red Lion. If you had only stayed in the jungle and not come to the village, you could have lived.

*(**ATTAR, TEM, SUTU, VORASEE**, and the **MONKEY** enter stage left.)*

**MONKEY:**
I told you, there he is.

*(**TEM** crosses over to **KOBA**.)*

**TEM:**
Koba, are you all right?

**KOBA:**
Yes, Mother, I am fine.

**ATTAR:**
Look, my son has killed the great Red Lion! I could not be more proud.

**KOBA:**
Yes, I killed the Lion, but I do not feel happy about it.

**VORASEE:**
Why do you suppose the Red Lion came to the village to hunt?

**ATTAR:**
He came for food, of course.

**VORASEE:**
For food, yes. But food for himself? Listen. Do you not hear it?

**SUTU:**
Hear what, Vorasee?

*(**VORASEE** crosses over to upstage right and peers down behind the bush.)*

**VORASEE:**
Hear this, Sutu.

*(**KOBA** and **SUTU** cross over to join **VORASEE**.)*

**SUTU:** *(Bending down to pick up something.)*
Oh, the poor little things.

*(**SUTU** stands cradling a newborn lion cub in her arms. **KOBA** also bends down and picks up another cub.)*

**VORASEE:**
This is why the Red Lion came to hunt in our village. No doubt we killed the mother of these young cubs hunting for food for our own children, and the Red Lion came to our village to hunt for food for his children. There was no evil in the lion's intent—only survival.

**SUTU:**
What will happen to his babies now?

**VORASEE:**
Without the Red Lion to protect them, there is no doubt a jaguar or leopard will find these cubs and eat them. This is the way of the wild.

**KOBA:**
No, I will not permit it. I am responsible for them now. I did not understand the Red Lion's purpose. I should have left him alone to tend to his children. I will raise these young cubs until they are old enough and strong enough to be on their own. By myself I cannot bring balance back to this land, but I can help in this one small way.

*(The rumble of thunder can be heard in the background.)*

**VORASEE:**
Listen once again. . . . Do you hear the wonderful sound?

**ATTAR:**
The rains are coming.

**TEM:**
Glorious day! The rains are returning.

**ATTAR:**
And perhaps all the animals will return with the rains, and this land will be plentiful for all.

**SUTU:**
Praises to you, Koba. By killing the Red Lion you have brought us luck. You have brought back the rains.

**KOBA:**
I have done nothing to bring the rains. That came from a greater power than I have—even with my magic spear.

**ATTAR:**
Magic spear?

**KOBA:**
Vorasee prayed over my spear and turned it into a magic weapon. It is how I was able to best the Red Lion.

**VORASEE:**
Young Koba, I did not place magic powers over your spear, I merely put courage in your heart. You killed the Red Lion with your own skill and bravery. You have come to be a true warrior on this day. And by unselfishly vowing to raise the young lion cubs so that they too may live to hunt one day, you have come to be a true man. I stand with pride to know such a brave and wise young man.

**KOBA:**
Thank you, Vorasee. I am honored by your words.
*(As he cuddles the baby lion cub.)*
Come, little cub, we will take you home.

*(**KOBA** exits stage left. **VORASEE, ATTAR**, **TEM**, and **SUTU** follow, leaving the **MONKEY** alone perched on the turntable at stage right.)*

**MONKEY:**
Well, maybe there is hope for these humans after all. Although it always seems to be the young people who bring this hope. I do not know what happens to them when they grow up. Perhaps I will never know. Perhaps I am not supposed to know. But there must be a purpose in it somewhere. . . .

*(The stage right turntable turns around to hide the **MONKEY**. After a beat, the **VULTURE** enters stage left. He cautiously approaches the **RED LION**, then climbs on top of it and sits looking out towards the audience. In the background, more thunder is heard, and lightning is seen as the horizon turns to red. Then all fades to black.)*

*(Curtain.)*

END OF KOBA AND THE RED LION

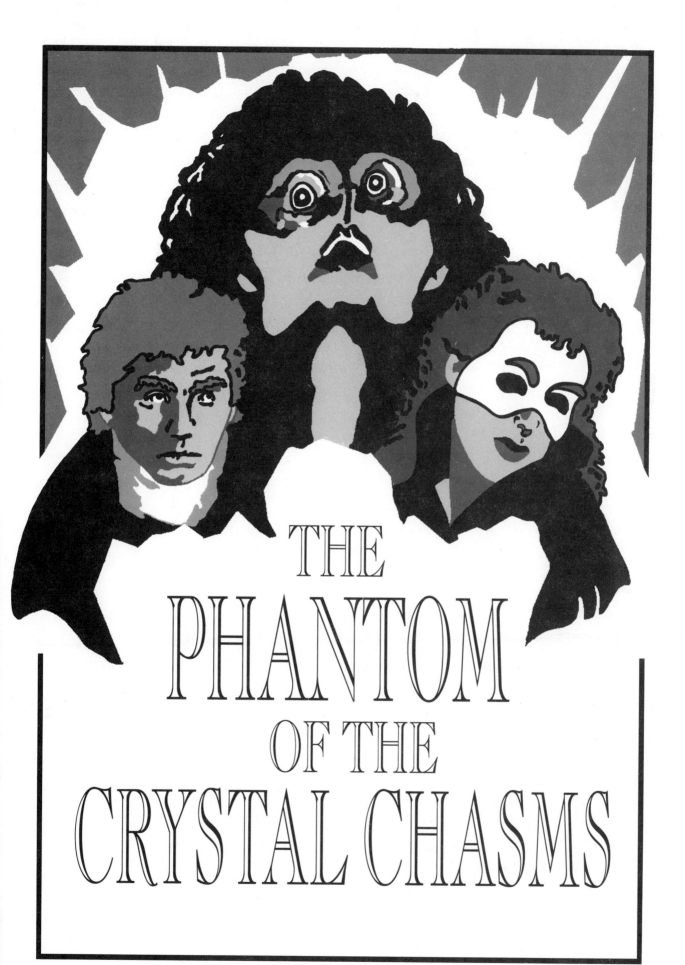

# THE PHANTOM
## OF THE
# CRYSTAL CHASMS

# The Phantom of the Crystal Chasms

### A Space Masque by Joan Garner

## CAST OF CHARACTERS (m=male   f=female)

SCOUT (f)         OMAR (m)         PHANTOM (f)         PASSELL (f)
JENNINGS (m)      RYAN (m)         DEVON (f)

## CHARACTER AND COSTUME DESCRIPTIONS

(The following costume suggestions are for a stylized/operatic production.)

**SCOUT:** Scout is self-assured, direct, and judgmental. She won't take any guff, and she always speaks her mind. Scout wears sweaters and heavy mountain-climbing clothing. Climbing boots.

**JENNINGS:** Jennings doesn't like himself very much; therefore, he doesn't like his life or anything associated with it. He seeks thrills and adventure because he's bored. Jennings wears clothing similar to Scout's.

**OMAR:** One gets the impression that Omar is more a follower than a leader. He should be a big man. Omar wears a bulky outfit of wool and fur like the Tibetan mountain people do. Fur boots.

**RYAN:** Ryan is a good guy but doesn't adjust well to adversity. He panics when placed in a stressful situation. Ryan wears an outfit like Scout's and Jennings's.

**PHANTOM:** The Phantom's life has contained many injustices, so she has turned hard and cruel. Her movements are slick and sinister, and her emotions are always exaggerated. The Phantom wears an elegant costume of shimmering gown and cape of darker, rich colors. Colored stockings and sequined slippers. She also wears a white mask that covers most of her face. Hair should be long, black, and lush.

**DEVON:** Devon is a subservient sort, one who will cower and run away more than stand her ground. She is there primarily to act as a segue from one scene to another and to clarify matters. Devon wears a tattered outfit similar to Omar's. Fur boots.

**PASSELL:** Passell is like the Phantom; her emotions go beyond the norm. However, Passell does not hate and will not fight for what she believes is her right. Passell wears a magnificient gown and cape like the Phantom's, but with more color and sequins. Colored stockings and sequined slippers. Passell wears a mask that covers the upper part of her face. Hair should be very long and lush, but of a color other than black.

**Scene Design for *The Phantom of the Crystal Chasms***

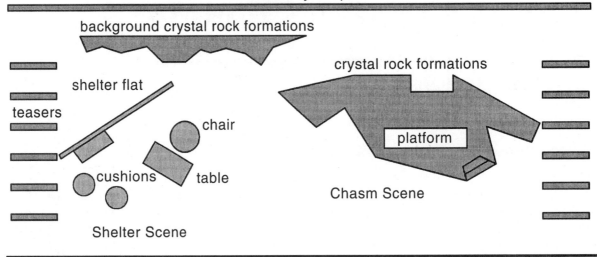

Apron

## SET

The set as suggested is bigger than usual to assist in the overall grand opera feel.

## PROPS

backpacks, crystals, dagger, laser gun.

## AS A STUDY LESSON

*The Phantom of the Crystal Chasms* is designed specifically to explore melodrama. The characters' emotions are all on the surface and are played as high pathos. Because of the brevity of the play, the actors will be required to quickly establish their characters and play it through with little change in intent. Jennings and the Phantom are bad. Ryan is good. Scout and Passell are somewhere in-between.

## AS PERFORMANCE

This play will do well by itself or grouped with the others. This is another play that would do well as contest material, or as a term assignment.

## CONSIDERATIONS, EFFECTS, AND AFFECTS

Special effects are used a great deal in this play. However, if you look closely, most of the effects are accomplished by lighting. If a full lighting complement is unavailable, a spotlight or other portable pieces of equipment (strobes) will do as well.

This should be a highly stylized production, with costumes and sets being as magnificent as the characters and situation.

# The Phantom of the Crystal Chasms

**SET:** The stage is divided into two distinct playing areas:
1) At stage right is the Cabin Scene, which is the interior of a small outpost. It is very rustic, with the only visible item of comfort being a fireplace. A table with chairs sits out from the walls, and large cushions rest on the floor near the fireplace. The window is frosted over.
2) At stage left is the Chasm Scene, which consists of sharp jutting rock formations of crystal rising up along the back. They split in the corner, leaving a crack wide enough for a person to slip through. In front of the formations is a platform that looks like a big, flat crystal rock. The platform is approximately table height and may have a few steps built in for access from floor to platform. This structure should blend in with the rest of the crystal-like scenery. The entire formation should be built in such a way that the rock climbers may begin their ascent from center stage and quickly disappear behind it. The Chasm Scene should look cold, stark, and unfriendly; as the Cabin Scene should look sparse, dull, and unmaintained.

**AT RISE:**
Morning, May 17, 7814. A cold day on the planet Chaseon.

**SCOUT** sits on a cushion near the fireplace. A backpack sits at her side. There is another backpack on the table. **SCOUT** rocks back and forth, waiting impatiently. **JENNINGS** enters stage right. He plops down in a chair, disgusted. **SCOUT** is self-assured, direct, and judgmental. She won't take any guff, and she always speaks her mind. **JENNINGS** doesn't like himself very much; therefore, he doesn't like his life or anything associated with it. He seeks thrills and adventure because he's bored.

**JENNINGS:**
Nothing—not one bread crumb or box of stale cereal to eat. I've never seen a place so completely empty. I'm surprised there's toilet paper in the bathroom.

**SCOUT:**
The brochure said to bring your own provisions.

**JENNINGS:**
Provisions for the climb, not food to keep you from starving to death while you're waiting for late-arriving team members. And look at this place—it's just a shack thrown up in the middle of nowhere.

**SCOUT:**
We were told conditions would be primitive. It's part of the appeal, isn't it?

**JENNINGS:**
Yes, yes, I've seen the same literature on the trip, but I haven't memorized it like you have.

**SCOUT:**
I just believe in being prepared, that's all.

**JENNINGS:**
Well, if you're so prepared, I bet you packed extra provisions.

**SCOUT:**
And what if I have?

**JENNINGS:**
Then give me a grain bar or meat stick.

**SCOUT:**
No.

**JENNINGS:**
Why not?

**SCOUT:**
I don't like you, that's why not.

*(**JENNINGS** looks surprised, then laughs uproariously.)*

**JENNINGS:**
You're all right, kid. Maybe a little skinny for my taste, but you're all right.

*(**OMAR** enters with **RYAN** stage right. One gets the impression that **OMAR** is more a follower than a leader. **RYAN** is a good guy but doesn't adjust well to adversity. He panics when placed in a stressful situation.)*

**OMAR:**
We finally have our stray team member.

**RYAN:** *(Slipping his backpack off.)*
The shuttle broke down just outside the stratosphere. We had to call for a backup. I'm sorry I'm late. Have you had to wait long?

**JENNINGS:**
Only all morning.

**SCOUT:**
It hasn't been all morning. More like an hour.

**OMAR:**
Well then, let me introduce everyone. The young lady is Scout—she comes to us from Tacus Solstice, as does Jennings here. Our newcomer is Ryan, who is from Dubury Summit. And of course you all know me. I'm Omar, your guide. Before we begin our climb today up Peak 4, it's important you know a few things about this wondrous planet called Chaseon.

**JENNINGS:** *(Grumbling.)*
Oh, good, yet another delay.

**OMAR:**
Chaseon is the fifth planet out from our sun Rigel. Chaseon has a mass of 2 sextillion, 38 quintillion short tons. But the planet's core is not composed of magnetic metallic material, like other planets, and it hasn't a shell or mantle layers encircling the core.

**JENNINGS:**
We've all had to attend astrogeology class in school, Omar. We don't need a refresher course now.

**OMAR:**
Oh, but I think you do. I believe you must appreciate and respect the mountain before you climb it, and in order to do that, you should know what it's composed of.

**JENNINGS:**
All right, but how about cutting out all of the technical mumbo jumbo? Chaseon is solid crystalline matter. On the far side of the planet—the side that never sees the sun—they quarry the crystal to make fuel composites. On this side—the side that only sees the sun four of its eight hours of day—are huge crystal mountains with deep ridges and chasms, thus the planet's name, Chaseon. You're next, Scout.

**SCOUT:**
Uh, okay. What makes Chaseon irresistible to mountain climbers is that you can't climb up a mountainside with conventional methods. Antigravity harnesses can't operate in the atmosphere; the fuel mixture clumps and clogs the fuel line. The air pressure automatic boring pitons don't work because the crystal is so smooth, the spike slips out the minute it goes in. And you can't use a piolet to chip the rock away because the crystal is too hard. So the only way to climb up . . .

**JENNINGS:**
. . . is to go hand and foot. No safety cables, no harnesses, just you and the mountain. And because it's all so smooth and slippery, getting your footing and holding on is just about impossible, making it the ultimate high-risk thrill sport. One false move, and you're plunging down an 800-foot chasm and falling onto solid rock. You're history.

**SCOUT:**
Ryan, is this your first climb on Chaseon?

**RYAN:**
Yeah. I didn't know everyone here had been on this trip before. Maybe I should stay behind. I'd probably slow you up.

**JENNINGS:** *(Grabbing for his backpack.)*
Smart thinking, kid, and awfully considerate. You stay here. We'll be back before nightfall.

**OMAR:**
Stop issuing commands. You're not the team leader here; I am. Ryan paid his money to come on this climb just like you did, and he's coming with us whether you like it or not. Besides, he's an experienced climber on Dubury Summit.

**JENNINGS:**
Dubury Summit ain't Chaseon. He's going to fall into the icy deep and break his neck as sure as I'm standing here. Of course, he'll be lucky if he just breaks his neck and dies. Then he won't have to face—that other thing.

**RYAN:**
What other thing?

**JENNINGS:**
You don't know?

**RYAN:** *(To OMAR.)*
What's he talking about?

**OMAR:**
Nothing. He's being a pain in the neck, that's all.

**SCOUT:**
Don't pay any attention to him, Ryan.

**JENNINGS:**
Must be something to it if they're protesting so much.

**RYAN:**
What something?

**JENNINGS:**
The monster that lurks down in the pit of the caverns just below Peak 4.

**RYAN:**
Monster.
*(He laughs.)*

**JENNINGS:**
Uh-huh. Laugh, my boy—go ahead. It's just a story told over a warm fire with a mug of hot coffee in your hand. But it's amazing how the story persists and grows. The Phantom of the Crystal Chasms, it's called. Maybe it's not a monster per se, but there's something down there—something that's strong and powerful. The miners talk about it all the time.

**RYAN:**
Get out of here.

**JENNINGS:**
That's right, don't believe me. You're better off on the peaks if you're not frightened. But when you do fall and start screaming for help because the Phantom is coming after you, don't expect us to rush down and save you. Everyone says the cries stop before they get there anyway. And when they finally descend to the caves, all they find are pieces of equipment: a pair of goggles, a lone glove. . . . Ask Omar about the last time we went down to retrieve a fallen climber. Ask what we found.

**OMAR:**
Come on, we're losing daylight.

**JENNINGS:**
No, no, no. Tell ol' Ryan here what you found of that Turner guy. Come on, he paid his money, he might as well get the full treatment.

**SCOUT:**
You're a sadist, Jennings.

**JENNINGS:**
Yeah, but I've paid my money just like everyone else. I get to have a little fun out of this. Tell him about Turner. Tell him, Omar, or I will. Go on.

**OMAR:**
Turner fell off Peak 4 near the base. The side we climb up is called the Lansing Slip, and there's a narrow chasm that follows alongside it. The opening is not especially deep. If you fell in it, you'd have a good chance of surviving. Turner lost his footing there and plummeted down. He was able to call back up to us and tell us he thought his leg might be broken, but that's all we heard, so we started down after him. When we were about halfway, Turner started crying for help—that something was after him. He was yelling and kind of babbling, panicky-like. All we could make out were the words "trying to kill me."

**JENNINGS:** *(Coaxing.)*
And?

**OMAR:**
And the word "phantom." But that doesn't mean anything. I'm sure he was delirious. I suspect his injuries were more severe than he had thought.

**JENNINGS:**
When we got down there, all we found was his backpack. We searched all night and all the next day, but couldn't find any traces of Turner or anyone else. If there is a Phantom down there, it sure does well by its name.

**SCOUT:**
It's just a story. I've climbed this mountain seven times, and I've never heard or seen this Phantom.

**RYAN:**
What makes you think I'd believe anything he says? He's just having his fun.

**JENNINGS:**
That's right, sweet little Scout, I'm just trying to loosen things up. Don't believe me. But tonight, Ryan, when you're safe and snug back in your own little bed on Dubury Summit, if you happen to hear a noise, don't be surprised to find the Phantom hovering over you. *(Making a sound like a ghost.)*
Ooooooo.

**SCOUT:**
You're not funny, Jennings.

**RYAN:** *(Chuckling.)*
Oh, he's a little funny. Come on. Let's go before the Phantom shows up here.

*(SCOUT, JENNINGS, and RYAN gather their things and follow OMAR out stage right. The lights dim to pitch black. Then a single light comes up; a bright streaming light that shines directly onto the platform in the Chasm Scene. There stands the PHANTOM. It is a woman who looks quite spectacular. You can't see most of her face because a white mask covers it. The PHANTOM'S life has contained many injustices, so she has turned hard and cruel. Her movements are slick and sinister, and her emotions are always exaggerated. The PHANTOM stands for a moment simply staring at the audience; then she begins to laugh devilishly. When she raises her arms toward the light source, flashes of color begin to snap all around her, and small exploding sounds are heard over her laugh, which becomes louder, then dies as the flashing stops and the light dims back to black. After a pause, the lights return to normal, showing the CLIMBERS upstage center at the base of the crystal formations. The PHANTOM is gone.)*

**OMAR:** *(Beginning to climb up.)*
This is Peak 4. It's a relatively simple climb, but most think it's the prettiest climb on the planet.

**JENNINGS:**
Yep, it's the bunny hill.

**SCOUT:**
Jennings, do you think you might cut out the smart remarks for a little while?

**JENNINGS:**
Gosh, Scout, sweetheart, I don't think I can.

**SCOUT:**
Stay close to me, Ryan. I'll show you the places to step as we go up this cluster.

**RYAN:**
Thanks.

**JENNINGS:**
My, my, how cozy. Would you like us to leave you two alone?

**SCOUT:**
Shut up, Jennings.

**JENNINGS:**
Darling, our first lover's quarrel.

**OMAR:**
Jennings, you take up the rear.

**JENNINGS:**
Aye, aye, Captain. Finally we're getting this show on the road.

*(The **CLIMBERS** start up the formation and quickly disappear behind it. They make enough noise to be heard from onstage, and it's loud enough to rouse the **PHANTOM**, who enters stage left. She steps towards the platform looking upward toward the noise. **DEVON** also enters stage left and joins the **PHANTOM** in looking up. **DEVON** is a subservient sort—one who will cower and run away more than stand her ground. She is there primarily to act as a segue from one scene to another and to clarify matters.)*

**DEVON:**
What is it?

**PHANTOM:**
They're up top again. Almost every day now there's someone climbing around up there. Apparently these mountains have become very popular.

**DEVON:**
The miners say someone has set up a climbing exhibition on this side of the planet. People come from the neighboring habitats to spend their vacations crawling all over the mountains.

**PHANTOM:**
The miners say that, do they? And what do the miners say of me?

**DEVON:**
Well, most of them think you don't exist. But there are others who believe you make a good story, what with your mystical powers and face . . . I mean, your mask.

**PHANTOM:**
You mean my face. My hideous, horrifying face. What do you think of all this, Devon?

**DEVON:**
You know me, miss. I don't think much of anything at all. That's what you like about me, remember? It's why I'm the only one allowed down here to bring you food and supplies.

**PHANTOM:**
Yes, my good little girl, Devon. You're my only link with the outside world and reality. Little Devon, the only human being I ever speak to.

**DEVON:**
There's Passell, miss.

**PHANTOM:** (*Angrily.*)
I told you never to let her name pass your lips. Passell is too special for the likes of you to speak of. I live for her and will do whatever is necessary to keep my daughter happy. She is of a higher level than both of us. If you refer to Passell again, I'll burn you to a crisp with the power of the crystals. Do you understand?

**DEVON:** (*Terrified.*)
Yes, miss. Please, miss, I didn't mean anything by it. Please, miss.

**PHANTOM:** (*Passive once again.*)
There, there, Devon. You mustn't tremble and shake so, you'll start a cave-in.

**DEVON:**
Thank you, miss. I'll be good.

(*The noise up top begins again.*)

**PHANTOM:** (*Exploding.*)
Aaauuhhh! I must do something about these interlopers! I must liberate this planet from these unwelcome visitors.

**DEVON:**
But how?

**PHANTOM:** (*Thinking.*)
The blackness of night. They do not come when the sun sleeps. I will blacken the skies, and they will be gone.

**DEVON:**
But miss, you can't do that. Your powers are great indeed, but not powerful enough to make the sun disappear.

**PHANTOM:**
I will take the clouds overhead and stir them around until their thickness blocks out the rays of the sun and darkness will cover the mountain. Unable to see their way, the climbers will have to retreat back down the mountain.

(*The **PHANTOM** climbs up onto the platform and raises her arms up towards the sky.*)

**PHANTOM:** (*Continued.*)
Mighty power of the crystals, make the sun no more today. Take the power from these walls and reach upward. Climb high into the sky and touch the clouds, that they may do your bidding.

(*The single light overhead comes up as the flashing lights and sounds come back like before. But as the lights continue to flash, the regular lights begin to dim.*)

**PHANTOM:** (*Continued.*)
Clouds above, swallow the sun and hide its light from our eyes. Make the day night that darkness may reign once more!

(*The normal light fades to black, and the single overheard light and flashing lights follow, leaving the entire stage black. After a beat, we hear **SCOUT** scream and **RYAN** yell for help. Then it sounds as if someone has fallen; then, nothing. Gradually the single light comes up,* *and we see **RYAN** lying on the platform [with backpack propping him up] in front of the **PHANTOM**, who watches him carefully. **RYAN** is unconscious.)*

**DEVON:**
Is he dead?

**PHANTOM:** *(Kneeling by **RYAN**.)*
No. But it will only be a matter of time.

*(**RYAN** stirs.)*

**DEVON:**
Look. He's waking up.

*(**RYAN** shakes the unconsciousness away and opens his eyes to see the **PHANTOM** hovering over him.)*

**RYAN:** *(Recoiling all he can.)*
Holy—what is this? Who are you?

**PHANTOM:**
More to the point, who are you? You're trespassing down here.

**RYAN:** *(Wincing in pain.)*
Help me.

**PHANTOM:**
Are you in much pain?

**RYAN:**
I just fell off a mountain—what do you think?

**PHANTOM:**
Can you move?

**RYAN:**
No. It feels like both my legs are broken, and my neck is killing me. I need help!

**PHANTOM:** *(Standing.)*
Your agony is of little concern to me.

**RYAN:**
Are you just going to stand there and watch me die?

**PHANTOM:**
I have considered the possibility.

**RYAN:**
What kind of heartless, faceless witch are you?

**PHANTOM:**
Witch, am I?

*(The **PHANTOM** kneels by **RYAN'S** side while pulling a black crystal from a pocket. The crystal is attached to a cord that she puts around **RYAN'S** neck. **RYAN** falls back upon his backpack in excruciating pain, then fumbles to get the crystal off, but passes out before he can remove it.*

*PASSELL enters stage left and stops upon seeing the* **PHANTOM** *and* **RYAN** *on the platform.* **PASSELL** *is dressed similarly to the* **PHANTOM** *and also wears a mask, but it is apparent that she is younger than the* **PHANTOM**. **PASSELL** *is like the* **PHANTOM**; *her emotions go beyond the norm. However,* **PASSELL** *does not hate and will not fight for what she believes is her right.)*

**PASSELL:**
Mother, what are you doing?

**PHANTOM:** *(Looking back.)*
Relieving him of his pain.

**PASSELL:**
You're killing him!

**PHANTOM:**
He's intruding.

**PASSELL:**
He's hurt. Leave him alone.

**PHANTOM:**
Who are you to tell me what to do?

**PASSELL:**
I am blood of your blood, and I'm asking you to spare this young man.

*(The* **PHANTOM** *pauses, then retrieves the black crystal from around* **RYAN'S** *neck. She then crosses down the platform and passes by* **PASSELL** *on her way out.)*

**PHANTOM:**
Be careful, Passell. Be careful of what you say to your mother—of how you speak to *this* mother.

*(The* **PHANTOM** *exits stage left with* **DEVON**. **PASSELL** *watches them leave, then steps up onto the platform and kneels by* **RYAN'S** *side. She takes her cape off and covers him with it to keep him warm. The movement awakens* **RYAN**, *and he tries to move away upon seeing* **PASSELL**.*)*

**RYAN:**
No, don't—please!

**PASSELL:**
Calm yourself. I mean you no harm.

**RYAN:**
You're not the other one. . . . Who are—
*(He grabs a leg.)*
—the pain!

**PASSELL:**
I can take the pain away.

**RYAN:**
Then do it—do something—anything!

**PASSELL:**
Gladly, but there are conditions.

**RYAN:**
What? You want to bargain with me now?

**PASSELL:**
If I relieve the pain and heal your injuries, you must stay down here with me.

**RYAN:**
Stay down here? But I don't know you, and I have no idea what you even look like.

**PASSELL:**
Is my appearance so important to you, even at a time like this?

*(**PASSELL** pulls on one of **RYAN'S** legs, and he yells in pain.)*

**RYAN:**
All right! Just stop the pain.

**PASSELL:** *(Tugging on **RYAN'S** leg some more.)*
Do you promise to stay with me?

**RYAN:**
Yes, I promise!

*(**PASSELL** pulls a clear crystal from a pocket and places it around **RYAN'S** neck. Once the crystal is around his neck, he begins to relax, and his breathing slows. **PASSELL** takes **RYAN** and holds him in her lap as the single light overhead dims to dark and the lights over the Cabin Scene come up to full. **OMAR**, **SCOUT**, and **JENNINGS** are in the cabin. **JENNINGS** is sitting, **OMAR** stands by the window looking out, and **SCOUT** paces.)*

**SCOUT:**
We have to do something.

**JENNINGS:**
Do what? He's gone, just like Turner.

**SCOUT:**
There's a chance that he's still alive.

**JENNINGS:**
Right, and I'm the emperor of Tacus Solstice.

**OMAR:**
We'll go back up at first light. There's nothing we can do for him tonight. All we can pray for is that he's mobile enough to get to his backpack. If he can get to his survival kit, there's a good chance we'll find him alive in the morning.

**JENNINGS:**
We? What's this *we* business?

**OMAR:**
We'll need your help to lift him up and out.

**JENNINGS:**
Well, isn't that too bad.

**SCOUT:**
What's the matter, Jennings, afraid of running into the Phantom?

**JENNINGS:**
Don't be ridiculous.

**OMAR:**
We can't save Ryan without you. Please.

**JENNINGS:**
Geez. You just better be ready to head out the second that sun hits the horizon. But I tell you, the only thing we're going to find is a crumpled body of a boy from Dubury Summit.

*(The lights fade in the Cabin Scene, and the single light over the platform comes back up. PASSELL continues to hold RYAN until he awakens and sits up.)*

**PASSELL:**
How are you feeling?

**RYAN:**
Much better. The pain's all gone.
*(He rubs his shoulders and legs.)*
The legs are a little weak, but they feel pretty good.

**PASSELL:**
Your legs should strengthen in a day or two.

**RYAN:**
How did you do it? How did you heal my broken legs so fast?

**PASSELL:**
The crystals hold great power. Once you know how to harness and manipulate their vast energy, you can do many things.

**RYAN:** *(Holding out the crystal around his neck.)*
The other crystal . . .

**PASSELL:**
The crystals hold an undefined power. In our hands it may be a constructive or destructive power—a healing or a killing power.

**RYAN:**
The other one with a mask . . .

**PASSELL:**
. . . is my mother. She has had a hard and difficult life that has distorted her personality as much as it has distorted her face. I have seen an evil grow within her, and it saddens me.

**RYAN:**
She tried to kill me.

**PASSELL:**
But she didn't.

**RYAN:**
I bet because you stopped her.

**PASSELL:**
Yes, I stopped her.

**RYAN:**
Why?

**PASSELL:**
What she was doing was wrong. Please don't stare at me like that. You have no idea how it torments me.

**RYAN:**
Why? What's the matter with your face? Why do you wear the mask?

**PASSELL:**
Can you only see the mask? Can you see nothing else?

**RYAN:**
Do you have a birth defect, or were you in an accident or something?

**PASSELL:**
Do not ask about the mask. We may discuss whatever you like, but not the mask.

**RYAN:**
What's your name again?

**PASSELL:**
I am Passell.

**RYAN:**
How did you come to this place?

**PASSELL:**
I have always been here with my mother. I have been nowhere else.

*(Beat.)*

**RYAN:**
Passell—about that promise I made. I was in a great deal of pain and would have promised anything. You understand, don't you? You really don't expect me to stay down here with you, do you? I have a life on Dubury Summit. I have my family.

**PASSELL:**
Your family will grieve for a while, thinking you have perished in a climbing accident, but their mourning will ease in time.

**RYAN:**
But I haven't perished. I'm alive.

**PASSELL:**
You promised to stay with me.

**RYAN:**
I know I promised, but I made that promise under duress. Surely you can't hold me to it. Be reasonable.

**PASSELL:**
Yes, I didn't expect you to keep your promise—I only hoped you would. It's so lonely down here. I have Mother, but . . . When I saw you, I thought I might finally have a friend to talk to.

**RYAN:**
Why not come back to Dubury Summit with me?

**PASSELL:**
I couldn't possibly.

**RYAN:**
Why not?

**PASSELL:**
The mask! And mother.
*(She moves away from him.)*
When you're stronger, I'll show you the way out of here. Until then, I'll try not to trouble you further.

*(PASSELL begins to exit stage left when the PHANTOM enters and stops her daughter.)*

**PHANTOM:**
Passell, what's wrong?

**PASSELL:**
I am wrong—no more than that. I am wrong.

*(PASSELL exits sadly. The PHANTOM watches her leave, then turns towards RYAN angrily.)*

**PHANTOM:**
You have hurt my daughter.

**RYAN:**
I'm sorry.

**PHANTOM:**
You're sorry? Is that all you can be? Simply sorry? I should have killed you last night when I had the chance. Then my Passell wouldn't know this heartache.

**RYAN:**
She wanted me to stay down here with her in this godforsaken place. How could I do that?

**PHANTOM:**
You can't stay because you're repulsed by our faces, aren't you?

**RYAN:**
It's all of this—and the faces. What are you hiding? Are you so ugly it takes a mask to make you presentable?

**PHANTOM:**
You are a cruel and heartless man.

**RYAN:**
No, I'm not—I'm honestly not. It's just that all of this is so bizarre and unreal. How can I believe any of it is actually happening? For all I know I'm hallucinating—delirious from the fall.

**PHANTOM:**
Well, if you're hallucinating, you won't feel this.

*(The **PHANTOM** pulls out a dagger and lunges towards **RYAN**. **RYAN** yells and catches the **PHANTOM'S** arm before she can plunge the dagger into his heart. As they struggle, **RYAN** grabs the **PHANTOM'S** mask and pulls it off to reveal a terribly disfigured face. The **PHANTOM** draws back screaming and trying desperately to get her mask back, but **RYAN** holds it out of her grasp, so she quickly covers her face with her cape and huddles in the background. The screaming brings **OMAR**, **SCOUT**, and **JENNINGS** rushing in stage right and **PASSELL** and **DEVON** rushing in stage left.)*

**OMAR:** *(As he enters.)*
We heard a—Ryan, you're alive!

**PASSELL:** *(As she enters.)*
Mother!

*(**PASSELL** hurries towards the platform, but before she reaches the top, **JENNINGS** pulls out a laser gun and shoots her. **PASSELL** falls between **RYAN** and her mother.)*

**RYAN:** *(Crawling towards **PASSELL**.)*
What did you do that for? Are you crazy?

**JENNINGS:**
I thought she was going to—I don't know—there was this screaming—then there's these stories and she comes rushing in. I thought . . .

*(**JENNINGS** drops his gun as he sees the **PHANTOM**, who has crawled over and taken **PASSELL** in her arms.)*

**PHANTOM:**
What have I done? You were my only joy. I lived for you. Everything I did was for you. What do I do now?

**RYAN:**
I'm sorry. I didn't mean for her to . . .

**PHANTOM:**
Go away. Leave us alone.

*(The **PHANTOM** rests **PASSELL** on the platform, moves back a little, pulls out her black crystal, and holds it high in the air above her before putting it around her neck.)*

**PHANTOM:** *(Continued.)*
This will end my pain.

*(The lights fade as the single light overhead becomes brighter and the flashing lights come on again with the sounds. After a moment, the **PHANTOM** slumps back, and the lights and sounds return to normal. **OMAR** steps over to help **RYAN** off the platform and to his feet.)*

**OMAR:**
Come along, Ryan. We need to get you to a hospital. We'll inform the authorities of this once we're up top again.

**RYAN:**
It's all a terrible nightmare.

**SCOUT:**
Ryan, it's all right now. You can tell us all about it once you've regained your strength.

**DEVON:**
Here, I know a quick way to the surface. I'll show you out.

**OMAR:**
Who are you?

**DEVON:**
I'm Devon. I work as a miner in the quarry. I brought food to Passell and her mother.

**OMAR:**
Please take us there. Ryan needs to see a doctor.

**RYAN:**
That won't be necessary. I'm a little weak, but I feel fine—well, as fine as I can be under the circumstance.

**JENNINGS:**
Do you think they'll arrest me? It was an accident.

**SCOUT:**
Oh, shut up, Jennings.

*(All begin to exit stage left.)*

**RYAN:**
Wait a minute.

*(RYAN leaves OMAR and crosses back to PASSELL. He looks at her a moment, then gently takes her mask off. He steps back in surprise and appears confused and upset.)*

**RYAN:** *(Continued.)*
She's beautiful. She's the most beautiful woman I've ever seen. Why did she wear the mask? Why did she deceive me?

**DEVON:**
Passell wore the mask so her mother wouldn't feel like such a freak. She wanted you to see her goodness and spirit, not her physical beauty. For Passell, if you love only beauty, your love is false and unwanted.

**JENNINGS:**
Let's get out of here. I think I'm going to be sick.

*(OMAR, JENNINGS, SCOUT, and DEVON exit stage left. Momentarily, SCOUT reenters and crosses to RYAN.)*

**SCOUT:**
Ryan, please, let's go. There's nothing more we can do here. You'll feel better once we're back home.

**RYAN:** *(Still infatuated with* **PASSELL***.)*
What was I so afraid of? What scared me to death when I didn't even know what was under the mask?

**SCOUT:**
Sometimes the real horror lies within our own imaginations. The monsters we make up in our dreams can be much more fierce and hideous than anything the universe might ever conceive. Come on, Ryan, it's over.

**RYAN:**
That's what her mother said. Go on, I'll be along in a minute.

**SCOUT:**
But Ryan . . .

**RYAN:**
Go on now and leave me alone.

**SCOUT:**
She's dead, Ryan.

**RYAN:**
And you're insensitive. Get out of here!

*(Miffed,* **SCOUT** *storms out stage left.* **RYAN** *stares at* **PASSELL** *for a moment, then returns to her and holds her up in his lap. He removes the crystal from around his neck and places it around* **PASSELL'S** *neck.)*

**RYAN:**
I wish this could work for you. . . . Powers of the crystals, bring this innocent woman back to life!
*(He searches upward, and the lights dim except for the bright light that shines down from overhead. He looks back down at* **PASSELL***, but nothing happens.)*
Oh, Passell! I didn't know what I had. I'm sorry.

*(After another moment,* **RYAN** *carefully lays* **PASSELL** *back on the platform, then exits stage left. After a beat the lights begin to flash again, as when the power of the crystals was working, but after the display, the two women continue to lie still on the platform. Eventually the light overhead also fades to black.)*

*(Curtain.)*

## END OF THE PHANTOM OF THE CRYSTAL CHASMS

# Winds of Silk

### *A Minispectacle by Joan Garner*

## NOTES

In reading this play, a simple method in remembering who's who in this very large cast is that all of the SPICE FAMILY female names end in "-LEE," except for SELMA. The males of the RICE FAMILY, and also including PAPA-SAN SPICE, end in "-LO." And the villagers' names end in "-LU."

There are three cast lists:

The **CAST OF CHARACTERS (First Arrangement)** is the way the play is written. The play was specifically designed for a large cast of children and teens. Also, all the characters in the play have at least one line to say, and each has a certain amount of action to perform on stage.

The **CAST OF CHARACTERS (Second Arrangement)** modifies the characters to include more female roles. As it is usually the case that more girls audition for plays than boys (or are involved in school theatre), this play can be easily adapted to accommodate this possibility.

The **CAST OF CHARACTERS (Third Arrangement)** reduces the number of players to a smaller cast size. Some characters can double up with the line load and action. This reduces the number of players from 40 to 26.

The letters "m" and "f" indicate male or female. If an asterisk accompanies the (m) symbol, it means that the character could be female as easily as male. *See the cast list (first arrangement). Accompanying the character's name is the age category (e.g., child, teen, adult). This indicates the character could be made up as, or cast to be, either a child, teen, and so on.

## CAST OF CHARACTERS (First Arrangement)

| | | |
|---|---|---|
| (f) | REFLECTION OF THE MIRRORS | (Adult) |
| (m)* | THE GREAT SEA SPIRIT | (Adult) |

### THE SPICE FAMILY

| | | |
|---|---|---|
| (m) | PAPA-SAN TO-LO | (Adult) |
| (f) | MAMA-SAN SAY-LEE | (Adult) |

### THE RICE FAMILY

| | | |
|---|---|---|
| (m) | PAPA-SAN RO-LO | (Adult) |

### THE SPICE FAMILY SISTERS

| | | |
|---|---|---|
| (f) | BAY-LEE | (Child) |
| (f) | DAY-LEE | (Child) |
| (f) | FAY-LEE | (Preteen) |
| (f) | GAY-LEE | (Preteen) |
| (f) | JAY-LEE | (Teen) |
| (f) | MAY-LEE | (Teen) |
| (f) | PAY-LEE | (Teen) |
| (f) | RAY-LEE | (Teen) |
| (f) | TAY-LEE | (Teen) |
| (f) | SELMA | (Preteen) |

### THE RICE FAMILY BROTHERS

| | | |
|---|---|---|
| (m) | BO-LO | (Child) |
| (m) | MO-LO | (Child) |
| (m) | PO-LO | (Teen) |
| (m) | SO-LO | (Teen) |
| (m) | VO-LO | (Teen) |

### MAJOR VILLAGE CHARACTERS

| | | |
|---|---|---|
| (m)* | MINISTER RU-LU | (Adult) |
| (f) | MADAME YU-LU | (Adult) |
| (m) | MASTER SU-LU | (Adult) |
| (m)* | VU-LU | (Teen) |

### THE PIRATES

| | | |
|---|---|---|
| (m) | CAPTAIN MAX | (Adult) |
| (f) | LADY LULU | (Adult) |
| (m) | WICKED WILLY | (Adult) |
| (f) | FANCY FLORA | (Adult) |
| (m) | CRAZY CLYDE | (Adult) |

THE VILLAGERS

| | | | | | | |
|---|---|---|---|---|---|---|
| (m)* | JU-LU | (Adult) | | (f) | QU-LU | (A/T) |
| (m)* | DU-LU | (Adult) | | (f) | TU-LU | (A/T) |
| (f) | FU-LU | (A/T) | | (f) | KU-LU | (A/T) |
| (f) | GU-LU | (A/T) | | (f) | HU-LU | (A/T) |
| (f) | MU-LU | (A/T) | | (m)* | ZU-LU | (A/T) |
| (m)* | BU-LU | (A/T) | | | | |

Number of males in the cast = 18        Number of females in the cast = 22  **=40**


## CAST OF CHARACTERS (Second Arrangement)

| | | |
|---|---|---|
| (f) | REFLECTION OF THE MIRRORS | (Adult) |
| (f) | THE GREAT SEA SPIRIT | (Adult) |

THE SPICE FAMILY

| | | |
|---|---|---|
| (m) | PAPA-SAN TO-LO | (Adult) |
| (f) | MAMA-SAN SAY-LEE | (Adult) |

THE RICE FAMILY

| | | |
|---|---|---|
| (m) | PAPA-SAN RO-LO | (Adult) |

THE SPICE FAMILY SISTERS

| | | |
|---|---|---|
| (f) | BAY-LEE | (Child) |
| (f) | DAY-LEE | (Child) |
| (f) | FAY-LEE | (Preteen) |
| (f) | GAY-LEE | (Preteen) |
| (f) | JAY-LEE | (Teen) |
| (f) | MAY-LEE | (Teen) |
| (f) | PAY-LEE | (Teen) |
| (f) | RAY-LEE | (Teen) |
| (f) | TAY-LEE | (Teen) |
| (f) | SELMA | (Preteen) |

THE RICE FAMILY BROTHERS

| | | |
|---|---|---|
| (m) | BO-LO | (Child) |
| (m) | MO-LO | (Child) |
| (m) | PO-LO | (Teen) |
| (m) | SO-LO | (Teen) |
| (m) | VO-LO | (Teen) |

MAJOR VILLAGE CHARACTERS

| | | |
|---|---|---|
| (f) | MINISTER RU-LU | (Adult) |
| (f) | MADAME YU-LU | (Adult) |
| (m) | MASTER SU-LU | (Adult) |
| (f) | VU-LU | (Teen) |

THE PIRATES

| | | |
|---|---|---|
| (m) | CAPTAIN MAX | (Adult) |
| (f) | LADY LULU | (Adult) |
| (m) | WICKED WILLY | (Adult) |
| (f) | FANCY FLORA | (Adult) |
| (m) | CRAZY CLYDE | (Adult) |

THE VILLAGERS

| | | | | | | |
|---|---|---|---|---|---|---|
| (f) | JU-LU | (Adult) | | (f) | MU-LU | (A/T) |
| (f) | DU-LU | (Adult) | | (f) | TU-LU | (A/T) |
| (f) | FU-LU | (A/T) | | (f) | KU-LU | (A/T) |
| (f) | GU-LU | (A/T) | | (f) | HU-LU | (A/T) |
| (f) | MU-LU | (A/T) | | (f) | ZU-LU | (A/T) |
| (f) | BU-LU | (A/T) | | | | |

Number of males in the cast = 11        Number of females in the cast = 29  **=40**


## CAST OF CHARACTERS (Third Arrangement)

| | | |
|---|---|---|
| (f) | REFLECTION OF THE MIRRORS | (Adult) |
| (m)* | THE GREAT SEA SPIRIT | (Adult) |

THE SPICE FAMILY

| | | |
|---|---|---|
| (m) | PAPA-SAN TO-LO | (Adult) |
| (f) | MAMA-SAN SAY-LEE | (Adult) |

THE RICE FAMILY

| | | |
|---|---|---|
| (m) | PAPA-SAN RO-LO | (Adult) |

| THE SPICE FAMILY SISTERS | | | THE RICE FAMILY BROTHERS | | |
|---|---|---|---|---|---|
| (f) | GAY-LEE | (Preteen) | (m) | MO-LO | (Child) |
| (f) | JAY-LEE | (Teen) | (m) | PO-LO | (Teen) |
| (f) | RAY-LEE | (Teen) | (m) | SO-LO | (Teen) |
| (f) | TAY-LEE | (Teen) | | | |
| (f) | SELMA | (Preteen) | | | |

| MAJOR VILLAGE CHARACTERS | | | THE PIRATES | | |
|---|---|---|---|---|---|
| (m)* | MINISTER RU-LU | (Adult) | (m) | CAPTAIN MAX | (Adult) |
| (f) | MADAME YU-LU | (Adult) | (f) | LADY LULU | (Adult) |
| (m) | MASTER SU-LU | (Adult) | (m) | WICKED WILLY | (Adult) |
| (m)* | VU-LU | (Teen) | (f) | FANCY FLORA | (Adult) |
| | | | (m) | CRAZY CLYDE | (Adult) |

| THE VILLAGERS | | | | | |
|---|---|---|---|---|---|
| (m)* | JU-LU | (Adult) | (f) MU-LU | | (Adult) |
| (m)* | DU-LU | (Adult) | (f) QU-LU | | (Adult) |
| (m) | ZU-LU | | | | |

Number of males in the cast = 14      Number of females in the cast = 12   **= 26**

Modified (Second Arrangement—more female roles)

Number of males in the cast = 9      Number of females in the cast = 17   **= 26**

In this modified arrangement where the characters are eliminated, their lines can be given to the remaining characters. In the case of the minor Villagers, they can double for the Pirates:

JU-LU can be CAPTAIN MAX      MU-LU can be LADY LULU
DU-LU can be WICKED WILLY      QU-LU can be FANCY FLORA
ZU-LU can be CRAZY CLYDE

## PROPS

fishing nets, baskets, mats, paddles, kites, pearls, pouches, flowers, food, drink, lanterns, spyglass, trays, fans, bamboo poles, crumpled paper, pirate flag, seashell, swords, packets of glitter, fountain pole, rainbow pole, gong, poles with mirrors, poles with wind chimes, tom-tom, laundry basket, towels, buckets, Selma cutout on pole, rolls of silk, streamers, pillow, bell, kite pole, tables, chairs.

## AS A STUDY LESSON

The emphasis of *Winds of Silk* is production, not acting. It is called a minispectacle because of the many special effects, fanciful costumes, colorful set, and special lighting. This play will help acting students interact with all the production elements and members of the stage crew, who are often considered secondary in a theatre production. *Winds of Silk* should help the actors gain new respect and appreciation for all aspects of a production as they work with this play's many features.

## AS PERFORMANCE

*Winds of Silk* is a full-length play for children. It is approximately 70 to 80 minutes in length and could fit into the school's theatre production schedule nicely.

## CONSIDERATIONS, EFFECTS, AND AFFECTS

All the special effects are easily done and explained within the play.
The more color and pizzazz put into this play, the better it will be.
Because the spyglass will be used to conk people over the head, it is suggested that it be made of cardboard and foam.

**Scene Design for *Winds of Silk***

Mountain/Sky Flat

foothills flat

foothills flat

steps up to and platform for the Great Sea Spirit

pass-through to execute the various poles

top of waterfall (painted on flat)

Mercantile flat

Rice house flat

Spice house flat

sliding door

sliding door

swinging doors

porch

half flat (only rises 3 to 4 feet)

bottom of waterfall (painted on flat)

Madame Yu-Lu's Junk

foothills flat

Sampans come in through here

bay/ocean

footdock

beach/land

Pagoda Platform

Shrine of the Great Sea Spirit

proscenium

proscenium

proscenium

Apron

# Winds of Silk

**SET:** The entire stage is the small fishing village of Rising Red Sun on an island in the South Seas. The sky is a bright blue, and green mountains with snowcapped peaks loom in the distance. Foothills stand closer in, with a waterfall tumbling into the ocean at the left (perhaps above the Junk). The foreground is two-thirds sandy beach and one-third sea. Two small rice paper and wood houses stand side by side to the right. These houses belong to the **SPICE FAMILY** and the **RICE FAMILY** respectively. Another larger building, made of tattered shingles and wood planks, sits to the left of the houses, center stage. This is the Red Sun Mercantile, where fishermen prepare their nets on the long porch in front and women clean the catch of the day inside.

[The Mercantile structure shows a definite Western influence in design. It is actually a facade to a saloon of the Old West. In fact, swinging saloon doors decorate the entrance, and the word "Mercantile" is painted over faded, weatherworn "Saloon" lettering on the sign over the porch. To one side of the word "Saloon" is also a faded, weatherworn painting of a mug of beer, and under that it reads "Beer—Two Bits."]

Directly to the left and down from the Mercantile stands a small footdock (half step up—6" high) running alongside the shore. The footdock serves as a dividing line between the sand and water. All boats coming to shore will tie up at the footdock. An old dilapidated Junk is already tied up at the end of the footdock next to the Mercantile—upstage. The Junk belongs to **MADAME YU-LU**, who keeps store goods inside. A piece of sailcloth hangs over the Junk reading "Madame Yu-Lu's Dry Goods."

To the far right stands the Shrine to the Great Sea Spirit, a *torii* (gateway) with a large gong placed in its center. Attached to the left and right of the Shrine's *nuki* (crosspiece) are colorful streamers. A small altar for offerings stands below the gong. Pretty flowers adorn the altar.

[Later, **REFLECTION OF THE MIRRORS**, on her Pagoda Platform, will be rolled to the far left to offset the Shrine to the Great Sea Spirit.]

If there is an apron that the Shrine and Pagoda Platform pieces can be placed on, so much the better.

The set should be two-dimensional and painted as if it exists inside an *ukiyo-e* (oriental wood-block color print) painting.

**AT RISE:**
As the curtain opens, a spotlight falls on **REFLECTION OF THE MIRRORS** downstage center. She is dressed in a sparkling metallic kimono, bejeweled and spectacular. Her hair and makeup are those of a geisha. **REFLECTION OF THE MIRRORS** kneels on a pillow atop a moderately tall platform adorned to look like a miniature pagoda.

Two **PAGODA ATTENDANTS** [JU-LU and DU-LU; males] stand stoically on either side. On either side of the **PAGODA ATTENDANTS** stand two **MIRROR STANDARD-BEARERS** [FU-LU and GU-LU; females] holding up poles with strings of tiny mirrors dangling from the top. These mirrors should reflect and sparkle in the spotlight. Behind the **PAGODA ATTENDANTS** and **MIRROR STANDARD-BEARERS** are four **CHIME STANDARD-BEARERS** [MU-LU, NU-LU, TU-LU, and KU-LU; females] who hold poles with wind chimes attached. The **CHIME STANDARD-BEARERS** are hidden in the darkness at the moment, as is the rest of the stage behind **REFLECTION OF THE MIRRORS**. The **STANDARD-BEARERS** and **ATTENDANTS** are **VILLAGERS**.

[Clothing for most of the village people is simple, worn, and of drab colors. The village people wear felt sandals or slippers or go barefooted, depending on their station in the community (e.g., **MINISTER RU-LU** and **MASTER SU-LU** would probably wear felt sandals, whereas **VU-LU** would go barefooted).]

As the curtain opens, the sound of a gong is heard, and **REFLECTION OF THE MIRRORS** raises her head to the audience. She will remain in a reverent, bowed position, with hands folded.

**REFLECTION OF THE MIRRORS:**
Welcome, most honorable guests. Welcome to our theater. We would like to tell you a story of long ago. It is a story of good and evil. It is a story of bravery and courage. It is a story of spirits and deities. I am Reflection of the Mirrors, and this story is called *Winds of Silk.*

*(The gong is struck once again as the lights come up to full on the entire stage. The CHIME STANDARD-BEARERS and MIRROR STANDARD-BEARERS shake their poles so that the mirrors sparkle and the chimes chime. The two PAGODA ATTENDANTS wheel the Pagoda Platform and REFLECTION OF THE MIRRORS to stage right in front of the Shrine of the Great Sea Spirit, while the STANDARD-BEARERS cross over and line up on the footdock. This opens up the center to show the village in the background.)*

**REFLECTION OF THE MIRRORS:** *(Continued.)*
We ask you please, most honorable guests, to imagine our setting to be a small fishing village—the village of Rising Red Sun.

*(A red circle cutout rises from behind the mountains to hang in the blue sky. All look back to see the sun rise, and they bow towards it. BU-LU hits the gong once again. Then REFLECTION OF THE MIRRORS turns back to address the audience again.)*

**REFLECTION OF THE MIRRORS:** *(Continued.)*
We ask you to imagine that this village of Rising Red Sun is resting on a tiny island in the Pacific Ocean. It is not a rich village and everyone works very, very hard.

*(Two VILLAGERS come out of the Mercantile: HU-LU [female] sits on the porch and begins cleaning the fish in her basket; ZU-LU [male] picks up a fishing net to mend. MAMA-SAN SAY-LEE comes out of the Spice house, crosses with her basket of laundry downstage to the footdock, and proceeds to wash her clothes in the water.)*

**REFLECTION OF THE MIRRORS:** *(Continued.)*
But the people of this village are most content. Each member of the village has a job to do. The men fish in the sea, and the women tend to their households. The children of the village play.

*(BO-LO races on stage from the right, being chased by MO-LO, who has an oriental hand-held tom-tom. BO-LO and MO-LO RICE are young, mischievous boys. The tom-tom makes a lot of noise, and the two young boys laugh and jump up and down in amusement. PAPA-SAN RO-LO comes out from the Rice house. PAPA-SAN RO-LO is very old and looks as if he's ready to fall down.)*

[The children and young people of Rising Red Sun are dressed in more colorful outfits than their elders. The tom-tom is a drum with ball and string attached. When the ball is swung around, it makes a thumping noise when it strikes the drum part.]

**PAPA-SAN RO-LO:**
Hey, you crummy kids, you make too much racket! You want the whole village to come down on this house? You be quiet!

**BO-LO** and **MO-LO:** (*Bowing to their father.*)
Yes, honorable Papa-san.

(*PAPA-SAN RO-LO* begins to cough and wheeze. **HU-LU** and **ZU-LU** scurry over to stand on either side of **PAPA-SAN RO-LO**. They take hold of his arms to hold the old man up, and help **PAPA-SAN RO-LO** back into the Rice house.)

**REFLECTION OF THE MIRRORS:**
If you please, Papa-san Ro-Lo is a very old man on his last chopsticks.

(*Once **PAPA-SAN RO-LO** is gone, **BO-LO** bangs the tom-tom at **MO-LO** again. The boys run back out to the right, laughing.*)

**REFLECTION OF THE MIRRORS:** (*Continued.*)
It is a peaceful village of long ago. There is not much excitement, good or bad. People of Rising Red Sun live simply and happily until, one day—*this* day. . . .

(*BU-LU* bangs the gong, then exits stage right. The **PAGODA ATTENDANTS, JU-LU** and **DU-LU**, roll the Pagoda Platform and **REFLECTION OF THE MIRRORS** to stage left, opposite or parallel to the Shrine of the Great Sea Spirit. The **CHIME STANDARD-BEARERS, MU-LU, NU-LU, TU-LU,** and **KU-LU**, shake their chimes and exit offstage right, while the **MIRROR STANDARD-BEARERS, FU-LU** and **GU-LU**, step over to the Pagoda Platform and place their mirror poles in supports built into the back of the Pagoda Platform. They then step back to the Mercantile along with **JU-LU** and **DU-LU** to join in the scene and work. In time, **MU-LU, NU-LU, TU-LU** and **KU-LU** will come out of the Mercantile as **MO-LO** and **BO-LO** reenter from stage right to sit with the ladies on the porch of the Mercantile. When all is settled, **MAMA-SAN SAY-LEE** stands with her laundry basket, stretches her back, and calls out . . .)

[From now on, normal lighting will dim and a special light will come up to highlight **REFLECTION OF THE MIRRORS** whenever she speaks a long narrative. Also, action in the background will freeze unless otherwise noted. When **REFLECTION OF THE MIRRORS** finishes her dialogue, the lighting will return to normal while the action resumes.]

**MAMA-SAN SAY-LEE:**
Gay-Lee! May-Lee! Ray-Lee! Where are those girls?

(*From over the foothill flat, stage right, a pole is lifted up with four brightly colored paper dragon and butterfly kites attached. The pole is pumped up and down to give the impression the kites are flying.*)

[The kites are small, to appear as if they are at a distance, and their tails fan out to the left, looking as if the wind has caught them. Strings for the kites loop to the right and disappear down behind the foothill flat.]

**MAMA-SAN SAY-LEE:** (*Continued.*)
(*Looking back at the kites.*)
There they are, playing with their kites again.
(*Shouting as loudly as she can.*)
You girls come home! There are chores to do!

(*MAMA-SAN SAY-LEE* steps into the Spice house.)

**REFLECTION OF THE MIRRORS:**
Of course, the children of the village do not play all the time. They are also taught the work of their elders, for one day, this will be what they will do. They will work hard, raise their own families, and celebrate the fortunes of life. This is how it has been for many generations and how it will be for many more. You work, you love, you live . . .

*(The kite pole comes down as the Sampan [raft-type boat] is pulled in up to the footdock by VO-LO and SO-LO, two of the teen RICE BROTHERS. They tie the Sampan up at the footdock. On the Sampan, among the tangled nets and baskets of fish, stands MASTER SU-LU, and another, PO-LO, a third RICE BROTHER. Two village men, JU-LU and DU-LU, come down to help haul baskets up and into the Mercantile.)*

[A rope is attached to each front end of the Sampan. There is another set of ropes on the back of the Sampan for pulling the boat back out to sea—offstage left. **MASTER SU-LU** is one member of the village who is more nicely dressed. He is dressed like a *daimyo* (noble lord).]

**JU-LU:**
Did you have a good catch this morning, Master Su-Lu?

**MASTER SU-LU:**
Yes, we did, honorable Ju-Lu. These Rice boys will make fine fishermen.

**DU-LU:**
Good to hear it. Their father will be most pleased.

**REFLECTION OF THE MIRRORS:**
If you please, presenting the five sons of the House of Rice . . .

*(The five boys cross downstage and stand proudly in a row while work continues behind them. Each boy bows to the audience as REFLECTION OF THE MIRRORS calls out his name.)*

**REFLECTION OF THE MIRRORS:**
Bo-Lo, Mo-Lo, Po-Lo, So-Lo, and Vo-Lo.

**MASTER SULU:**
Come, boys. We will get these fish to the Mercantile, then head out again this afternoon to catch more.

*(The RICE BROTHERS help MASTER SU-LU carry baskets of fish from the Sampan into the Mercantile, while the SPICE SISTERS come frolicking in from stage right. They hold four large kites—replicas of the four smaller ones on the kite pole. Following behind the nine SPICE SISTERS is a tenth sister, SELMA. Her sisters haven't let her play with the kites, and she enters sad and dejected.)*

**MAY-LEE:**
Why did Mama-san have to call us now? Just when we had our kites up in the wind.

**TAY-LEE:**
We're always being called away from our fun. It isn't fair.

**REFLECTION OF THE MIRRORS:**
If you please, presenting the *ten* daughters of the House of Spice . . .

*(The **SPICE SISTERS** cross downstage and line up in a row. Like the **RICE BROTHERS**, each bows when **REFLECTION OF THE MIRRORS** calls out her name.)*

**REFLECTION OF THE MIRRORS:** *(Continued.)*
Bay-Lee, Day-Lee, Fay-Lee, Gay-Lee, Jay-Lee, May-Lee, Pay-Lee, Ray-Lee, Tay-Lee, and— Selma.

*(As the **SPICE SISTERS** cross back, **TAY-LEE** drops the tail of her kite, and **SELMA** bends down to pick it up for her. **TAY-LEE** quickly pulls it away.)*

**TAY-LEE:**
Don't touch my kite, Selma.

**SELMA:**
I only wanted to help you hold it off the ground so it wouldn't get dirty, honorable sister Tay-Lee.

**TAY-LEE:**
Well, don't. Don't come near my kite ever again, do you hear me?

**PAY-LEE:**
That goes for our kites, too. We don't want you touching anything of ours.

*(Striking a superior pose, the **SPICE SISTERS** cross stage left to join those at the footdock and Mercantile. Heartbroken, **SELMA** wanders over and sits on the steps of the Shrine of the Great Sea Spirit.)*

**SELMA:**
I only wanted to help.

**REFLECTION OF THE MIRRORS:**
Poor little Selma. The Spice girls will not play with their sister because her name is different from all the other names in the village.

*(**PO-LO** steps down from the Mercantile to join the **SPICE SISTERS**.)*

**PO-LO:**
Good morning, honorable Spice sisters. You are well, I hope?

**RAY-LEE:**
We are well, honorable Po-Lo—especially Jay-Lee.

*(The girls giggle. **PO-LO** smiles and holds **JAY-LEE'S** hand. She blushes and smiles back.)*

**REFLECTION OF THE MIRRORS:**
If you please, Spice sister Jay-Lee has a whopping big crush on Rice brother Po-Lo.

**JAY-LEE:**
I would be most pleased if you would join us for our evening meal, Po-Lo.

**PO-LO:**
Oh, that would be wonderful, Jay-Lee. But I couldn't accept unless the invitation was for my brothers and honorable father as well.

**JAY-LEE:**
I will ask Mama-san if this is all right with her.

**PO-LO:**
Yes, please do.

*(JAY-LEE crosses over to the entrance of the Spice house and waves back to PO-LO, who has crossed back to join his older brothers and MASTER SU-LU on the Sampan. VO-LO and SO-LO pick up the ropes on the other side of the boat and pull it back out to sea, stage left. The SPICE SISTERS watch the Sampan go out to sea and wave good-bye.)*

**RAY-LEE:** *(Mimicking PO-LO and making fun of her sister.)*
Yes, pleeeeaaase.

*(The sisters laugh until MAMA-SAN SAY-LEE comes to the door of the Spice house.)*

**MAMA-SAN SAY-LEE:**
You girls come inside and clean these mats. Come on, now.

*(The sisters groan and exit into the Spice house. SELMA is left alone on stage sitting on the steps of the Shrine of the Great Sea Spirit.)*

**SELMA:** *(Straightening the flowers on the altar.)*
Oh, Great Sea Spirit, could you tell me what is wrong with me? Why do my sisters dislike me so? I have done nothing to them. I help them whenever I can and I love them all very much. So why don't they play with me or talk to me? It makes me most unhappy, Great Sea Spirit.

*(After a pause, PAPA-SAN TO-LO enters stage right carrying a basket of berries and roots.)*

**PAPA-SAN TO-LO:**
Daughter Selma, what are you doing at the Shrine of the Great Sea Spirit all by yourself?

**SELMA:**
My sisters hate me, Papa-san.

**PAPA-SAN TO-LO:**
Oh, I am sure they do not, my daughter.

**SELMA:** *(Crying.)*
Yes, they do. They never let me play with them. They call me names and pull my hair, but most of the time they act as if I'm not there at all. They hate me because I'm different. My name isn't Fay-Lee or May-Lee. They hate me because my name is Selma.

**PAPA-SAN TO-LO:**
It is not easy to be different, daughter. However—at the same time—it is quite special, too.

**SELMA:**
I don't want to be special. Everyone makes fun of me.

**PAPA-SAN TO-LO:**
The Minister of Wisdom once told me: "To ride upon another cloud is to fly very high."

**SELMA:**
What does that mean, Papa-san?

**PAPA-SAN TO-LO:**
Well, I do not know, but it sounds very wise, does it not? The Minister of Wisdom is always saying wise things, and I do not think anyone in the village ever understands him. This is why he is the Minister of Wisdom—a man to be respected most highly.

**SELMA:**
Yes, Papa-san.

**PAPA-SAN TO-LO:**
There is one more thing I'd like to tell my special daughter.
*(He wraps his arms around her.)*
Do you know I love you very much?

**SELMA:** *(Smiling through her tears.)*
Yes, Papa-san.

*(SELMA and PAPA-SAN TO-LO hug as MAMA-SAN SAY-LEE ushers the other SPICE SISTERS outside. They carry gakyzukas [straw mats] and straw paddles to beat the mats clean with. The girls are not happy about having to do this chore.)*

**GAY-LEE:**
But, we just cleaned these mats last week, Mama-san.

**MAMA-SAN SAY-LEE:**
Mats need to be cleaned every week. You do not want to live in a dirty house, do you?

**GAY-LEE:** *(Grumbling under her breath.)*
I wouldn't mind it.

*(MAMA-SAN SAY-LEE thumps GAY-LEE on the head and exits back into the Spice house. The girls proceed to beat the mats, but it is a halfhearted effort.)*

**FAY-LEE:**
Work, work, work. It's all we ever do.

**JAY-LEE:**
I'm going to grow old and gray very fast if I have to keep doing all this work. Po-Lo won't ever look at me again.

**TAY-LEE:**
Good. Then Po-Lo can look at *me*.

*(TAY-LEE laughs, so JAY-LEE thumps TAY-LEE on the backside with her paddle. The girls go back to their wearisome work when PAPA-SAN TO-LO crosses to them with SELMA.)*

**PAPA-SAN TO-LO:**
What is this? So many frowning faces. Why are my daughters so unhappy?

**RAY-LEE:**
It's all this work we have to do, Papa-san. It's not fair.

**PAPA-SAN TO-LO:**
We all must share in the work, daughter. What if I stopped bringing roots and berries down from the mountains for everyone in the village? Where would I get the money to buy your clothes? What if your mama-san stopped cooking? You would go hungry. We all must share because we are a family. We all work, and we all benefit from this work.
*(He puts a gentle arm around SELMA.)*
Come, Selma.

**TAY-LEE:**
Why doesn't Selma have to work?

**PAPA-SAN TO-LO:**
If you girls will not let Selma play with you, why should she be expected to help with your chores? This is a family, my daughters. We must learn to share the fun times as well as the not-so-fun times.

**SELMA:**
I will stay and help my sisters, Papa-san. I don't mind.

**PAPA-SAN TO-LO:** *(Giving **SELMA** another hug.)*
Ah, you are such a good daughter, Selma. You make me proud.

*(**PAPA-SAN TO-LO** exits into the Spice house. The sisters give **SELMA** dirty looks.)*

**PAY-LEE:** *(Mimicking **SELMA**.)*
"I will stay and help my sisters, Papa-san."

**RAY-LEE:** *(Also mimicking **SELMA**.)*
"I don't mind."

**PAY-LEE:**
You make us look bad in front of Papa-san. We lose face.

**SELMA:**
I didn't mean to. I thought you would like me to help. If we all help, the work will get done faster.

**TAY-LEE:** *(Mimicking **SELMA**.)*
"If we all help, the work will get done faster." Well, here.
*(**TAY-LEE** throws a mat over to **SELMA**.)*
You do *my* mat.

**MAY-LEE:** *(Taking **TAY-LEE'S** lead and also tossing her mat over at **SELMA**.)*
Yes, you do my mat, too.

*(Soon the other sisters pile all the mats in front / on top of **SELMA**.)*

**TAY-LEE:**
Share in our work, Selma—like Papa-san's precious girl.

*(**MAY-LEE** gives **SELMA** a whack with her paddle and the other girls follow suit. When they think they have given **SELMA** enough of a whacking, they laugh and exit stage right. Weeping, **SELMA** bends down, picks up a mat, and begins beating it.)*

**REFLECTION OF THE MIRRORS:**
It is a sad day for Selma. Most days are sad days for the girl. When you are different, others do not understand. When they do not understand, they do not like you, and you become an outcast. If those who do not understand Selma would only take the time to get to know her, they would see that Selma is not so different after all. Everyone needs to be loved and treated respectfully no matter what their name is, whether they are rich or poor, and no matter what they look like. There is good and bad in each of us. This is what makes the world go around.

*(The lighting of normal day dims as other lights begin to flash about, and a rumbling sound is heard. **SELMA** looks back and stands in awe at the sight. A puff of smoke appears over the waterfall, and when the smoke clears, you see the **GREAT SEA SPIRIT** standing above / on the waterfall. Lights swirl over him [rotating gobo] giving the impression of waves moving across his body.)*

[The **GREAT SEA SPIRIT** is an ominous-looking creature—loud and boisterous—with a brightly colored, billowy costume. Long, white hair trails behind him to the ground, and he wears heavy makeup. The **GREAT SEA SPIRIT** should look like a character out of a kabuki drama.]

**GREAT SEA SPIRIT:**
Why do you not run away, girl? Are you not terrified at the spectacle of me?

**SELMA:**
I see you are a great thing. I see you are very big and powerful. But somehow, I see you are not something to be afraid of.

**GREAT SEA SPIRIT:** (*Upset.*)
No? No? Do you not know I could squash you with the flick of my finger?
(*He flicks his fingers, and the lights flash again and thunder rumbles.*)
Do you not know I could wipe your whole village off the face of this little island with the furrow of my brow?

(*A wind whips up from the sea and blows against the Junk and* **SELMA**.)

[The sound of wind can come from a recording, or by cast and crew members offstage making a whooshing sound. The Junk can be shaken from behind to show that the wind has picked up.]

**SELMA:**
Yes, Great One. I see you are strong and magnificent. Still, there is something about you I do not fear.

**GREAT SEA SPIRIT:**
You are a most brave subject. I like that. But do you not know who I am, girl?

**SELMA:**
I only know you are a wondrous thing to behold. However, I think only our Minister of Wisdom would be wise enough to know who you are.

**GREAT SEA SPIRIT:**
You just prayed to me a moment ago, girl. You prayed to me, and I have come to see you.

**SELMA:** (*Dropping her mat and happily stepping toward the* **GREAT SEA SPIRIT**.)
Yes, I know who you are now. You are our Great Spirit of the Sea. You are the one who watches over our village to see no harm comes to us. And you give us fish from the waters that we may live and prosper. Yes, I know you very well, Great One. You are the one in my prayers every night. Thank you, Great Spirit. Oh, thank you for hearing my prayers and coming to see me.

**GREAT SEA SPIRIT:**
What is your problem, child? Why do I only hear sorrow in your voice as it floats over my colorful coral reef? Why do I feel your many teardrops fall upon the whitecaps of my mighty ocean waves?

**SELMA:**
Oh, Great One, I'm not liked by my sisters because they say I'm different. I will do anything for them to like me, Most Honorable Spirit. If I knew how to change so they would like me, I would.

**GREAT SEA SPIRIT:**
The Minister of Wisdom once said: "To change oneself to the fancy of the world is to change the world to the fancy of one."

**SELMA:**
What does that mean, Great Sea Spirit?

**GREAT SEA SPIRIT:**
I do not know, but it sounds very wise, does it not?

**SELMA:**
Yes, Great One—most wise.

**GREAT SEA SPIRIT:**
I will study your predicament, little—little?

**SELMA:**
My name is Selma, Great Sea Spirit.

**GREAT SEA SPIRIT:**
Selma?

**SELMA:** *(Almost ashamed of her name.)*
Yes, Honorable One.

**GREAT SEA SPIRIT:**
Well then, little Selma. I will study your predicament and see if there is a way I can help you.

**SELMA:** *(Kneeling before the **GREAT SEA SPIRIT**.)*
Oh, thank you, Most Generous One.

*(**SELMA** kowtows to the **GREAT SEA SPIRIT**. The lights flash, the Junk shakes, and smoke billows up over the **GREAT SEA SPIRIT**. When the smoke leaves and the lights return to normal day, the **GREAT SEA SPIRIT** is gone. Jubilantly, **SELMA** picks up a mat and begins cleaning it. With this activity under way, **MADAME YU-LU** comes out from her Junk. She stumbles and fumbles, topsy-turvy.)*

**MADAME YU-LU:**
My heart! My heart! I am dying—my heart! What is coming of this day? I sit in my junk and get tossed about like I am nothing but a small pebble of sand on a long and narrow beach—nothing but a tiny grain of rice in acres and acres of rice paddies—nothing but a minute drop of water in the huge ocean—nothing but . . .
*(Noticing **SELMA**.)*
Selma, child, what has come across these waters just now? What has rolled in with the tide? What has skipped along the dale? What has gone with the wind?

**SELMA:**
Oh, nothing to be afraid of, Madame Yu-Lu. It will not harm you.

**MADAME YU-LU:**
It felt like the fury of the Great Wind Spirit that had come upon this island once before. You are young and do not know such rage as that which comes from the Great Wind Spirit. The Great Wind Spirit can whip up a most fearsome gust and send it across our tiny island. It happened before, not so long ago. It was a terrible wind that took our village and put a little bit of it here and a little bit of it there. We were days in finding all of the pieces so we could put it back together again. We even found some things that were not a part of our village to begin with.
*(Pointing back to the Mercantile.)*
You see the Mercantile? It is a most strange building, no? We know not where it came from, but when we finished putting it back together, we got this. It comes from a faraway land, we think. Somewhere where they have a S-A-L-O-O-N. Saloon with beer for two bits. So you

can well understand why I am afraid of these fierce winds. If you think these ferocious winds are coming again, you will tell me, no?

**SELMA:**
Yes, Madame Yu-Lu. I will tell you.

**MADAME YU-LU:**
Bless you, child. You are a good girl. Tell your Mama-san to stop by and see me. I have new material in from the mainland. It is very pretty—maybe for a very pretty girl like you.

**SELMA:**
Oh, no, Madame Yu-Lu. I'm not pretty.

**MADAME YU-LU:**
Who says this? Who says you are not a pretty girl? You tell them to come see me. I will set them straight on the matter in no time. Why, you are as pretty as a picture—as pretty as a rose—as pretty as the stars—as pretty as . . . Well, you are.

**SELMA:**
Thank you, Madame Yu-Lu. You are most kind.

**MADAME YU-LU:**
Thank *you*, little Selma. You tell your Mama-san about my material, now.

**SELMA:**
Yes, I will.

(*MADAME YU-LU exits back into her Junk. SELMA picks up a mat or two and exits into the Spice house. Enter MINISTER RU-LU, the Minister of Wisdom, with VU-LU, the village idiot. VU-LU has a bandage over his left hand.*)

**MINISTER RU-LU:**
My boy, my boy, how many times must I tell you not to stick your hand in the beehive?

**VU-LU:**
Three?

**MINISTER RU-LU:**
Three what?

**VU-LU:**
Three times you have to tell me not to stick my hand in the beehive? This is a math problem? Maybe the answer is four.

**MINISTER RU-LU:**
No, this is not a math problem. Why must I tell you time and again not to stick your hand in the beehive?

**VU-LU:**
Because I don't get it the first time?

**MINISTER RU-LU:**
No, no. Why do you *not* stick your hand in the beehive?

**VU-LU:**
Because I will get stung.

**MINISTER RU-LU:**
Very good, Vu-Lu.

**VU-LU:**
But how do I get the honey if I don't stick my hand in?

**MINISTER RU-LU:**
You put on a glove and scoop the honey out with a spoon.

**VU-LU:**
The honey is in the glove?

**MINISTER RU-LU:**
No. The honey is in the beehive. You wear the glove to keep from getting stung.

**VU-LU:**
From the spoon?

**MINISTER RU-LU:**
From the bees!

**REFLECTION OF THE MIRRORS:**
If you please, we wish to present to you the most honorable Minister of Wisdom, Ru-Lu.

(***MINISTER RU-LU*** *bows before the audience.*)

**REFLECTION OF THE MIRRORS:** (*Continued.*)
We also wish to present to you the most worrisome Vu-Lu, the village idiot.

**MINISTER RU-LU:**
Bow, Vu-Lu.

**VU-LU:**
What?

**MINISTER RU-LU:**
You have just been introduced to our honorable guests. You should bow to show your respect.

**VU-LU:** (*Pulling up his shirt to find his "respect."*)
Why would our most honorable guests want to see that?

**MINISTER RU-LU:** (*Forcing **VU-LU'S** head down.*)
Bow!
(*Addressing the audience.*)
You must forgive Vu-Lu. The boy is a little slow.

**VU-LU:**
I know I am a little *low*. You're pushing my head down, so I'm *low*.

**MINISTER RU-LU:** (*Raising **VU-LU'S** head back up.*)
Slow, Vu-Lu. You are a little *slow*.

**VU-LU:**
Oh, no, Minister. I run very fast.

**MINISTER RU-LU:**
Not that kind of slow, Vu-Lu.

**VU-LU:**
What kind do you mean?

**MINISTER RU-LU:**
I mean . . . You see, young friend, I am afraid you are not working with all your oars in the water. There is an old saying: "He who cannot find sense enough to come in from the rain is one who will be forever soggy."

**VU-LU:**
But that is how I clean my clothes. When it rains, I stand in it and wash my clothes. This way I never have to take my clothes off.

**MINISTER RU-LU:**
There is some logic in that, Vu-Lu. Although it frightens me to think that there is some logic in that.

**VU-LU:**
What do you mean, Minister?

**MINISTER RU-LU:**
I mean that perhaps I am the dimwitted one, and you are the wise man. Come, Vu-Lu, we must gather flowers for this evening's offering to the Shrine of the Great Sea Spirit.

(*MINISTER RU-LU* and *VU-LU* exit stage right as the nine *SPICE SISTERS* come out of the Spice house.)

[The five older **SPICE SISTERS**, **JAY-LEE**, **MAY-LEE**, **PAY-LEE**, **RAY-LEE**, and **TAY-LEE**, wear dark stretch clothing and caps. Their hair is drawn up under their caps, and they have little canvas pouches tied around their waists. **BAY-LEE**, **DAY-LEE**, **FAY-LEE**, and **GAY-LEE** carry towels. **PAY-LEE** and **RAY-LEE** carry buckets of water—droplets of blue paper—while **JAY-LEE**, **MAY-LEE**, and **TAY-LEE** carry knives.]

**PAY-LEE:**
Come on, everyone. We'll go to the coral reef today. We haven't been to the coral reef for a long time. Maybe we'll find oysters there, and maybe we can find an oyster with a pearl in it.

**JAY-LEE:**
Oh, I would like to find a pearl. How special that would be.

**MAY-LEE:**
How special any of us would be if we found a pearl.

**TAY-LEE:**
Yes, the whole village would honor me. I would be famous.

(*SELMA* hurries out of the house wearing the same black stretch diving outfit as the five older girls.)

**SELMA:**
I will come with you, please. I can dive very well. I will help you dive for pearls.

**PAY-LEE:**
You're not serious. You dive for pearls? Don't make us laugh.

**RAY-LEE:**
You must be most skillful to dive for pearls, Selma. You must hold your breath under water for a very long time. You must know how to find oysters and pry them open to see if a pearl is inside. You can't do these things.

**SELMA:**
I can too. Papa-san has taught me how.

**RAY-LEE:**
So you know how to dive for pearls. What makes you think you can come with us?

**TAY-LEE:**
Ray-Lee is right. I will be the one to find a pearl. You must be favored by the Great Sea Spirit to find pearls. A pearl is very rare and special. When I find the pearl, I will be honored, and there will be a big celebration to give thanks to the Great Sea Spirit and *me*. How could you ever think the Great Sea Spirit would favor *you*, Selma. You are nothing. You are a silly little girl, and I hate you.

*(TAY-LEE laughs while PAY-LEE and RAY-LEE dump the droplets of water from their buckets on top of SELMA'S head. The girls laugh, thumb their noses at SELMA, and exit beyond the footdock stage left. SELMA falls to her knees crying and dejected again.)*

**SELMA:**
Why do they hate me so?

*(A thundering voice comes from offstage.)*

**GREAT SEA SPIRIT:**
Because they are mean and nasty little girls!

*(SELMA pops her head up and looks all around.)*

**SELMA:**
Who said that? Is there someone here, please?

*(Normal lighting dims and, as before, other lights begin to flash, and the smoke billows up above the waterfall. The GREAT SEA SPIRIT returns with all of his special effects.)*

**GREAT SEA SPIRIT:**
I have returned, Selma. I think I know how to teach your sisters a lesson in goodwill and humility. I think I can help you.

**SELMA:**
Oh, Great Sea Spirit, I would be ever so grateful.

**GREAT SEA SPIRIT:**
Your sisters are looking in the wrong spot to find a special pearl. They look in the sea where the oysters are. But other creatures of the sea eat many of the oysters. You cannot find that special pearl in the sea. But you can find an extraordinary pearl under this waterfall.

**SELMA:**
Under the waterfall you are standing on?

**GREAT SEA SPIRIT:**
Yes, Selma.

**SELMA:**
Great Sea Spirit, I don't wish to argue with you, but the waterfall is fresh water. The oysters we know of are found in sea water.

**GREAT SEA SPIRIT:**
Yes, but one oyster slipped in with a big tide that roared over the beach and landed in the pool of the waterfall. This oyster has been in the pool for many years and has grown very large. Inside this oyster you will find a very large and very special pearl. When you show this pearl to your sisters, they will respect you for being in favor with the Great Sea Spirit.

**SELMA:**
Is it not dangerous to dive into the pool from the waterfall?

**GREAT SEA SPIRIT:**
It is most dangerous. If you want the respect of your sisters badly enough, you will risk it. You must show yourself worthy to gain such a prize, Selma. If you are brave enough, and you show me your courage by diving into the pool of the waterfall, I will favor you with a giant pearl.

**SELMA:**
You will be with me, Great Sea Spirit?

**GREAT SEA SPIRIT:**
I will be with you, little Selma.

**SELMA:**
Then I'm not afraid.

*(**SELMA** exits stage right. The **GREAT SEA SPIRIT** puffs up and roars forth as thunder and lightning flash around him.)*

**GREAT SEA SPIRIT:**
Oh, hear me, spirits of the world. I am the Great Sea Spirit, and I am here to tell one and all: respect all things whether fish, bird, animal, air, soil, or human. You are here, they are here. No matter where they come from—no matter where you come from—all are here. All have the right to be here. You should respect all things, and all things should respect you.

*(Another flash, another display of special effects, and the **GREAT SEA SPIRIT** is gone.)*

**REFLECTION OF THE MIRRORS:**
And so Selma went up into the mountains to stand before the waterfall.

*(A spotlight follows the action above the foothills flat and waterfall flat. A small cutout on a stick of **SELMA** in her black stretch outfit moves along top of the foothill flat as if it were walking towards the waterfall. The cutout stops at the edge of the waterfall.)*

**REFLECTION OF THE MIRRORS:** *(Continued.)*
The waterfall is very tall and very powerful. The water at the bottom tumbles over and over. One can easily drown in the waterfall, Selma thinks as she stands above it. Selma also thinks of her sisters and of the Great Sea Spirit giving her this chance to dive for a giant pearl. She cannot disappoint the Great Sea Spirit, who is helping with her most tormenting problem, no matter how frightful the churning waters appear. So Selma gathers every ounce of courage she has, takes a deep breath, closes her eyes, and dives from the top of the waterfall into the swirling pool below.

_(The cutout figure of **SELMA** dives down from the top of the waterfall. The swirling water effect that previously covered the **GREAT SEA SPIRIT** swirls over the waterfall now.)_

**REFLECTION OF THE MIRRORS:** _(Continued.)_
How brave Selma is to risk her life like this—to dive into the treacherous waterfall. When she hits the foaming water, the impact almost forces all the breath out of her body, but Selma forges on. Down, down she swims to the bottom of the pool, holding her breath for ever so long. As she swims towards the edge of the pool, Selma spots the magnificent oyster peacefully resting between mossy rocks, just as the Great Sea Spirit had said—a giant oyster as big as Selma. She quickly busies herself, taking a knife and prying at the oyster. Selma works and works, the seconds passing rapidly, the air in her lungs wanting to burst forth. She wants to surface and take another breath of fresh air, but Selma fears she might not find the oyster again on a second dive, so she works harder and faster. Finally, the oyster opens and inside is a most magnificent giant pearl.

_(The wave light over the waterfall turns to a brilliant, almost blinding intensity.)_

**REFLECTION OF THE MIRRORS:** _(Continued.)_
It is a pearl as big as your hand. It is a pearl perfectly round and precious. It is a pearl that glimmers as brightly as the stars. It is a wondrous treasure for Selma, and she carefully snatches it from the oyster, tucks it in her pouch, and swims to the top of the pool. Then Selma climbs out of the swirling waters and lies on the sandy beach in front of the waterfall to rest. But before she heads back to the village of Rising Red Sun, Selma kneels and prays to the Great Sea Spirit—many thanks. And to show his approval, the Great Sea Spirit creates a colorful rainbow that rises from the churning waterfall up to the blue sky above.

_(A cutout rainbow on a pole rises from the bottom of the waterfall and reaches up into the blue sky. The rainbow will stay there until **SELMA** rejoins her sisters back at the village downstage.)_

**REFLECTION OF THE MIRRORS:** _(Continued.)_
This is a most special day for Selma. It is a day of miracles.

_(The bright lights remain on the rainbow for a moment until the **SPICE SISTERS** reenter stage left. **TAY-LEE** is the center of attention as she holds a small cloth in her hands. The other sisters huddle around her.)_

[It shouldn't be necessary for **JAY-LEE**, **MAY-LEE**, **PAY-LEE**, **RAY-LEE**, and **TAY-LEE** to be wet—merely give the impression that they have been in the water by having them remove their caps and towel off as they enter.]

**FAY-LEE:**
May I see it again, Tay-Lee? Please, may I?

**TAY-LEE:**
You've already seen it once, Fay-Lee.

**FAY-LEE:**
I know, but it is so wondrous. Might I see it again?

**MAY-LEE:**
Yes, please? May we see it again, Tay-Lee?

**TAY-LEE:**
Oh, very well.

*(**TAY-LEE** removes the cloth and holds a small pearl in her hand. Her sisters ooh and aah.)*

**JAY-LEE:**
What a prize you have found, Tay-Lee. There will be a great celebration tonight. We must tell the whole village of your pearl.

**TAY-LEE:**
Yes, everyone must know that I'm the only one in favor with the Great Sea Spirit.

*(**SELMA** enters from the right. She is excited.)*

**SELMA:**
Sisters, guess what has happened to me?

**PAY-LEE:**
We couldn't possibly care what has happened to you, Selma. Look, Tay-Lee has found a pearl. She's in favor with the Great Sea Spirit.

**SELMA:**
Oh, that's wonderful, Tay-Lee.

**TAY-LEE:**
Yes, but we all knew *I* would be the one to be favored by the Great Sea Spirit, didn't we, sisters?

*(All agree.)*

**SELMA:**
I'm very happy for you, Tay-Lee. May I see it?

**TAY-LEE:**
Well, I suppose.

*(**TAY-LEE** shows the pearl to **SELMA**. All of the sisters ooh and aah again.)*

**SELMA:**
Oh, what a splendid pearl, indeed. A most splendid pearl. But look.
*(Reaching into her pouch.)*
I, too, have been favored by the Great Sea Spirit.

**MAY-LEE:**
You?

**SELMA:**
Yes, I went diving by myself and I also found a pearl.

**PAY-LEE:**
You're lying.

**TAY-LEE:**
Now, now, sisters. If Selma says she found a pearl, then she found a pearl. But it can't be as wondrous as mine. I know that.

**GAY-LEE:**
Let's see your pearl, Selma.

**SELMA:**
Oh, yes. I'm so glad you want to see it.

(*SELMA pulls out a cue-ball size pearl from her pouch. The sister's eyes grow wide and they all stand there aghast.*)

**FAY-LEE:**
Oh, Selma. Wherever did you find a pearl like that?

**SELMA:**
Under the waterfall.

**RAY-LEE:**
What? But there aren't any oysters under the waterfall. The waterfall is fresh water.

**SELMA:**
Well, I know that, but you wouldn't let me dive with you in the ocean, so the waterfall was the only place for me to go.

**GAY-LEE:**
You dove into the waterfall. How brave of you, Selma.

**PAY-LEE:**
Weren't you afraid of drowning?

**SELMA:**
A little.

**JAY-LEE:**
Selma, it is the most magnificent thing I have ever seen.

**GAY-LEE:**
Yes, it is. You are surely favored above all others on this island for the Great Sea Spirit to give you such a pearl. I'm glad I have you for a sister, Selma.

**SELMA:**
Oh, thank you, Gay-Lee.

**FAY-LEE:**
Me, too. You are as special as Papa-san has said.

**TAY-LEE:**
It's a fake. No pearl is that big.

**SELMA:**
I assure you, Tay-Lee, my pearl is as genuine as yours.

(*The Sampan comes back in with the **RICE BROTHERS** aboard and **MASTER SU-LU**.*)

**VO-LO:** (*Ringing the bells on the Sampan and calling towards the Mercantile.*)
We have returned with more fish, honorable friends!

(*A few **VILLAGERS** come out of the Mercantile to join the brothers. **PO-LO** and **SO-LO** cross over to the **SPICE SISTERS**. As they do, **TAY-LEE** quickly stuffs her pearl into her pouch and grabs **SELMA'S** giant pearl.*)

**PO-LO:**
Jay-Lee, did you ask your Mama-san if we might have the evening meal with you?

**JAY-LEE:**
Oh, Po-Lo, the entire village will be celebrating tonight!

**SO-LO:**
Why is that?

**TAY-LEE:** *(Before JAY-LEE can tell of SELMA'S find.)*
Look what I found!

**FAY-LEE:**
But Selma . . .

*(TAY-LEE pushes FAY-LEE aside and gives PO-LO SELMA'S pearl. VO-LO crosses over to see what's going on.)*

**VO-LO:**
You found that giant pearl, Tay-Lee?

**TAY-LEE:**
Yes, I did.

**SELMA:**
But I . . .

**TAY-LEE:**
Go finish cleaning those mats, Selma. No one is interested in what you have to say.
*(Turning back to the crowd.)*
Yes, I found this giant pearl. The Great Sea Spirit has favored me.

**SELMA:**
Please, Tay-Lee, *I* . . .

**TAY-LEE:**
Go on, Selma. No one wants to listen to you. Go on!

**MAY-LEE:**
Yes, isn't it a glorious pearl *Tay-Lee* found. We must have a celebration in honor of Tay-Lee.

**SO-LO:**
Oh, yes.
*(Calling over to the Sampan and to all behind him.)*
Come everyone! Tay-Lee has found the most stupendous pearl in all creation!

*(The VILLAGERS come in from all directions and gather around TAY-LEE with excitement as SELMA crosses back over to the Shrine of the Great Sea Spirit, once again in tears. This time GAY-LEE follows and sits with SELMA, placing a comforting arm around her. FAY-LEE, BAY-LEE, and DAY-LEE also cross to join SELMA.)*

**MINISTER RU-LU:**
With a pearl this big, this village is truly in good grace with the Great Sea Spirit and all spirits that rule the world!

**MASTER SULU:**
Come one and all! We must tell Mama and Papa Spice of their very special daughter, Tay-Lee.

*(The VILLAGERS exit into and around the Spice house as MADAME YU-LU stops to talk to SELMA.)*

**MADAME YU-LU:**
Little Selma, why are you crying? Are you not happy for your sister? A pearl that size shows good fortune for this village.

**SELMA:**
I am happy the village has found good fortune, Madame Yu-Lu.

**MADAME YU-LU:**
Good. Come along then, or you will be left out of the fun.
*(As she exits stage right.)*
We are going to trip the light fandango—put on the Ritz—have a hot time in the old town tonight!

**GAY-LEE:**
I'm sorry, Selma. I'm so very sorry.

**SELMA:**
Thank you, Gay-Lee.

**FAY-LEE:**
We would have told everyone that you were the one to find the pearl, Selma, but who would believe us?

**SELMA:**
It's all right, Fay-Lee. That you know who is right and who is wrong, and that you are here by my side, is a great comfort to me. Your caring is all I need.

**GAY-LEE:**
I could never understand why my sisters dislike you so. You're not so different from us. I'm sorry for ever having made fun of you and for leaving you out of our games. I was afraid if I insisted you join us, they wouldn't let me play either. But now, after what they did to you, I don't want to play with them anymore. We will play together—you and me, Fay-Lee, Bay-Lee, and Day-Lee—if that is all right with you.

**BAY-LEE** and **DAY-LEE:**
We love you, Selma.

**SELMA:**
Oh, and I love you all so much, too.
*(SELMA hugs her sisters and is happy once more.)*
It really doesn't matter who found the pearl. The village is happy, and I want us all to be a part of the fun and celebration.

**FAY-LEE:**
Yes! We can have as much fun as that mean ol' Tay-Lee! Why, we can have *more* fun because we know who *really* found the wonderful pearl!

*(The girls dance and skip cheerfully into the Spice house.)*

**REFLECTION OF THE MIRRORS:**
And so Selma is very happy. It doesn't matter to her so much that Tay-Lee claimed to have found the giant pearl, even though Selma risked her life to get it. Selma believes her reward to be Gay-Lee, Fay-Lee, Day-Lee, and Bay-Lee, who want to share sisterly things with her now. To Selma, this friendship is more valuable than any pearl in the world—no matter how big—no matter how splendid.

*(The **VILLAGERS** enter from all points, stringing Japanese lanterns here and there, setting up makeshift tables, and spreading out trays of food and drink for the celebration. The red sun in the background comes down as the lights dim a little to indicate evening.)*

**REFLECTION OF THE MIRRORS:** *(Continued.)*
It is now night. The whole village comes to pray at the Shrine of the Great Sea Spirit for favoring their village with such a gift, and to honor Tay-Lee for finding the pearl.

*(The **VILLAGERS** are eating, talking gaily, and having a good time. After a moment, **PAPA-SAN TO-LO** stands before the village and raises his cup. **BU-LU** steps up to the shrine and bangs the gong to get everyone's attention.)*

**PAPA-SAN TO-LO:**
Honorable guests. I raise my cup in many thanks to the Great Sea Spirit for blessing this village with his precious gift from the sea.

*(The **VILLAGERS** reverently bow their heads toward the Shrine of the Great Sea Spirit.)*

**PAPA-SAN TO-LO:** *(Continued.)*
And I salute my lovely daughter Tay-Lee for having such good favor come to her.

*(The **VILLAGERS** salute Tay-Lee, except for **SELMA, GAY-LEE, FAY-LEE, DAY-LEE,** and **BAY-LEE,** who quietly sit and look at one another knowingly.)*

**PAPA-SAN TO-LO:**
In honor of having such good friends, and as a part of this celebration tonight, I have asked my beautiful daughters to dance for you.

*(The **VILLAGERS** enthusiastically applaud as **JAY-LEE, MAY-LEE, PAY-LEE, RAY-LEE,** and **TAY-LEE** step downstage in front of everyone with their Japanese fans. They dance to a recording of "Japanese Sandman" or the like. When they finish, the **VILLAGERS** applaud again, and the girls bow and go back to join the others as **PAPA-SAN RO-LO** steps up before everyone to make an announcement. **BU-LU** bangs the gong again and the village falls quiet.)*

**PAPA-SAN RO-LO:** *(Still applauding and watching the **SPICE SISTERS** move off.)*
Very nice—very nice—lovely little ladies . . .
*(**PAPA-SAN RO-LO** begins to cough and wheeze again, and **HU-LU** and **ZU-LU** step to either side of the old man to hold him up.)*
Now my sons will perform . . .
*(Cough, cough.)*
. . . will perform . . .

*(**PAPA-SAN RO-LO** nods off and slumps in **HU-LU** and **ZU-LU'S** hold. The **VILLAGERS** appear surprised and concerned.)*

**MASTER SU-LU:** *(Stepping out.)*
What has happened?

**MADAME YU-LU:** *(Stepping out.)*
Oh, dear. You do not suppose that he—that poor Papa Ro-Lo has . . .

**MINISTER RU-LU:** *(Stepping out.)*
. . . passed on to the heavens above?

**MASTER SU-LU:**
Well, he *is* a very old man.

*(**MADAME YU-LU** steps down to stand in front of **PAPA-SAN RO-LO**. She looks at him carefully, then . . .)*

**MADAME YU-LU:**
Ro-Lo!

**PAPA-SAN RO-LO:** *(Startled, he awakes and continues his speech.)*
. . . ah, the bamboo dance in honor of—in honor of . . .

*(**PAPA-SAN RO-LO** nods off again. This time the entire village shouts out "**RO-LO!**")*

**PAPA-SAN RO-LO:** *(Continued.)*
*(As he awakes.)*
. . . beautiful Tay-Lee.

*(The **VILLAGERS** sigh in relief and applaud as **ZU-LU** and **HU-LU** drag **PAPA-SAN RO-LO** back to his seat. **SO-LO**, **VO-LO**, and **PO-LO** step downstage with bamboo poles. They dance and swing the bamboo shoots around to the rhythm and music of "In a Persian Market" or the like. When they finish, the **VILLAGERS** applaud and **MINISTER RU-LU** steps out to make an announcement. **BU-LU** bangs the gong again.)*

**MINISTER RU-LU:**
For this special occasion, Vu-Lu has prepared a poem. He would like to recite it to you now.

*(The **VILLAGERS** are a little leery about this, and **MINISTER RU-LU** must coax **VU-LU** out of the crowd. **VU-LU** will recite his poem directly to the audience and ask his questions to the audience after his poem. He will include the **VILLAGERS** when required.)*

**VU-LU:** *(Pulling from his pocket a crumpled piece of paper with a poem on it.)*
Uh—if you please—a poem for this most special occasion.

*(Reciting)*
What a wonderful, wonderful thing to see,
A pearl so rare and as big as me.
How grand and nice it surely must be,
To snatch a pearl up from under the sea.

I honor the one who found this great pearl,
A gift that did quite overwhelm us.
The Spirits give grace to the special Spice girl,
Respectfully so, sweet—Tay-Lee.

*(The **VILLAGERS** groan.)*

**VU-LU:** *(Continued.)*
I know, I know. I am so sorry, but I could not find a word that rhymes with "overwhelm us." I could not even find a word that sounds like "overwhelm us." I went through the alphabet—

alm us, belm us, celm us, delm us—but I could not find a word that sounds like *elm us*. Do you know of a word that would fit this poem?

*(**VU-LU** waits for a response from the audience. Hopefully, that response will be "Selma.")*

**VU-LU:** *(Continued.)*
What did you say? Did you say Selma?
*(He looks back to the **VILLAGERS**.)*
They tell me Selma.

*(Addressing the audience again.)*
True, Selma does sound a little like overwhelm us . . .
*(He looks at his paper and marks it with a pencil.)*

*(Reciting.)*
I honor the one who found this great pearl,
A gift that did quite overwhelm us.
The Spirits give grace to the special Spice girl,
Respectfully so, sweet Selma.

Yes, that will work better, but it does not go with the poem. We do not honor Selma tonight. We honor Tay-Lee, for Tay-Lee is the one who found the giant pearl.

*(The audience should argue the fact with **VU-LU** at this point.)*

**VU-LU:** *(Continued.)*
Tay-Lee is not the one who found the pearl? You say Selma found the pearl?

*(**VU-LU** awaits further input from the audience.)*

**VU-LU:** *(Continued.)*
Oh, I think you are sadly mistaken. I may not be the smartest person on this island, but Tay-Lee is the one who found the pearl.

*(As the audience may argue further, **MINISTER RU-LU** will step up and address the audience.)*

**MINISTER RU-LU:**
With so many people saying Selma is the one who found the pearl, we will have to take their words under advisement. We will heed your words, most honorable guests, and look into the matter further. We thank you. We thank you very much for bringing this matter to light.

*(**MINISTER RU-LU** and **VU-LU** bow and go back to the others as the lights fade on the village while they continue to celebrate.)*

**REFLECTION OF THE MIRRORS:**
Yes, we are truly thankful to you for telling one and all that Selma is the true Spice sister to find the pearl. Although the village celebrates the rest of the night, questions are asked, and Tay-Lee's claim that *she* took the pearl from the oyster is now in doubt.

*(While **REFLECTION OF THE MIRRORS** speaks these next few lines, the **VILLAGERS** clear away the celebration decorations and exit to their respective houses, and so on. **VO-LO** and **SO-LO** take the Sampan back out to sea with **MASTER SU-LU**. This leaves the stage dark and empty.)*

**REFLECTION OF THE MIRRORS:** *(Continued.)*
Three days pass. No one has come forward to say Selma is the one who found favor with the Great Sea Spirit, but it is of no matter to Selma. Selma is content to have a few of her sisters to play with, the villagers are proud to have been blessed by the Spirits, and the Minister of Wisdom is happy that Vu-Lu has not stuck his hand in the beehive again. News of the giant pearl spreads above the ocean waves from island to tiny South Sea island. Although the people of the South Seas are a little envious that Rising Red Sun and not their own village has found favor with the Great Sea Spirit, they are happy for their island neighbors—except for a group of unsavory characters sailing about the island waters. A band of villainous, thieving, despicable, rough-and-ready, loathsome, pilfering pirates hear of the great find and come to the island to see the pearl for themselves, and to steal it from the village.

*(The lights come up as the red sun cutout is placed back in the sky. Entering on another Sampan come **CAPTAIN MAX** and his thieving pirate gang: **LADY LULU**, **WICKED WILLY**, **FANCY FLORA**, and **CRAZY CLYDE**. **CAPTAIN MAX** stands up front in a pose similar to that of George Washington crossing the Delaware. He is looking through a spyglass while **LADY LULU** and **FANCY FLORA** huddle close behind him. **WICKED WILLY** and **CRAZY CLYDE** pull the Sampan in by the ropes. Unlike the **RICE BROTHERS**, this pair of sloppy pirates haul the Sampan in too fast. **CAPTAIN MAX** stands at the helm hollering for them to stop while **LADY LULU** and **FANCY FLORA** just holler in general.)*

[The group wear worn pirate outfits that are pretty much a grab bag of fashion and style. However, it appears as if they are striving to look their best, although the result is more bizarre than impressive. The Sampan the fishermen use can be the same Sampan now used by the **PIRATES**. The sail may be changed, and a pirate flag can be placed on the mast.]

**CAPTAIN MAX:**
Avast, me hearties! Halt! Slow down! Whoa, you stupid oafs! STOP!

*(The Sampan rams against the footdock. **LADY LULU** and **FANCY FLORA** fall on top of **CAPTAIN MAX**. **WICKED WILLY** and **CRAZY CLYDE** look back and laugh.)*

**LADY LULU:** *(Trying to right herself.)*
Get your bloomin' carcass off me, Flora. You weigh a ton.

**FANCY FLORA:** *(Climbing off **LADY LULU**.)*
Oh my, I'm crumpling Her Worship, how careless of me.

*(**FANCY FLORA** and **LADY LULU** stand. They dust themselves off and make themselves presentable.)*

**CAPTAIN MAX:** *(As he scurries to his feet and grabs **CRAZY CLYDE** by the collar.)*
Didn't you hear me say avast?

**CRAZY CLYDE:**
Blimey, Cap'n, I thought you said "go fast!"

*(**CAPTAIN MAX** conks **CRAZY CLYDE** on the head with the spyglass.)*

**CAPTAIN MAX:** *(Looking back to find **WICKED WILLY** on the footdock.)*
Willy, take the pirate flag down and tie off the ship before we lose it with the tide.

**WICKED WILLY:**
*Boat*, Cap'n. It's a *boat*—it ain't no ship—and it's a leaky boat at that.

**CAPTAIN MAX:**
Aye, sad to say. But I'm gettin' me a ship shortly, lad. If we find that giant pearl we heard spoke of, I can muster me a fleet of ships, and you'll be my first mate—how does that sound?

**WICKED WILLY:**
I'll *be* your first mate? What am I now?

**CAPTAIN MAX:**
You're a pain in my backside, that's what you are.

**WICKED WILLY:**
Well, you can promise me the moon, but we have to get that pearl first. We've been wandering from island to island for days now, and still no blasted pearl.

**CRAZY CLYDE:** *(Pulling a seashell from his pocket.)*
I found a pretty seashell.

**CAPTAIN MAX:** *(Conking **CRAZY CLYDE** on the head again with his spyglass.)*
Pretty seashells are a dime a dozen, you loony. We need to find us that rare and valuable giant pearl.

**CRAZY CLYDE:** *(Cradling his seashell.)*
I like my seashell.

**LADY LULU:**
I'm so happy for you.

**FANCY FLORA:**
We've been to so many villages, and not one has had a decent manicurist to do my nails. Do you suppose this is the village of Rising Red Sun?

**CAPTAIN MAX:**
Could be—could very well be. Lady Lulu, what say it here on this sign?

**LADY LULU:**
It says, "Mercantile." It also says "Saloon" and "Beer—Two Bits."

**WICKED WILLY:**
A pub—booze! Bless my soul, civilization at last!

*(**WICKED WILLY** heads for the Mercantile, but **CAPTAIN MAX** stops him.)*

**CAPTAIN MAX:**
Wait, lad. You can't be gettin' yourself all tanked up. Remember our plan?

**WICKED WILLY:**
Ah, Cap'n. If you won't let me take up with my usual ways of plunderin' and torchin', can't ya at least let me have one little drink? Huh? Come on, Cap'n, whaddaya say?

**FANCY FLORA:**
How would that look—you s'posn to be a respectable gen'lman and all?

**WICKED WILLY:**
Ah, I ain't no respectable gen'lman. Never wanted to be—never will be.

**CAPTAIN MAX:**
You have to try and be, lad. It's part of the plan.

**WICKED WILLY:**
Well, it's a stupid plan if'n you ask me. It'll never work, and we'll never get that pearl. For all we know, this ain't even the island.

**CAPTAIN MAX:**
You have a terribly negative attitude, lad. If I had such a cynical disposition, I wouldn't be where I am today.

**WICKED WILLY:**
And just where is that, Cap'n? You ain't got a ship. You hardly got a seaworthy boat. You're just as well off as I am, which ain't sayin' much.

**CRAZY CLYDE:** *(Pulling his seashell out of his pocket again.)*
We've got a nifty seashell.

*(CRAZY CLYDE offers CAPTAIN MAX the seashell. CAPTAIN MAX merely looks at it for a beat, then bops CRAZY CLYDE on the head with the spyglass.)*

**FANCY FLORA:**
I don't care what you think, Wicked Willy. I think Cap'n Max has a snappin' good plan.

**CRAZY CLYDE:**
So do I.

**WICKED WILLY:**
Who asked you?

**CRAZY CLYDE:**
Nobody's, but I'll say my piece if'n I want to. Captain Max is the smartest bloke in these parts, and if he says the plan will work, it'll work. Uh, Cap'n, exactly what *is* the plan, anyway?

**CAPTAIN MAX:**
You're hopeless, Clyde. We're posing as respectable English merchants looking for a village to set up a shipping line to and from the Far East. That's why we're wearing these fancy duds—to look respectable. And the ladies are with us to give a touch of elegance to the operation.

*(LADY LULU and FANCY FLORA pouf their hair and try to look beautiful. It isn't easy.)*

**WICKED WILLY:**
Blimey, if these two bags of feathers are s'posed to give us a touch of elegance, we're in big trouble.

**FANCY FLORA:**
Hey, I take reference to that.

**LADY LULU:**
*Offense*—take *offense* to that, you dummy.

**FANCY FLORA:**
Oh, all right. Just because you've had letterin' and the rest of us ain't, you don't have to hold it over our heads.

**CAPTAIN MAX:**
Ladies! Gentle ladies, we're refined folk, remember?

**FANCY FLORA:**
Oh, yeah. The height of notability, we are.

**WICKED WILLY:**
You're the height of something.

*(FANCY FLORA smacks WICKED WILLY with her purse.)*

**LADY LULU:**
If the village thinks we're respectable, honest people, then they'll take us into their confidence and maybe tell us where that pearl is.

**FANCY FLORA:**
That's why we're all gussied up like this—so's we appear like decent folk. So you can't be goin' into no bar for a snort or two. How would it look if one of the major stockholders dashed off to get crocked the minute he steps off the ship?

**WICKED WILLY:**
Boat! It's a lousy, stinkin' little boat!

**LADY LULU:**
Shhhh, you'll wake everyone up.

**WICKED WILLY:**
I don't like it. I don't like it one bit. I want to go back to doin' what I do best—choppin' off fingers and burnin' orphanages to the ground!

**CRAZY CLYDE:**
Quiet! You'll wake everyone.

*(CAPTAIN MAX conks CRAZY CLYDE on the head again with the spyglass to shut him up. As he does this, MADAME YU-LU comes out of her Junk.)*

**MADAME YU-LU:**
Noise? Noise so early in the morning? Are we having another celebration—are we going to burn the candle at both ends—are we going to boogie-woogie—are we going to party down?

**CAPTAIN MAX:** *(Attempting to look presentable, he bows while grandly doffing his hat.)*
Ah, madame, how glad we are to make your acquaintance.

**MADAM YU-LU:**
Who are you? I have never seen you before. We have strangers on the island.

*(Enter PAPA-SAN TO-LO and MINISTER RU-LU from the right with GU-LU, MU-LU, NU-LU, QU-LU, and KU-LU.)*

**MINISTER RU-LU:**
We were on the mountain and saw a boat dock at our harbor. As it did not look like Master Su-Lu's Sampan, we came to see who it was.

**CAPTAIN MAX:** *(Crossing to MINISTER RU-LU with extended hand.)*
You must be the head of this charming little village. You look so smart and—wise. I'm Cap'n Max—I mean, Maxwell Kumquat of the British Bombay Company.

**CRAZY CLYDE:**
Maxwell Kumquat? Blimey, what a name.

*(WICKED WILLY snatches CRAZY CLYDE up and holds a hand over CRAZY CLYDE'S mouth to shut him up. Meanwhile, CAPTAIN MAX is trying to shake MINISTER RU-LU'S hand, but MINISTER RU-LU bows instead, so CAPTAIN MAX bows, then MINISTER RU-LU bows, then CAPTAIN MAX. This continues for a moment until CRAZY CLYDE wiggles free of WICKED WILLY, crosses over, takes CAPTAIN MAX'S spyglass, and bops CAPTAIN MAX on the head. CAPTAIN MAX stops bowing and looks angrily at CRAZY CLYDE as he snatches the spyglass back.)*

**CRAZY CLYDE:** *(Continued.)*
Works rather well, don't it?

**CAPTAIN MAX:** *(He turns to continue his conversation with MINISTER RU-LU.)*
Sir, we are wealthy merchants touring your lovely little islands down in the South Pacific here. We've come to see about opening a trade route between Great Britain and the South Seas.

**MADAME YU-LU:**
Oh, I am a merchant, too. See? "Madame Yu-Lu's Dry Goods." That is me.

**CAPTAIN MAX:**
Aye, I see that. Most impressive, madame, most impressive indeed, ain't it—uh, *isn't* it, friends?

*(The PIRATES agree on cue.)*

**CAPTAIN MAX:**
Oh, where are my manners? Allow me to introduce you to my gang—uh, colleagues. Everyone, this is the lovely Lady Lulu.

**LADY LULU:** *(Curtsying to the VILLAGERS.)*
Happy to meet you, I'm sure.

**MADAME YU-LU:**
Are you a real lady of royal blood?

**CAPTAIN MAX:**
Why, of course she is. I'm sure there's some royal blood in there.

**CRAZY CLYDE:**
Somewhere.

*(CAPTAIN MAX bops CRAZY CLYDE on the head with the spyglass.)*

**CAPTAIN MAX:**
And this is Crazy Clyde. He really ain't—isn't crazy. He's just—high-strung.

*(CRAZY CLYDE takes MINISTER RU-LU'S hand to shake and tries to pry the ring off the MINISTER'S finger. When MINISTER RU-LU shouts in pain, CAPTAIN MAX bops CRAZY CLYDE again. This time, CRAZY CLYDE collapses to the ground and passes out before them.)*

**CAPTAIN MAX:** *(Stepping over CRAZY CLYDE to escort FANCY FLORA to the front.)*
This is Fancy Flora. She used to entertain in the best back alleys—I mean, the best *theater* houses in London.

**GU-LU:**
A performer. We have dancers here. Perhaps you can dance with our young ladies.

**FANCY FLORA:** *(Not especially thrilled by the prospect.)*
Oh, yes. I can't wait.

**CAPTAIN MAX:**
And finally, my partner in crime—uh, business, Wicked Willy.

**MINISTER RU-LU:**
Wicked?

**CAPTAIN MAX:**
Uh, yes—it's a nickname, you see—picked up at the charity balls at the Royal Pavilion. Have you heard of the Royal Pavilion?

**MU-LU:**
Sorry, we have not.

*(CRAZY CLYDE awakens and crawls to join LADY LULU.)*

**CAPTAIN MAX:**
It's a very rich place—only us wealthy merchants and noble chaps can go there. You see, William here has this nasty habit of outbidding everyone in the palace during charity auctions—thus his name, Wicked Willy.

**WICKED WILLY:** *(Doffing his hat like CAPTAIN MAX did earlier.)*
Howjado, Guv'nor.

**QU-LU:**
My, my—to have such important people gracing our little village. We are truly honored.

**CAPTAIN MAX:**
Ah, shucks, we ain't—we're no big deal. We're mighty honored that you're honored, but we haven't done nothin' to merit your praises. We're but humble servants of Her Majesty, Queen Victoria, God bless her.

*(The PIRATES strike a pose of humility, but it's a pretty feeble attempt.)*

**WICKED WILLY:**
The Cap'n is right, Guv'nor. We ain't anyone special—not the likes that might be favored by great spirits and such, are we?

**LADY LULU:**
Heavens, no. Why we haven't even met a body that has maybe been favored by the spirits of these parts.

**CAPTAIN MAX:**
Uh, you wouldn't happen to know of someone like that, would you? Someone special and, uh . . .

**PAPA-SAN TO-LO:**
I have a daughter who has found grace with the spirits.

**CAPTAIN MAX:**
What? Noooo. Your daughter, you say? Why, that can't be.

**WICKED WILLY:**
Someone on this very island? Someone who's maybe just a stone's throw away? Oh, I don't believe ya, Guv'nor. I mean no disrespect, but a body like that must be livin' in a palace, or somethin' like that.

**PAPA-SAN TO-LO:**
No, no, gentlemen, I assure you my daughter is in this house right here. She is sleeping, for it is still early in the morning, but when she awakes, I will see if she would like to meet you.

**CAPTAIN MAX:**
Oh, kind sir, you are such a good man, but we couldn't possibly impose. . . . Although it would be a great honor to meet the likes of one in favor with the spirits, we dare not impose.

**PAPA-SAN TO-LO:**
No imposition, good people. No imposition at all.

**CAPTAIN MAX:**
Isn't this a great day for us, gents and ladies? My, my.

*(The* **PIRATES** *agree.)*

**WICKED WILLY:**
Say there, Guv'nor. What did this daughter of yours happen to do to be in favor and all?

**PAPA-SAN TO-LO:**
The Great Sea Spirit gave her a wondrous pearl from the sea.

**CRAZY CLYDE:**
A pearl as big as me?

**MINISTER RU-LU:**
Yes, a giant pearl.

**CRAZY CLYDE:**
That's it, Cap'n! We found it!

*(The* **PIRATES** *quickly pile on top of* **CRAZY CLYDE** *to shut him up, then* **CAPTAIN MAX** *explains.)*

**CAPTAIN MAX:**
How embarrassing. Never mind him. The man's a bit daft, and he babbles at times. Think nothing of it. His words don't mean a thing.

**LADY LULU:** *(As she joins* **CAPTAIN MAX.***)*
You were speaking of a pearl? How extraordinary. Where is it?

**MINISTER RU-LU:**
We have hidden it from the sight of mere mortals. We fear the temptation of seeing such a treasure would be too great.

**CAPTAIN MAX:** *(Disappointed.)*
Oh, yes—of course. You're right—dishonest blokes may show up here and try to steal it away from you. That wouldn't be right. No, sir. That wouldn't be right.

**MADAME YU-LU:**
You come see my junk. I have many sale goods inside. We could make a good merchant team, I think.

**CAPTAIN MAX:**
Merchant? Oh, right. Yes, I want to see your *junk*, madame. But we've traveled far and would like to rest a bit, if you don't mind.

**MADAME YU-LU:**
This is not a problem. I am always in. You can come by any time—we aim to please—the customer is always right—our store is your store. You will see, I have a good store.
*(MADAME YU-LU begins to depart.)*
I have a top-notch store—second to none—best for less—only game in town.

*(MADAME YU-LU exits into her Junk.)*

**KU-LU:**
If you will excuse us, please. We will prepare a meal for you, if you like.

**FANCY FLORA:**
Oh, that's sweet. Thank you kindly.

**QU-LU:**
And I will tell the House of Rice. They will want to hear of this splendid news.

*(PAPA-SAN TO-LO exits into the Spice house, and QU-LU exits into the Rice house. The other VILLAGERS disperse into the Mercantile and offstage right to leave the PIRATES alone and sitting on the footdock. All are quite disappointed.)*

**LADY LULU:**
So they have the pearl hidden.

**FANCY FLORA:**
What rotten luck.

**WICKED WILLY:**
Wha'd you expect—that they'd give it to us on a silver platter?
*(Pantomiming like a squire with a silver platter in his hand.)*
"Here you go, milady, a nice big pearl for you. We were just holdin' onto it 'til you came to steal it." I say we burn the place down and sift through the ashes. It's bound to be around here somewhere.

**CRAZY CLYDE:**
The smart-lookin' chap said it be hidden from the sight of mere mortals.

*(CAPTAIN MAX bops CRAZY CLYDE on the head with the spyglass.)*

**WICKED WILLY:**
Wait a minute, the dunce may have something there.

**FANCY FLORA:**
What do ya mean?

**WICKED WILLY:**
"Hidden from sight of mere mortals."

**LADY LULU:** *(Getting an idea as she looks over to the Shrine.)*
Yeah, it makes sense that they'd put it someplace holy-like—someplace like in honor of the one that favored the village with the pearl in the first place.

*(LADY LULU crosses to stage right to eye the Shrine of the Great Sea Spirit. As she does, WICKED WILLY follows, and so do CAPTAIN MAX and FANCY FLORA. CRAZY CLYDE also follows, but doesn't understand what they're talking about.)*

**WICKED WILLY:** *(Catching on to LADY LU-LU'S thoughts.)*
Aye, someplace where they might pray.

**CAPTAIN MAX:** *(Also catching on.)*
Someplace where they would offer humble thanks.

*(The PIRATES look back at the village to see if anyone is watching, then they charge for the Shrine of the Great Sea Spirit. They scratch and fight to get into the altar. Flowers fly up and out. The ladies scream, and the men grunt and curse. Finally, CAPTAIN MAX crawls out from under the others, holding the giant pearl before him and laughing, pleased with himself.)*

**CAPTAIN MAX:** *(Continued.)*
Ha, here she be!

*(The other PIRATES stop fighting and huddle around CAPTAIN MAX.)*

**CAPTAIN MAX:** *(Continued.)*
What a sight to behold.

**FANCY FLORA:**
Blimey, Cap'n, it's the biggest thing I've ever set me eyes on.

**CAPTAIN MAX:**
And it's mine—all mine.

**WICKED WILLY:**
All yours?

**CAPTAIN MAX:**
*Ours*—all ours, naturally.
*(He stands.)*
We better hurry off now, before those dumb peasants come back.

*(The PIRATES scramble to the Sampan.)*

**CAPTAIN MAX:** *(Continued.) (As he stands at the bow of the boat.)*
Cast off! Set sail! Full speed ahead. Cap'n Max has finally found his fortune!

*(LADY LULU and FANCY FLORA scream and laugh in delight while WICKED WILLY and CRAZY CLYDE pull the Sampan back out to sea, stage left.)*

**REFLECTION OF THE MIRRORS:**
Now the pearl is stolen. The village of Rising Red Sun hid the pearl from sight, but they did not hide it well enough to escape the greedy pirates who found the precious gift and sailed away with it. Now the village has lost its valuable treasure and will surely lose face with the spirits of the World. How terrible for Rising Red Sun. How terrible to lose face.

*(PAPA-SAN TO-LO reenters from the Spice house with MAMA-SAN SAY-LEE and the ten SPICE SISTERS. KU-LU and MINISTER RU-LU come out of the Rice house with PAPA-SAN RO-LO and the RICE BROTHERS. The other VILLAGERS come out from everywhere. All are quite excited as they carry trays of food and look around expecting to find the strangers.)*

**PAPA-SAN TO-LO:**
They were here but a moment ago. Where did they disappear to?

**MAMA-SAN SAY-LEE:**
Are you sure they were people from Bombay?

**PAPA-SAN TO-LO:**
This is what they said. They were from Bombay Company, but where are they now? They said they were tired and wanted to rest.

**VU-LU:** (*As he looks over to the Shrine of the Great Sea Spirit and begins tugging on* **MINISTER RU-LU'S** *sleeve.*)
Minister Ru-Lu . . .

**MU-LU:**
This is most strange.

**VU-LU:**
Please, Minister Ru-Lu . . .

**NU-LU:**
And their Sampan is gone. They must have sailed away.

**TU-LU:**
Most strange. Did they not say they wanted to rest, and did they not accept our hospitality when we offered food?

**DU-LU:**
I understand those Europeans can be an independent lot.

**VU-LU:**
Please, everyone listen to me. What has happened to the Shrine of the Great Sea Spirit?

(*The* **VILLAGERS** *look over and gasp in horror, then cross over to the Shrine of the Great Sea Spirit.*)

**TU-LU:**
Oh, no. What has happened here?

**GU-LU:**
What has happened to the altar?

**MINISTER RU-LU:** (*Inspecting the altar closely.*)
The pearl is gone!

**NU-LU:**
What?

**QU-LU:** (*Confirming* **MINISTER RU-LU'S** *findings.*)
The giant pearl is gone from the altar!

**JU-LU:** (*Looking back toward the sea and adding two and two together.*)
And the boat belonging to the strangers is gone!

**DU-LU:**
Do you suppose?

**MU-LU:**
Suppose that the merchants took the pearl?

**KU-LU:**
It is a good thing to suppose.

**JU-LU:**
Maybe they were not merchants after all.

**TU-LU:**
Maybe they were telling us tall tales.

**GU-LU:**
If they were not merchants—if they were not who they said they were—who were they?

**NU-LU:**
But they wore fancy clothes. They appeared to be well-off. Why would they want the pearl?

**QU-LU:**
They wore the fancy clothes to make us believe they were wealthy merchants.

**MADAME YU-LU:**
I knew it! I knew they were not merchants the minute I laid eyes on them—the minute I sized them up—the minute I looked them over. They are not merchants, they are pirates!

*(The **VILLAGERS** gasp in horror again.)*

**PAPA-SAN RO-LO:**
Oh, no. How horrible.
*(He coughs and wheezes.)*

**MU-LU:**
What do we do now? How do we get the pearl back?

**MASTER SU-LU:** *(Drawing his samurai sword.)*
We will go to war, that is what we will do. I will outfit my Sampan to battle the pirate ship, and when we find them, we will take them prisoner and get the pearl back.

*(Most approve of this idea.)*

**MINISTER RU-LU:**
We cannot do that.

**MASTER SU-LU:**
Why not?

**MINISTER RU-LU:**
We cannot get back what was not ours to begin with. The pearl belongs to the Great Sea Spirit, and if the spirit wants the pearl back, he will get it.

**KU-LU:**
But how can the Great Sea Spirit get his pearl from the pirates?

**MINISTER RU-LU:**
The Great Sea Spirit has many powers. He will find a way. It was our good fortune to have the pearl for the brief time that we did. We must remember this and the happy times the

pearl brought to our village. Besides, we still have a more valuable gift. We have Tay-Lee, who was favored by the spirits.

*(This seems to appease the **VILLAGERS**. However, at that moment, normal lighting dims and the special effects lights flash. A puff of smoke arises, and the **GREAT SEA SPIRIT** appears once more over the waterfall.)*

**GREAT SEA SPIRIT:**
I sense something is very wrong here! I sense fear and loss. I sense shame and regret. What has happened to this village?

**MADAME YU-LU:**
Who is this? What is this? Oh, dear. We are doomed. Doomed!! This is it—it's all over—the final inning—the jig is up—it's curtains—we're history!

*(The **VILLAGERS** are frightened and kowtow before the **GREAT SEA SPIRIT**—all except **SELMA**.)*

**SELMA:** *(To the others.)*
Don't be afraid. He will not harm you. This is the Great Sea Spirit we pray to.

**MADAME YU-LU:** *(Tugging at **TAY-LEE'S** sleeve.)*
Why did you not know this?

**TAY-LEE:**
I . . . He . . .

**GREAT SEA SPIRIT:**
Silence! Why does everyone bow and fail to show his face to the Great Sea Spirit? Why does everyone feel ashamed except Selma? What is going on here? Where is the giant pearl I gave this village? What has happened to it?

**MINISTER RU-LU:** *(Slowly rising.)*
Oh, Great One. We have lost the pearl. We lose face.

**GREAT SEA SPIRIT:**
How did you lose the pearl?

**MINISTER RU-LU:**
We are not certain of the details, but we believe a band of pirates might have gained our confidence, then stole away with it.

**PAPA-SAN TO-LO:** *(Standing.)*
Yes, if you please, Great Sea Spirit. We put the pearl inside the altar as an offering to you, and when we came out of our houses, the pearl was gone and so were the merchants—or so they said they were merchants.

**GREAT SEA SPIRIT:**
Then you are not guilty of neglect, but of trusting strangers. You cannot be too trusting of strangers, for their ways and attitudes may differ from yours. Do not stop being kind and courteous to all things, but this does not mean you should not be cautious and careful, too.

**MINISTER RU-LU:**
Yes, Great Sea Spirit. How wise your words are.

**GREAT SEA SPIRIT:**
They are? The Minister of Wisdom thinks I am wise?

**MINISTER RU-LU:**
Oh, yes, Great Sea Spirit—very wise.

**GREAT SEA SPIRIT:** *(Pleased.)*
Well, how about that.
*(Angry again.)*
But my pearl has been stolen! How dare they steal anything from me! I will bring them back, those pilfering pirates. With one mighty gust of wind from my brother the Wind Spirit, I will bring the pearl back to this island! Stand back! My fury is about to be seen!

*(All hurry to their knees and cover their heads with their arms.)*

**GREAT SEA SPIRIT:** *(Continued.)* *(Pumping himself up while grandly spreading his arms outward.)*
Brother Wind Spirit, I call on you to make a mighty wind. Churn these waters and whip a storm across this land. Bring back the vessel carrying the thieves who stole my pearl!

*(Thunder rumbles and the skies turn dark as a wind whips up from the sea.)*

[To indicate wind, the actors will pantomime as if a wind is forcing them back, to and fro, etc. The harder the wind (coming up later), the more movement.]

*(After a moment, the Sampan carrying the **PIRATES** comes rolling back [pushed/heaved back] and slams into the footdock. The **PIRATES** go flying and land in front of the **VILLAGERS** in a heap. The winds diminish, and the lighting comes up to normal. The **GREAT SEA SPIRIT** is gone. The **VILLAGERS** stand and form a semicircle around the **PIRATES**. **CAPTAIN MAX** looks up sheepishly as he sees the disapproving eyes of the **VILLAGERS**.)*

**CAPTAIN MAX:**
Why, hello there. Quite a little blow we just had, wasn't it?
*(He stands as the other **PIRATES** huddle behind him for protection.)*
Was just on our way around your island to see the sights when this gale comes up and whisks us back into the harbor here—imagine that.

**MINISTER RU-LU:**
Captain Kumquat, do you know what has happened to our giant pearl?

**CAPTAIN MAX:**
What giant pearl? Oh, the giant pearl you were telling us of. No, can't say that I do. Has something happened to it?

**MASTER SU-LU:** *(Swinging his samurai sword at **CAPTAIN MAX**.)*
You know very well what has happened to it. You stole it!

**CAPTAIN MAX:**
Stole it? Us? I wouldn't go around callin' perfect strangers thieves and robbers like that. Where are your manners?

**MASTER SU-LU:**
Where is the pearl?

**LADY LULU:**
We haven't the foggiest.

**PAPA-SAN TO-LO:**
Please. We do not ask for ourselves. We do not want the pearl, for the pearl is not ours to have. However, the loss of the pearl has made the Great Sea Spirit very angry, and we fear to think what he might do if he does not get the pearl back.

**FANCY FLORA:**
So much fuss over a little bobble, I must say.

**CAPTAIN MAX:**
Listen, I can respect your beliefs and all that, but you can't expect us to believe some spirit from the sea is goin' to do something terrible just because one of his jewels is missin'. I mean, he must have thousands of 'em rollin' around on the ocean floor. What's one little pearl?

*(The wind begins to pick up from the sea again.)*

**MINISTER RU-LU:**
You do not understand.
*(Sensing that a storm is nearing.)*
Do you not feel it? A great storm is coming this way. We have displeased the Great Sea Spirit, and he and all the other spirits are bringing their wrath upon this island.

**MADAME YU-LU:**
Oh, terror of terrors! What will become of us now? It's coming—it's on its way—any minute now—in no time at all.

**HU-LU:**
What are you talking about?

**MADAME YU-LU:**
The big wind—the blasted blow—the dastardly draft—the blustery breeze. It's coming to get us. All will be destroyed!

*(The **VILLAGERS** gasp and panic as the wind increases and the skies darken.)*

**QU-LU:**
Quick, Minister Ru-Lu, what do we do?

**MINISTER RU-LU:**
We pray for forgiveness. Everyone pray to the Great Sea Spirit and to all the spirits to forgive our simple souls.

**GU-LU:**
I know! I know! Tay-Lee Spice can pray to the Great Sea Spirit.

**MU-LU:**
Yes, she has found favor with the Great Sea Spirit. If she prays to him, he will stop the wind.

*(The **VILLAGERS** think this is a good idea.)*

**MINISTER RU-LU:**
Yes, perhaps that will appease the Great Sea Spirit. Tay-Lee, you must kneel before the Shrine of the Great Sea Spirit and pray for his forgiveness.

**TAY-LEE:**
But I can't pray to the Great Sea Spirit.

**MAMA-SAN SAY-LEE:**
Please, Tay-Lee. You must try for everyone's sake.

*(The wind beings to pick up now as paper articles/tissue paper cutouts of leaves and such blow in from the sea.)*

[These pieces of paper, branches, and all can come from stage left and over and offstage right by having them attached to poles carried behind the Junk, Mercantile, etc. The articles will appear over the Junk, Mercantile, and houses and dance as if the wind is blowing them in and out.]

*(The older **SPICE SISTERS** huddle around **TAY-LEE** as she reluctantly goes to the shrine, kneels, and starts praying.)*

**TAY-LEE:**
Oh, Great Sea Spirit, I ask that you stop this wind from destroying this island. I ask . . .

*(The mast of **MADAME YU-LU'S** Junk topples over from the force of the wind. All shout in fear.)*

**MADAME YU-LU:** *(Rushing up to her Junk.)*
Ohhhhh, my boat! It will all be ruined!

**TAY-LEE:** *(Looking over at **MADAME YU-LU** and trying again.)*
Please, Great Sea Spirit . . .

*(A part of the sign over the Mercantile comes off and flies out to the right. These pieces are on poles, lifted off the building, and carried off over the houses so that they appear to be flying in the wind. **CAPTAIN MAX, WICKED WILLY,** and **CRAZY CLYDE** rush to their boat and tie it down.)*

**CAPTAIN MAX:**
Batten down the hatches, boys. It's going to be a humdinger of a blow!

**GAY-LEE:** *(Stepping forward.)*
Tay-Lee can't do it. She isn't the one in favor with the Great Sea Spirit!

*(Another piece of sign breaks off and flies out right. Another panicked cry from the **VILLAGERS**.)*

**FAY-LEE:** *(Stepping forward.)*
It's true! Selma is the one who found the pearl! Selma is the one in favor!

*(**GAY-LEE** and **FAY-LEE** pull **SELMA** to the shrine.)*

**GAY-LEE:**
Here, Selma, you try. You pray to your friend, the Great Sea Spirit. You must save us all.

**SELMA:**
Well, I will try.
*(**SELMA** kneels before the shrine.)*
Please, Great Sea Spirit, I know you do not want to hurt us. I know you are kindly and forgiving. You gave me the pearl that my sisters might respect me. You showed me where to find the pearl to help me become in favor with my family. You have done this, and I am most happy now. The pearl itself means nothing to me. The love of my sisters and family

means everything. It changes nothing now that the pearl is missing. What the pearl has done for this village is our greatest reward. Can you forgive us for losing it?

*(The skies thunder and roar and the **GREAT SEA SPIRIT** returns to his perch above the waterfall. The **VILLAGERS** kowtow as the **PIRATES** look back in amazement.)*

**CRAZY CLYDE:**
Jumpin' Jehoshaphat! Will you look at that!

**GREAT SEA SPIRIT:**
So—do they believe you now, Selma? Does the village believe that *you* are the one I favored and not that lying, mean, little Tay-Lee?

**MINISTER RU-LU:**
Oh, Great One, we are truly sorry. Our honorable guests tried to tell us that Selma was the one who found grace with you, but we did not listen. We lose face. Please, although we do not deserve it, please do not destroy our village.

**GREAT SEA SPIRIT:**
You have made me very angry!

**SELMA:** *(Crossing over closer to the **GREAT SEA SPIRIT**.)*
Please, Great Sea Spirit. I do not hold these people at fault. I love them. Can't you find it in your heart to forgive them too?

**GREAT SEA SPIRIT:** *(Softening a bit.)*
Well, I suppose.
*(Blustering once more.)*
But I am still plenty angry! We will see!

*(In a puff of smoke, the **GREAT SEA SPIRIT** is gone. The wind continues as things fly across stage.)*

**REFLECTION OF THE MIRRORS:**
So the Great Sea Spirit thinks upon it, and when he sees how happy Selma is and how sorry the villagers are for not believing that she was the girl who found the pearl and who is the true one in favor with the spirits, his anger lessens and he feels a warmth and compassion for the people of Rising Red Sun. With this feeling of generosity in his heart, he lifts up his mighty arms and turns the fierce, harmful wind into winds of silk.

*(A water fountain pole rises over the waterfall and bursts of glitter fly up and around it and sparkle in the increasing light. The wind dies down. In the meantime, during **REFLECTION OF THE MIRROR'S** speech, JU-LU, DU-LU, FU-LU, GU-LU, MU-LU, NU-LU, KU-LU, and QU-LU step over to the far left [in the sea], then JU-LU, DU-LU, FU-LU, and GU-LU take the end of four rolls of silk held by the others and run back to stage right stretching the strips of cloth out across the stage. They will then wave them up and down when **REFLECTION OF THE MIRRORS** says that the harmful winds turned into winds of silk. The **VILLAGERS** will shout for joy and applaud when this happens.)*

**REFLECTION OF THE MIRRORS:** *(Continued.)*
And the villagers pray many thanks for their good fortune and dance about in joy. And the men of the village put Selma up on their shoulders and parade her around for all to see and give thanks. There is much rejoicing and mirth.

*(Two of the bigger **RICE BROTHERS** hoist **SELMA** up on their shoulders. The others wave and take her hand as she is carried through the crowd.)*

**REFLECTION OF THE MIRRORS:** *(Continued.)*
But there is still one piece of business to take care of. There is still the matter of the giant pearl.

*(As **REFLECTION OF THE MIRRORS** makes this last statement, we see **CAPTAIN MAX** and his **PIRATES** trying to sneak back to their boat. **MASTER SU-LU** sees this and steps up to stop them.)*

**MASTER SU-LU:**
And just where do you think you are going?

*(The **VILLAGERS** stop their rejoicing and look over to the **PIRATES**.)*

**CAPTAIN MAX:**
I—well—there was so much merrymaking goin' on here, we thought it best to light out—uh—not wantin' to intrude and all.

**MASTER SU-LU:**
What of the pearl?

**CAPTAIN MAX:**
Now, Guv'nor, you're not wantin' that pearl. You told us so yourself. You told that very loud fellow up there with the long hair that this village don't want that pearl—it don't need it.

**FANCY FLORA:**
Right. Finders keepers, I always say.

**WICKED WILLY:** *(Drawing his sword.)*
I say to dash with 'em, Cap'n. We got the blasted pearl, let's run 'em through and light out to sea.

**MASTER SU-LU:** *(Drawing his samurai sword.)*
You'll have to go through me, you vile pirate!

*(**MASTER SU-LU** and **WICKED WILLY** face off and begin to battle until **SELMA** cries out.)*

**SELMA:**
Gentlemen, please!

*(**WICKED WILLY** and **MASTER SU-LU** turn to **SELMA**, who is lowered off the shoulders of the **RICE BROTHERS**. She meekly crosses over to **CAPTAIN MAX** and holds out her hands.)*

**SELMA:** *(Continued.)*
May I have the pearl back, please?

**CAPTAIN MAX:** *(Squirming and slowly turning to mush.)*
But, missy . . . You don't want . . . I could buy me a proper ship . . . I'll buy you something pretty too. Whadda' ya' say? I'll buy you a pretty lace bonnet, or a big colorful bumbershoot. Don't that sound nice?

**SELMA:**
The pearl, please.

**CAPTAIN MAX:**
But . . . But . . .

**SELMA:**
Please, sir.

**CAPTAIN MAX:**
Ah—drat!
*(He takes the giant pearl from his coat and looks at it one last time.)*
There goes my fleet of pirate ships. Here.

*(CAPTAIN MAX gives SELMA the giant pearl.)*

**WICKED WILLY:** *(Coming out of his boots.)*
What? Are you completely off your nut, Cap'n? It's ours!

**CAPTAIN MAX:**
Stand back, Willy. That's an order!

*(WICKED WILLY quickly lunges for SELMA and grabs her. He takes the pearl from her with one hand, wraps that arm around to hold her, and places the sword that the other hand holds at SELMA'S neck.)*

**WICKED WILLY:**
Everyone back or your precious little one here gets it.

*(The VILLAGERS scream in horror. WICKED WILLY slowly backs up to the footdock and toward the Sampan. In the meantime, CAPTAIN MAX whispers to MASTER SU-LU, and they disappear behind the crowd.)*

**WICKED WILLY:**
You think I'm goin' to be charmed by a little girl? Why I've had tykes like her for breakfast. Any of you tries something, I'll slash her pretty little throat.

**MINISTER RU-LU:**
Please, do not hurt our little Selma.

**WICKED WILLY:**
Think I'd fall for all this goodness bunk?
*(Mimicking.)*
"It isn't ours to give. I love everyone."
*(He eases onto the Sampan.)*
You people make me sick. Well, it's *my* pearl now, and I'm takin' it out to sea with your little Selma. If any of you come after me, I'll kill her, you hear!

*(CAPTAIN MAX and MASTER SU-LU come from behind the crowd and attack WICKED WILLY. WICKED WILLY turns SELMA loose to fight off CAPTAIN MAX and MASTER SU-LU, and she runs to PAPA-SAN TO-LO. After a mighty scuffle, MASTER SU-LU and CAPTAIN MAX have WICKED WILLY tied up in the ropes on the Sampan, and CRAZY CLYDE comes over and bops WICKED WILLY over the head with the spyglass for good measure.)*

**CRAZY CLYDE:**
Take that, you bad ol' pirate. Tryin' to hurt a poor little girl. You should be ashamed of yourself.

**CAPTAIN MAX:** *(Crossing back onto the footdock with MASTER SU-LU.)*
Say, you're a pretty strong one there, Samurai Sam.

**MASTER SU-LU:**
You are a masterful one yourself, Captain.

*(LADY LULU and FANCY FLORA cross over to SELMA.)*

**LADY LULU:** *(Kneeling down to tenderly embrace **SELMA**.)*
Are you all right, dearie?

**FANCY FLORA:**
He didn't hurt you, did he? Here—you dry your eyes now with my fancy kerchief. Everything will be all right.

**CAPTAIN MAX:**
We're awful sorry about this. We didn't mean for things to get so out of hand. To tell you the truth, this is the first time we've ever been pirating—not much for all this hacking and plundering, really.

**MINISTER RU-LU:**
What did you do before you became pirates?

**CAPTAIN MAX:**
Well, we—promise you won't laugh?

*(All promise.)*

**CAPTAIN MAX:**
I grew flowers. And Lulu and Flora sold 'em on the street for me. We found Clyde here in the sewer one cold winter's night. He hadn't had anything to eat for days and was almost gone from this earth. Sellin' flowers don't make much money, and I had a hard time just keepin' everyone fed. That's why we took up with these evil ways. We met Willy off the coast of India. He's truly a wicked one. We thought he might teach us how to be genuine pirates, but, well, it just don't seem to be in our nature to hurt people.

**MINISTER RU-LU:**
Why not stay here with us. We are not a rich people, but we have never gone hungry.

**LADY LULU:**
You'd want us here after what we tried to do to you?

**MINISTER RU-LU:**
Selma has forgiven us for not thinking she was the one who found the giant pearl. And the Great Sea Spirit has forgiven us for losing it. It seems only right that we should be grateful enough to forgive you as well.

**CAPTAIN MAX:**
Well now, we be humbled beyond all words here.

**FANCY FLORA:**
Yes, how ashamed we feel.

**CAPTAIN MAX:** *(To **FANCY FLORA**, **LADY LULU** and **CRAZY CLYDE**.)*
What do you say, ladies and gent?

*(**FANCY FLORA**, **LADY LULU**, and **CRAZY CLYDE** eagerly and excitedly shake their heads "yes.")*

**CAPTAIN MAX:**
Guv'nor, on behalf of these very grateful folk here, I say thank you. Thank you, good people. We accept your kindness.

**MASTER SU-LU:**
Good. Now we must decide what we are going to do about Wicked Willy.

**CAPTAIN MAX:**
No, leave him be.

*(All look surprised and puzzled.)*

**MASTER SU-LU:**
No?

**CAPTAIN MAX:**
He can wait. The first thing we should do is fix up the Shrine of the Great Sea Spirit and put the pearl back where it belongs.

**MINISTER RU-LU:**
Ah, yes.

*(The **VILLAGERS** sigh in relief. **MASTER SU-LU** pats **CAPTAIN MAX** on the shoulder, and they cross over and start to repair the Shrine with **MINISTER RU-LU'S** help. **JU-LU** and **DU-LU** cross over to **REFLECTION OF THE MIRRORS** and wheel the Pagoda Platform to the center of the stage, while the other **VILLAGERS** retrieve their chimes and mirror standards. The others pass out little packets of glitter.)*

**REFLECTION OF THE MIRRORS:**
So all is happy—all is right with the world. The village of Rising Red Sun is in good grace with the spirits, and Captain Max and his band are in good grace with Rising Red Sun. Somehow I do not think Captain Max and the others will ever steal again. Selma has taught them that crime does not pay—that goodness and giving will rise over selfishness and evil ways. The village has come to respect Selma greatly and hold her in high esteem, as she is the true one favored by the spirits. Tay-Lee has learned that a lie, no matter how big or small, is a bad thing. The village is happy again and will continue to fish and raise their families and be content with what they have. And now our story is over. We hope you have enjoyed our little offering. We wish to thank you for coming to our theater and we wish to say to you: Goodness and love can turn the worst things into the best things. Goodness and love can turn unpleasantness into beautiful . . .

**EVERYONE:**
Winds of Silk!

*(Those who pulled out and waved the strips of silk material before pick up the ends and do the same now. The other **VILLAGERS** throw their streamers and packets of glitter out into the audience. The lights flash and sparkle, the mirror and chime standards are shaken, and the **VILLAGERS** wave and tell the audience good-bye.)*

*(Curtain.)*

## END OF WINDS OF SILK

# About the Author

Joan Garner has been involved in theatre for over 20 years, participating in every aspect of play production while concentrating most heavily on theatre design. She has produced, directed, and acted, and most significantly, has been the production designer for over 40 plays, the majority of these being challenging musicals. She has also taught the art of set design and decoration, and has served on the board of directors at the community theatre level.

Joan has taken her interest in theatre a step further by writing six full-length plays to date, encompassing a variety of genres from farce to comedy to high drama. Two of these plays have won national playwrighting competitions and three have been produced.

Having returned to Colorado where she spent her youth, Joan resides in Littleton, and is currently Art Director for Libraries Unlimited, designing book covers, catalogs, and brochures. In her spare time she tinkers with a few ideas for novels, accepts freelance illustration and writing assignments, and enjoys creating fine art pieces and paintings.